Tony Hall was educated at King Edward's School, Edgbaston, Birmingham, and at Birkenhead School, Merseyside. He won an exhibition to Keble College, Oxford, where he read P.P.E. and edited the magazine *Isis*. In 1974, he joined the B.B.C. as a journalist trainee. He is now a senior producer on the Radio 4 programmes 'The World at One' and 'P.M.' He is married and lives in Twickenham.

Tony Hall

King Coal

Miners, Coal and Britain's
Industrial Future

Penguin Books

Penguin Books Ltd, Harmondsworth,
Middlesex, England
Penguin Books, 625 Madison Avenue,
New York, New York 10022, U.S.A.
Penguin Books Australia Ltd, Ringwood,
Victoria, Australia
Penguin Books Canada Ltd, 2801 John Street,
Markham, Ontario, Canada L3R 1B4
Penguin Books (N.Z.) Ltd, 182–190 Wairau Road,
Auckland 10, New Zealand

First published 1981

Copyright © Tony Hall, 1981

All rights reserved

Filmset, printed and bound in Great Britain by
Hazell Watson & Viney Ltd, Aylesbury, Bucks
Set in VIP Times Roman

For my father

Contents

Preface

The incentive for this book came from a radio programme I made involving delegates from the N.U.M. 'The trouble with you lot,' said one, 'is that you only come near us when we're threatening a strike. The rest of the time you couldn't give a toss.' It was a very fair challenge, and it was to fill in those blanks, to find out what had happened when the miners were not in the public eye, that I began the research which ended up as this book.

Let me begin with a disclaimer: it was a perilous task. I've never worked down a pit and so to that extent can never 'know' the industry in the same way as someone whose whole livelihood depends on it. Not only that, but miners are wary of outsiders, at least until they know what they're up to. Furthermore, they also have, more than any other industrial group, a tremendous grasp of their own history down to the minutest details, and don't need an outsider to tell them about their past. There is also another danger in writing any book which attempts to give a national view of events: in the coal industry more than any other, each area has different views and perspectives, and every pit within those areas has a totally different outlook and tradition. Generalizations become very dangerous, as well as potentially condescending, but as the questions I started out to answer were those of a layman, an outsider, some generalization was inevitable. The book's faults, I hope, are all those of an outsider trying to understand communities and an industry which men who've spent their whole lives in it still don't fully grasp.

Many people, throughout the coalfields, have helped to put me right. Members and officials of the N.U.M. have given up anything between ten minutes and three hours of their time to talk to me. Some are mentioned by name in the text, some are not, but to all of them, for their many kindnesses, go many thanks. I would, however, like to give my special thanks to the following: from the N.U.M., the President, Joe Gormley, and the Secretary, Lawrence Daly, as well as the former Secretary, Will Paynter, for one of the most stimulating conversations I had. At Euston Road, I would particularly like to thank David Branton and Trevor Pickup, but above all Steve Bundred, the research officer, and his assistant Kathy Falcoln, who put up with my presence for hours on end and sustained my work with tea and conversation. I would also like to record my thanks to Alex Eadie, M.P., who, by the unanimous agreement of everyone else I talked to at Westminster, knows more about the coal industry than any other M.P. in the House of Commons. At the National Coal Board, I would like to thank Clifford Shephard, until recently the Board member for industrial relations, the former Chairman, Lord Robens, and the Chairman of the Coal Board, Sir Derek Ezra, each of whom spared a great deal of his valuable time to talk to me. My special thanks, though, must go to Leslie Grainger, formerly the Board member for science, whose observations on his time at Hobart House helped me hugely. My thanks, too, to Jim McFarlane of the extra-mural department of Sheffield University, for all his help with the first-rate essays published in Chapter 2; they well repay reading in full. I would also like to thank my colleagues at the B.B.C., who, as the deadline for completion approached, put up with a 'part-timer' for a couple of months, and Neil Middleton of Penguins for his great encouragement in helping to sort out my initial thoughts. Though she told me not to, could I also thank my wife, Cynthia, who for the past two years and more has put up with this other thing, 'the book', and encouraged me all along the line.

There is, though, one person above all others to whom I owe an enormous debt of gratitude. Peter Tait, who until a year ago was branch secretary at Grimethorpe Colliery in South Yorkshire and one of Yorkshire's representatives on the National Executive Committee, is now the General Secretary of the Miners' International Federation. He, his wife Doris, and all his family have shown me great kindness and friendship over the past few years. Peter has gently guided me around some of the worst pitfalls that could have trapped an outsider, and given me insights and ingress into the world of the miner which I could not otherwise have obtained. Without his help, nothing like this book would have been possible. The good points in it are due to him, the failings wholly mine.

1. An Island Built on Coal

No one could have lived through the events of 1972 and 1974 without being aware of the power of coal. Anxiously, people scanned newspapers to see when their turn for a power cut was, and found predictions of apocalypse when the coal supplies eventually ran out. It was said that the old and sick were imperilled and industry was being dealt a mortal blow. The second miners' strike led to consequences so grave that the Government called an election to ask 'Who rules?', and they lost. Above all, civilized industrial society was seen to be frail and vulnerable.

In the midst of all this, most people wondered why coal was still so important. They had been told that coal was dirty, bulky and very much the fuel of the past. Most of the pits that produced it had been closed down, and the miners redeployed, trying to get their colliers' hands around the intricacies of light industry. So how could these men bring the whole country to a halt? What was more, from 1973 onwards, it appeared that coal was going to be the fuel of the future. Oil was too costly and was in danger of running out. Nuclear power was taking a long time to develop and aroused massive anxieties. King Coal looked set to rule again. But how had this come about?

The first great rise in the price of oil in 1973 produced a rash of reports extolling the future importance of coal. A little after the second great price rise, following the Iranian revolution in 1979, came the most authoritative study so far. The World Coal study, or W.O.C.O.L., was the result of collaboration between such diverse groups as Mitsui, Atlantic Richfield, the National Coal Board and Poland's Ministry of Mines, under the umbrella of the Massachusetts Institute of Technology. Having examined the state of the industry throughout the world, and looked at

13

potential demand for coal up to the turn of the century, the study concluded that only coal could provide 'the energy bridge to the future'.

Over 60 per cent of the world's reserves of coal, in other words coal that can be economically mined with today's technology, is found in just five countries: the United States (25·2 per cent), the Soviet Union (16·6 per cent), China (14·9 per cent), Australia (5 per cent) and Britain, which has just under 7 per cent of the world's reserves. In the Third World, India is by far the largest producer and consumer, though countries such as Colombia, Indonesia and Botswana may become significant exporters in the future.

The study predicts that between now and the end of the century, the demand for coal in the western industrialized nations will at least double and quite possibly treble in size. The major use will continue to be the generation of electricity, but the really significant rises in consumption will come from industrial users. And yet another new market could develop in the next decade with the use of coal to produce synthetic oil and gas. The result of this huge new demand will be a rapid increase in the world trade in coal; according to W.O.C.O.L., it could be up to three or five times its present size. The major importers will be Japan, Western Europe, especially France and Italy, and several newly industrializing countries such as South Korea, Taiwan and the Philippines. The really big exporters are likely to be Australia and the United States, though South Africa, Poland, Canada, the Soviet Union and China will also be significant. This new trade in coal will generate the building of new tankers, harbour facilities and a major expansion of the capacity of railways and inland waterways.

The study concludes that, unlike oil, reserves of coal are sufficient to allow a great expansion of its use well into the next century and beyond. By the early decades of the twenty-first century, renewable sources of energy should be coming into use on a significant scale. But it is in the next twenty years, until those sort of systems can be produced, that coal will be most vital. The technology for its safe and efficient use is already proven, unlike nuclear power. But, says the study, unless the decisions are made soon, the facilities will not be ready for the time, less than a decade away, when they will be needed.

So will these resources be developed? The dazzling future for coal has not escaped the notice of the major oil companies. The energy crisis demonstrated how the production of crude oil that provided the basis of their growth and power cannot last, so it appeared quite logical for them to diversify and acquire interests in coal production. And this, indeed, is what they have done. Shell, for example, maintains that the resources and effort needed to meet the forecast levels of international coal supply are beyond the capacity of the existing world coal industry: 'The major oil companies are among the few organizations that have the resources and expertise necessary to assist in the rapid development of an international coal business.' They expect to trade some 15 million tonnes of coal by 1983 from investments in Australia, South Africa and North America. The expertise of Shell International Marine is being used to develop the techniques for shipping coal economically, and research is going on into the possibility of sending coal by pipeline. Shell is also putting a great deal of money into new ways of using coal and burning it more efficiently. B.P. too is moving into coal, especially in Australia, South Africa and Canada. They are also carrying out joint studies with the National Coal Board into the possibility of converting coal into liquid fuels.

And what of governments? How do they view the future of coal? The message from the summit meeting of the O.E.C.D. countries, held in Venice in the middle of 1980, was that coal was here to stay. The seven nations committed themselves to a doubling of coal production and use within the next ten years. The great bulk of the increase would come from the United States, which has vast resources of coal, much of it easily accessible by open-cast mining. But for their part the British Government saw 'less immediate scope for further developing coal production and use in the United Kingdom than there is in other countries'. The result is that at a time of a great worldwide comeback for coal, there is great uncertainty within the industry in Britain. Have the lessons of the rundown of the industry in the

1960s been learnt? Or are we about to squander once more one of Britain's greatest national resources?

Coal was little used before the sixteenth century. Some was mined by the Romans in Northumberland to warm their troops on Hadrian's Wall, and, further south, to feed the sacred flame permanently burning in the Temple of Minerva at Bath, but its most common and rather ignominious role was as ballast for empty grain ships returning from Tyneside to the Fens. After the Romans left, there is scant trace of its use for the best part of 1,000 years. The Saxons and the Danes used wood, and the Domesday Book contains no reference to any coal-mine. It was not until a little after 1200 that coal-mining began to any serious degree, centred on the Tyne Valley and the area to the south, much of which belonged to the Bishop of Durham who was keen to promote development. It was from the North East that the coal trade started, the so-called 'sea coal' shipped to France, Flanders and London for use in lime-burning, salt-making and smithies. A Seacoal Lane, in fact, existed in London from the early thirteenth century. Nevertheless, the amount of coal hacked and dug from shallow pits and outcrops each year seldom exceeded about 15,000 tons. Timber was plentiful and cheap, so that the potential of coal remained unrecognized. Indeed, coal attracted so little general interest that it was commonly held in England and Belgium that coal was a form of vegetation that grew like a plant.

If there was ignorance about coal, then there was also a strong prejudice against it: coal was regarded as both noxious and disgusting. The coal used was of poor quality and gave off a choking, foul-smelling smoke, which, as most medieval housing was built without chimneys, led to consequences that were generally regarded as intolerable. In 1257, Queen Eleanor fled London because of the 'fumes of the sea coals'. Fifty years later a proclamation in the capital forbade the use of coal by lime-burners because 'an intolerable smell diffuses itself throughout the neighbouring places . . . to the annoyance of the magistrates, citizens and others'. Shakespeare conjured up the character of Master Seacole as a dirty, grubby fellow, and Stows Annals record that right up to the end of the reign of Elizabeth, 'the nice dames of London would not come into any house or room where sea coal was burned, or willingly eat of meat that had been roasted with sea coal fire'. Only through sheer necessity would people be persuaded to cast off such prejudices.

The rise of coal began in the reign of Queen Elizabeth the First, much earlier than is generally thought. During both her lifetime and that of her successor, James the First, the British countryside was stripped of trees and woodland, in part to meet the needs of a growing population for fuel, but also to fulfil the demands of manufacturing industry progressing and expanding more rapidly than ever before. Hardly an industrial process could be carried out without wood, and the demands were enormous. A man-of-war, for example, needed 4,000 great oaks to construct the hull, decks and fittings. As timber became less plentiful, so the price rose dramatically. It was an increase 'almost without precedent in the history of civilization', according to Professor Nev, writing in his book *The Rise of the British Coal Industry*. Small wonder then that the demand for an alternative fuel, coal, was so huge. To supply desperate needs there was a coal rush, a mad scramble for mining concessions as landed families and merchants ran up debts of thousands of pounds in the search for coal. Conmen toured the country offering to sink pits to see if there was coal where they knew perfectly well there was none. Unscrupulous pit-owners dug coal from beneath neighbours' fields, flooded rival pits with water and sabotaged pithead gear. Physical violence was commonplace, especially when there was too much coal on the market.

Within a century and a quarter of Queen Elizabeth's accession, coal production in the British Isles had increased fourteen times. By the middle of the seventeenth century, the annual output of one colliery on the Tyne probably exceeded the entire amount cut each year during the reign of Henry VIII from the whole of the Northumberland and Durham coalfield. It was nothing short of a revolution. In 1550 the area around Newcastle-upon-Tyne, for example, was still primarily agricultural, though there were a few pits on the banks of the river. By 1675 that same landscape was dominated by coal. Collieries had spread for several miles either side of the Tyne, coal wagons jammed the trackways, and the narrow mouth of the river was cluttered with hundreds of ships, all carrying coal. Similar developments were taking place in other coalfields, even those far from the sea. For the first time coal was being used as an important industrial fuel: for brewing, distilling, boiling sugar and soap, firing pottery and heating iron for rolling into sheets.

Coal also provided an important catalyst for commerce. The coal trade, mainly from Northumberland and Durham to the South East, an area of heavy and expanding population, brought wealth to London. Financiers grew rich on the money they lent to sink pits and to construct colliers to carry the coal. The tax on coal entering the port of London was used to fund the building of many of Sir Christopher Wren's churches, including St Paul's Cathedral. Coal merchants, lightermen, ship-builders, road hauliers and many more all made sure they did very well out of the trade. By 1681 about 587,000 tons were being shipped each year from the Tyne.

London had become so dependent on coal that by the end of the century an average citizen would expect to spend at least one tenth of his annual income on it, and even that to keep only one room warm for part of the day. The security of supplies was vital. During the civil war, Parliament foresaw 'many dangerous tumults and commotions' in London if the King were to maintain his control over Newcastle and its coal-pits. The capture of the city was seen as a priority, and when it occurred was greeted with great relief. Later in the century another threat, this time from pirates and privateers, was taken so seriously that armed convoys were arranged to ensure the safe passage of Tyneside coal. If the supply from Newcastle were stopped for any reason, the poor of London shivered. 'God bless Yorkshire and preserve the coal-pits,' exclaimed the Archbishop of York in 1685: necessity had overcome prejudice.

During the first half of the eighteenth century, coal commanded an importance never before achieved. In this respect, though, Britain was singular, producing about six times more coal than the rest of the world put together, her main commercial rivals, Holland and France, having little or none. The need for coal stimulated technology so that, for example, wagonways were developed to move it from pits to wharf, and larger ships to transport it by sea. The ever increasing depth of mines demanded innovation, and steam engines developed by Thomas Newcomen were used to pump water from as early as 1712. It was a remarkable breakthrough, as one awed traveller from the continent noted a few years later: 'In the coal-pits of Newcastle a single person can by means of an engine surprising and simple, raise 500 tons of water to the height of an hundred and eighty feet.' Coal was also first to promote forms of capitalistic organization new to Britain. Hitherto mines had been mainly small-scale, individually owned and worked by a handful of men. But as coal became less accessible and the costs of mining rose, so gradually control of collieries fell into the hands of larger and larger groups of men, associations better able to afford development. The split slowly developing between capital and labour deepened still further as mining enterprises employed salaried officials to supervise the work.

Above all, though, there was the enormous human cost of the growth of this industry: virtual slavery in Scotland, high risks of death from explosions, rock-falls or floods of water, and of course no compensation for the injured, maimed or deprived, the detritus of the coalfields. Miners had already gained a reputation for being tough, isolated, even brutish. They were 'desperate fellows', according to one contemporary spectator, 'which is seen by their attacking gaols to release any that are confined, but besides this . . . they know that ye kingdom cannot do without coals, and they know that other people cannot do their work'. That dependence, already strong, was to grow.

The Industrial Revolution, according to Professor Hobsbawm, marked the most fundamental transformation of human life in the history of the world. Cotton cities like Manchester multiplied tenfold in seventy years, their landscapes transfigured by mills five or six storeys high, towering over rows of squalid housing. A description of Manchester in 1814 records: 'The cloud of coal vapour may be observed from afar. The houses are blackened by it . . . the whole picture is a melancholic one.' In the first part of the Industrial Revolution, between 1770 and 1830, the output of coal quadrupled, not so much because of its use by industry, but rather because of its greater domestic use with the startling rise in the urban population that accompanied development. As late as 1842, two-thirds of all coal dug from British pits was burnt in the home. More people meant more hearths. But what of the impact of industrialization, as opposed to urbanization, on coal? Cheaper transport, following the opening of the first canal by the Duke of Bridgewater in 1761, as well as the development of new inventions, materials and processes, opened up a huge, new market for cheap finished goods, not only in Britain, but also, with the backing of government policies, worldwide. Nevertheless, despite the rapid changes in this period, cotton manufacturers did not adopt steam power as eagerly as is often thought. In fact even by 1838, one quarter of the industry's power was still provided by water. The really spectacular rise in the amount of coal mined, and its greatest impact on industry, were yet to come. Within a few years though, the transition of Britain to a fully industrialized country with enormous coal, iron and steel industries would be made.

Twenty-three million tons of coal were mined in 1830. By 1850, production had more than doubled. Six years later it had nearly trebled. By 1870, well over 100 million tons were mined each year, and at the end of the decade, the annual output of coal stood at 147 million tons. Within the space of half a century, coal was truly King and the men who were winning it had become politically and socially one of the most important and catalystic elements of the British working class.

Coal incubated its own revolution, for it was on the coalfields that the Railway Age began. The success of the Stockton and Darlington Railway, opened in 1825 by the Quakers to provide an outlet for Durham coal, attracted vast accumulations of capital gleaned from the first phase of industrialization. The dizzy height of railway mania was reached in 1846, when anyone with any savings at all joined in the boom, often putting money into ventures that even at the time were regarded as having little or no economic justification. Nonetheless the construction of the railways virtually created a steel industry and led to a huge increase in the demand for iron, all of which led to greater and greater need for coal. For coal, the railways provided the perfect market: it was fuel for the industry that built them, and power for the engines once they were finished.

The two decades after the Great Exhibition of 1851 were the zenith of Victorian prosperity. Solidly based on coal, industry grew at a rate that dwarfed anything that had gone before. The rise of iron manufacture was spectacular, following the development of the hot air blast and the steam hammer. Steel production was revolutionized by the invention of the Bessemer converter in 1850 and the open hearth furnace in the decade that followed. Factories turned more and more towards steam power and, after 1860, gas derived from coal became increasingly popular. Exports too expanded at an unprecedented rate, as other countries demanded the fruits of industrialization. Shipments of coal abroad rose from less than ¾ million tons in 1857 to over 13 million tons by 1873.

This era of prosperity lasted to the outbreak of the First World War. The figures for the production of coal show immense vitality: just over 110 million tons were dug in 1870 compared with more than 287 million tons in 1913, the largest amount of coal ever mined in one year. Exports of coal continued to rise too, from a little over 11 million tons in 1870 to over 73 million tons in 1913 or four-fifths of the volume of all British exports. Superficially, this performance is indeed impressive, yet with hindsight the harbingers of decline can only too well be seen, illustrating clearly the classic predicament of British industry in late Victorian times.

The consistently expanding demand for coal lulled the coal-owners into a sense of security about the future that did nothing to compel modernization and change. The huge increase in the output of coal up to 1913 was produced without the development of any significant labour-saving devices. True, improvements were made in the methods of conveying and winding coal, and in the ventilation of mines, but the actual cutting at the face was still done arduously by a naked or near-naked man hacking at the coal with a pick. The result was a startling fall in productivity. Despite an increase in the number of miners from approximately 200,000 in 1850 to well over a million by 1913, the amount of coal each man produced fell from an average of 319 tons a year in the early 1880s, to only 257 tons by 1913. By that date at least half, possibly two-thirds, of all coal mined in Britain came from pits planned before 1875, so that the miners were having to work progressively thinner and less productive seams. The fragmented ownership of the collieries also inhibited progress, as the multiplicity of small firms lacked the capital to develop a modern industry and instead indulged in a particularly senseless form of competition. For example, no agreement could be reached with the railways about a new double-sized coal-truck which had proved itself much more efficient than the existing one, because each company thought they would be taking too great a risk on something that would largely benefit the other. In the meantime, Britain's position as the world's main supplier of coal was becoming increasingly under threat from the coalfields of Germany and the United States, where amalgamations and rationalization were significantly much more common.

The First World War did nothing to arrest decline. The demand for coal was huge, yet colliery development was postponed, there were delays in obtaining plant and equipment, and, in the first year at least, a quarter of a million miners were enlisted into the armed forces. The more accessible and richer seams were worked furiously and left exhausted, and any incentive there might have been to modernize was taken away by the Government's decision to fix prices high enough to ensure that even the most inefficient colliery produced coal. The war did bring one important benefit to the miners, in the form of government intervention in the industry on a scale hitherto unprecedented. Decisions about coal production had become far too significant to be left to the numerous small coal-owners, and so by the end of the war they were left with only the day-to-day running of the pits as their responsibility. The miners found themselves with powers that were quite new to them. Growing unrest in the pits in 1915, and a short strike in South Wales, brought the personal intervention of Lloyd George and the virtual concession of all their demands. By 1918 they were involved in the management of the industry and were given flat-rate wage rises on a national as opposed to local level. Full well could the leader of the Welsh miners argue that 'the war drove us at least twenty-five years in advance of where we were in thought in 1914'.

But that situation was not to last long. In 1918 the miners asked for a substantial pay increase, a reduction in working hours and, arguing that the controls thought necessary in war were equally vital in peacetime, they declared that it was time for the industry to be nationalized. The Miners' Federation held a ballot to test opinion, and by a 5 to 1 majority the men voted in favour of a strike. Lloyd George was obviously worried about the consequences of the miners' decision, and persuaded them to delay while a Royal Commission looked into their claims. Judge John Sankey was given the task, and for the first time equal representation was given on a Royal Commission to both unions and employers. It is difficult to believe that anyone, least of all Lloyd George, expected a unanimous report, and in the event there wasn't one.

Sankey himself though, in the second part of his inquiry, made his recommendation clear: 'I recommend on the evidence before me that the principle of State ownership of the coal-mines be accepted.' Power would rest with a Minister of Mines, responsible to Parliament and advised by a standing committee of men who were elected by a National Mining Council. Six of the members of the standing committee would represent the workers, six the consumers and six the technical and commercial side of the industry. There would also be councils in each district, from whose members the National Mining Council would be drawn, and a local council to each pit. The reasons for his belief in nationalization were many, but were crystallized in one cardinal principle: 'Coal is our principal national asset, and as it is a wasting asset, it is in the interests of the State that it should be won and used to the best advantage.'

Nothing was done, and in March 1921 the collieries were returned to private ownership. Wage cuts were announced of a size that embarrassed even the Government, and when the miners understandably declined to accept them, the response from the owners was a lockout which began on 1 April 1921. The miners turned for support to the 'Triple Alliance' they had formed with the railwaymen and the transport workers. But having at first offered to go on strike, the other two unions went back on their word at the last moment, for reasons that they thought were perfectly fair. But the miners did not see it that way: the failure of the Triple Alliance was seen as a betrayal, and the day on which it happened – Friday, 15 April 1921 – went down in miners' history as 'Black Friday'. Left on their own, the miners were defeated and forced to accept the cuts in wages.

Events between 1922 and 1924 conspired to confirm the coal-owners' view that the wage cuts had worked wonders. Profits were at pre-war levels and exports were booming as never before. In fact, things were going so well that in 1924 a court of inquiry under Lord Buckmaster awarded the miners an increase in the minimum wage. What was largely ignored, though, was the fact that the coal industry's success was mainly due to the lack of competition in international markets. Germany's great coal-producing area, the Ruhr, had been occupied, and the United States coal industry had been hit by a strike. But once those two problems were solved, the British coal companies were exposed for the first time since the war as ageing and inadequate.

The turn-round from profit to loss was rapid. By the middle of 1925, about two-thirds of all collieries were operating at a loss, and a quarter of the industry's workforce was unemployed. Matters had been made even worse by the Government returning the pound to the Gold Standard, at the exchange rate that was good for very different conditions before the war. Our coal was now dearer than that of our competitors, so exporters had to lower the price or lose markets. Full well could Keynes argue that the miners were 'the victims of the economic juggernaut' engineered by the Treasury and the Bank of England.

The prescription of the coal-owners was depressingly familiar: they demanded a wage cut that would have effectively ended the minimum wage. This time the Trades Union Congress offered to support the miners, and the Government hastily came up with a compromise. A Royal Commission under Sir Herbert Samuel was set up to look at the future of the industry, and until it reported the Government agreed to subsidize the industry so that wages would stay the same. The day that this deal was announced, it was trumpeted as a victory for the miners – 'Red Friday', to assuage the memory of 1921.

The jubilation was shortlived. In March 1926, the Royal Commission gave its opinion. It recommended a lowering of wages to meet the immediate crisis, but in the longer term, at some unspecified date, amalgamations of colliery companies to derive the benefits from economies of scale. The coal-owners declared their opposition to any reorganization, but accepted the need for lower wages, and added a new demand for longer hours. It was obvious that the miners could not accept, so on 1 May 1926, the lockout began.

The General Council of the T.U.C. met the Prime Minister, Stanley Baldwin, and tried to persuade him to do something for the miners. But their negotiations broke down, and at midnight on 3 May, the General Strike began. At first it was a great success: large sections of British industry were paralysed, and the railways were at a standstill. But the response seems to have been too much for the General Council, who increasingly began to worry about the forces they had unleashed. They saw the gradual improvement of the Government's supply organization, and above all Baldwin's determination to defeat what he saw as an attack on the constitution. It was with some gratitude, therefore, that the T.U.C. seized on a memorandum produced by Sir Herbert Samuel, just back from holiday, which recommended wage reductions linked to firm guarantees for the reorganization of the industry. The memorandum carried no governmental authority whatsoever, was clearly anathema to the miners, and yet was accepted by the General Council of the T.U.C. The General Strike was over: the miners were on their own.

The wage cuts solved nothing. The longer hours only added to unemployment. The years of depression hit the miners much harder than any other section of the working class, and the hunger marchers were the living symbol of that. But for those lucky enough to keep a job in the pits, the future of the industry looked as black as the world outside. The pits were becoming more and more inefficient; the coal that they were producing was becoming less and less competitive. The colliery companies were too small, generally speaking, to carry out the sort of widespread changes that were necessary. Instead, they tried to load the burden of their inefficiencies onto the backs of the miners, by imposing wage cuts.

There were some attempts by the Government to encourage amalgamations and the setting up of cartels, but they achieved little. Their failure, and the failure of the industry, was shown most starkly in a report produced in 1936 by P.E.P. Its assessment was a devastating indictment of private enterprise and the suffering it had inflicted. The report showed that between 1913 and 1934, output per man-shift, a measure of productivity in coal mining, had increased in Poland by 63 per cent and in the Ruhr by 77 per cent; in Britain it had increased by just 7 per cent. One of the reasons for this dismal progress, said the report, was the failure to mechanize British pits. Collieries in the Ruhr won 97 per cent of their coal by mechanical means in 1934, compared with only 2 per cent in 1913. But by the same year, less than half of all the coal cut in Britain was won by machine. Another weakness, and, according to the report, a much more important one, was the small size of most of the colliery companies. In the mid 1930s there were still some 2,000 mines in Britain, raising an average yearly output of about 100,000 tons each. How could they compete successfully against pits like the German ones, which averaged just under a million tons a year, or the Dutch mines, which at that time averaged 2 million tons each?

Private enterprise had clearly failed, and the miners felt that the case for nationalization was now more unanswerable than ever. The Second World War helped to bring the demise of the coal-owners one step nearer. Coal production became so important to the war effort that the Government took full control over the mining and allocation of coal, though it left the day-to-day management of the pits in the hands of the owners. The workers were involved in the running of the industry by the formation of pit production committees, which were to help managers to secure the maximum possible output. This partial state control was not entirely successful, and how could it be? The industry was in a terrible state before the war even began, and a lot of power still rested with the colliery companies. But at least control by the Government made it very difficult for anyone except the coal-owners to contemplate a return to the previous state of affairs once the war was over. A report by the mining engineer, Charles (later Sir Charles) Reid, made such a move impossible.

The Reid Report declared: 'A vast programme of reconstruction of existing mines and the sinking of a number of new ones is now required.' Its final words were: 'There is no time to be lost.' The report said that the British mining industry had failed because it had been in a perpetual state of financial embarrassment and uncertainty about its future. Private ownership had resulted in an excessive number of ill-planned mines of inadequate capacity. Most of the colliery owners were opposed to amalgamations and had soured relations with their employees.

The report recommended fundamental changes in the layout of the majority of British pits, new methods of cutting the coal, increased use of machines and a 'revolutionary change' in the methods of hauling coal from the face to the surface. Central workshops serving groups of collieries were a necessity, and the surface areas of pits needed replanning. There should be a training scheme for new entrants into the industry, and ways should be found for managers to explain development plans and new ideas to the workforce. The mineworkers needed to have the security of an assured job and the knowledge that everything was being done to look after their health and safety. In return they should help to increase productivity and cut out unofficial strikes.

In fact, the Reid Report did not recommend nationalization. Reid believed that the existing colliery companies needed to be merged into units of greater and more efficient size. The conflicting interests of individual companies had to be brought together: 'A great pioneering task thus awaits the employer and the mining engineer, which is nothing less than the rebuilding of the industry on the most modern lines.'

The General Election of 1945 resulted in a government pledged to nationalize the coal industry. The Labour benches on 1 August 1945 were spilling over with euphoric M.P.s. As the Conservatives greeted their defeated leader with a chorus of 'For He's a Jolly Good Fellow', Labour backbenchers responded with 'The Red Flag'. The King's speech a fortnight later gave notice of a bill to establish public ownership of the coal industry, and on 19 December 1945 it was given a first reading. A year later, when the miners held their last conference under the old owners, the new General Secretary of the union, Arthur Horner, told the delegates:

I hope there will be an appreciation throughout the industry that things have changed, and that when you put the flags up on vesting day – when the flags go over the pits for the National Coal Board – it does mean something different. It is a tremendous change . . . it is not a change in name, it is a change that gives us the possibility of realizing things we have only dared dream about for years and years and years.

On 1 January 1947, control of the coal industry was vested in the National Coal Board.

For the whole of the first decade of its existence, the Coal Board could sell as much coal as it could produce. Coal was still in a virtual monopoly position as a supplier of fuel and power, and the demands on coal were enormous. But the Coal Board was also in an impossible situation, because as well as having to win as much coal as it could, it had at the same time to rebuild an industry which had been exhausted by decades of neglect.

An expansionary outlook dominated the Coal Board's thinking. In 1950, they published their 'Plan for Coal', which set out a programme of reconstruction for the industry. The plan showed that the Coal Board was aiming to produce 240,000,000 tons of coal a year by the early 1960s, which was about 43,000,000 tons more than when it took over. Six years later they revised their target a little, based on hard experience. In a new plan called 'Investing in Coal', they settled for a figure of 230,000,000 tons by the early 1960s. But their confidence in the future of coal was unshaken: 'The use of oil can be expected to continue to grow rapidly, and from 1960 onwards the nuclear power stations will begin to provide a new source of energy, but even in the longer term the problem of over-production of coal can scarcely arise.'

At the end of its first decade, the Chairman of the Coal Board, the former miners' leader Jim Bowman, wrote: 'Coal mining is not a Cinderella industry. It is the key to Britain's economic future.' He looked back with pride at the way that the Board had spent huge amounts of money on investment, well over £600 million in fact, and had made great progress with mechanization.

But although these trends were particularly encouraging, they were also having difficulties increasing the output of coal to match demand. One reason was the problem of attracting qualified men to join the industry. There was also the snag that pits that were relatively inefficient were kept in production simply to meet the incessant demands for coal. The result was a disappointing growth in productivity: output per man-shift grew by only about 14 per cent in the first decade, despite huge sums of investment. The figures for the amount of coal mined each year were equally disappointing. The annual production of coal rose in the first five years of nationalization to about 210 million tons, and thereafter stagnated. The shortfall was met by importing coal from abroad. By the mid 1950s it appeared more and more that coal was not capable of meeting the demands made upon it.

The pressure on coal meant that some large consumers looked elsewhere. The railways had been warned by the Ridley Committee in 1952 that they were wasting scarce fuel resources, and so, after a while, they began a programme to replace steam engines with diesels and, sometimes, electric locomotives. Electricity boards were also urged by the Government to convert power stations to burn oil instead of coal, and in 1955 they announced the details of the first programme of nuclear power stations to take some of the pressure off coal. What started as a slow shuffle soon became a stampede.

In 1957 the consumption of coal in Great Britain fell by just over 5,000,000 tons. The Coal Board shrugged their shoulders and said that a great deal of the fall was due to higher than average temperatures. There were also problems with the economy, people were using coal more efficiently, and some were turning to oil. Similarly, the Clean Air Act was beginning to have an impact on users. But all in all, the Board saw every reason to believe that the decrease in the consumption of coal was only a temporary setback.

The following year the demand for coal was lower still. For the first time since vesting day, the Coal Board decided to restrict their output: Saturday working was brought to an end and the recruitment of adult workers was in most cases stopped. But the Board continued to resist pressures to cut the productive capacity of the industry by closing pits on a large scale. They held talks with consumers about their future requirements and came up with a document called the 'Revised Plan for Coal'. The plan recognized that some of the hopes of three years earlier were not going to be met, but they still believed that by the mid 1960s Britain would need about 200 million tons of coal a year. But by the end of 1959 the total annual consumption of coal had fallen by over 30 million tons compared with three years earlier. Over the next couple of years it was to go up a bit, then down a bit, then up a little again. But the underlying trend was massively against coal.

The resulting fall in the production of coal was enormous. And the scale of the turn-around of the fortunes of coal seared the minds and vision of today's miners, as the hardships of the thirties did their fathers'. Statistics often blunt the edge of argument, but in this case they make the point as nothing else could. In 1957, just over 207 million tons of coal were brought out of Britain's pits. By 1965, the figure was 178 million tons. By 1970, it was just over 133 million tons. And by 1975, the total output from Britain's collieries stood at just 114·7 million tons. Over the same period, the number of pits had been reduced from 822 to 241, and the number of miners employed had fallen from 704,000 to 245,000. It was the most fundamental change the coal industry had ever undergone.

The proportion of Britain's fuel needs met by coal declined dramatically. After the war, nine-tenths of the country's energy came from coal: by the early 1970s, little more than a third did. The crown had been seized by oil. From the early 1950s, the price of oil had been falling, though there was a temporary respite in 1957 when the Suez Canal was blocked, and tankers had to make the longer trip around the Cape of Good Hope. But by 1960, the respective costs of oil and coal for electricity generation were almost the same. And as soon as coal lost its overwhelming price advantage, its many drawbacks became a very real handicap. Oil, for example, was cleaner than coal, easier to handle and had no ash to get rid of. Railways and industry shunned coal; householders put hardboard over their fireplaces, and warmed themselves in front of Magicoal fires. Only power stations increased their usage of coal. Successive governments tried to soften the blow, but nonetheless, by the early seventies, oil had become the dominant fuel in the British economy. The reign of King Coal, begun in the Industrial Revolution, had apparently come to an end.

Lord Robens, in his autobiography, quotes a senior official at the Ministry of Power as saying: 'You can forget about O.P.E.C. They will never amount to a row of beans.' A number of authoritative bodies, quite apart from the Coal Board and the N.U.M., had argued otherwise throughout the sixties and early seventies. In 1973, their beliefs were vindicated when the price of oil rose to levels hitherto unprecedented. In June 1970, the price of Saudi Arabian light crude oil was $1.80 a barrel. By the end of 1973, it had shot up to $11.65. The price of oil had risen more than five times, and for the economies of Western Europe, the era of cheap energy had gone for ever. And for the first time people began to ask, 'What happens when the oil runs out?'

The value of Britain's coal was suddenly transformed. The attitudes and policies that had dominated up to then were thrown out of the window. In the words of one expert from an oil company, it was the second coming of coal. Coal's new importance was recognized in the N.C.B.'s 'Plan for Coal', published in 1974, and agreed with the N.U.M. and the Government. The plan set in train a major investment programme to provide 42 million tons of new capacity by 1985. This would be done by extending the life of existing pits, and developing new collieries, for example at Selby in Yorkshire. Three years later another strategy was worked out, to see the industry through into the next century. 'Plan 2000' estimated that a reasonable figure for the demand for coal by the year 2000 was about 170 million tons, and to achieve that would require another substantial programme of investment. According to Sir Derek Ezra, the Chairman of the Board, the N.C.B. would have to undertake 'one of the most striking examples of industrial renewal in recent British economic history'.

More confirmation of the return of King Coal came in 1980 with the publication of a massive international report on the future of coal. The report argued that coal production throughout the world could increase by up to 200 per cent by the end of the century. Coal would be a 'bridge to the future', a resource that would get the world through the energy shortages that could threaten every economy in every country by the year 2000.

In this respect, Britain is particularly well placed. There are proved, workable reserves which are sufficient for 300 years, even at faster rates of production. At the same time, new technologies are being developed which will increase the potential use of coal. The fluidized bed combustion of coal, for example, will result in the burning of coal in a vastly more efficient manner in power stations and factories. The rise in the price of oil has also brought about a renewed interest in the synthetic production of fuels made from coal. As oil becomes more scarce and even more expensive, coal will also become more important in the production of chemicals. Few would doubt, in the midst of all this, that the future for coal in Britain is secure.

But will Britain meet the challenge? In the midst of confidence there is uncertainty. Developing coal takes a long time and is expensive. Will the present Government support the industry to carry out the investment it needs if coal is to be a major energy source for the future? At present the Government appears intent on withdrawing the operating grants to coal-mining in Britain, at a time when every other country is pouring money into development. Will the Government revive the mistakes of the sixties and early seventies, and base the future of our energy supplies on short-term considerations? Ordinary miners today are fearful that a new round of closures is about to be foisted upon them, just as in the 1960s. They wonder why, and come to the gloomy conclusion that it must be retribution for their victories of 1972 and 1974. At a time when the world outlook for coal is better than it has ever been, has Britain learnt the lessons of its past?

2. The Colliery

Almost every outsider who has been down a pit comes up and declares: 'Pay them whatever they ask.' At the end of a visit it would be an exceedingly fit person who was not completely exhausted. A little later comes the realization that at most he has spent only four hours underground; he has done no work and has simply been a spectator. Apart from that, the overriding need is for water, tea, beer – anything to quench a very strong thirst – and then for cleanliness. But even after a long shower, there is still a smell of coal, and dust stays in the nose, dirtying handkerchiefs for some days afterwards. Once back on the surface, it is almost impossible to relate the sunshine, green fields, trees and houses, to the work, the noise and dirt far below. Orwell, when he visited a pit, was left with an over-powering memory of hell: 'Most of the things one imagines in hell are there – heat, noise, confusion, darkness, foul air, and, above all, unbearably cramped space.' Therein lies the claim of the miners to be always a special case.

The day begins with a change of clothes. In the last couple of years, the N.C.B. have decided to supply men with a complete outfit for underground wear; boots, bright orange boiler suit, gloves, knee-pads, helmet and belt. In the lamp room, a self-rescuer is clipped to one side of the belt. It is heavy and cumbersome, but contains a mask that converts carbon monoxide into carbon dioxide in the event of a fire, and could keep a man alive for about an hour. On the other side of the belt is hung a heavy battery, which provides the power for the lamp that is clipped to the helmet.

The top of the shaft is reached through two doors that act as an airlock to control the circulation of air below. Inside, at the pit top or the 'bank', each man is issued with two brass tokens. One is handed in, and the other kept until the end of the shift so that if there is an accident an immediate tally can be made of those still missing. It is a salutory reminder, if one was needed, of the dangers of mining. Each man is searched for contraband; no cigarettes or matches are allowed, so many chew tobacco or take snuff. All carry snap-tins containing sandwiches, and water-bottles, whose contents are treasured as gold.

The cage is an iron box, with two or three levels to it, each with rails to take the mine-cars for which it was designed. It is impossible to stand up straight inside, and when a shift is being wound up or down they are very crowded. Bells ring. The gates slam shut and the cage drops a little. The next level is loaded, then more bells. A certain pattern of ringing means that men are being wound. The cage begins to drop fast and the air rushes past. But it is only when someone shines a light on the side of the shaft that the real speed of the descent can be appreciated. After about a minute of blackness, lights go past, and the cage comes to a halt. It bounces up and down gently: apparently it is quite natural for the steel rope to give a little. The cage has overshot, explains somebody. More bells, and the cage moves slowly up to the level of the pit bottom.

Dangling over a hole hundreds of feet deep is an experience that has its dangers. In 1973 a pit cage at Markham Colliery in Derbyshire plunged to the bottom of a 1,400-foot shaft. Eighteen men were killed and eleven seriously injured. The consultant at Chesterfield Royal Hospital told an inquiry that there were injuries the like of which they had never seen before: 'One man had his tibia driven right through the sole of his foot.' On the day of the disaster, the M.P. Eric Varley overheard a journalist asking a miner whether he had any comment to make. 'Yes,' came the reply. 'Remember this day when our next pay claim comes round.'

At pit bottom, a warm wind blows. There are offices belonging to deputies and other officials, as well as workshops for fitters and electricians, and the Deployment Board which tells men where they'll be working. From there, roadways lead off into the pit. The actual coal-face, though, is still some way off. In some pits the men walk to the face, but more usually they catch a paddy-train hauled by a locomotive or by rope. Even then, there could still be a long walk. Because so much time is often spent in travelling underground, a man may work for only five hours actually at the face. He cannot by law work any longer because there is a legal restriction on the number of hours any man may work below ground.

Coal is mined by driving two parallel roadways, or 'gates' as they are called, out into the seam. The coal-face runs between the ends of the two gates, a distance of possibly two hundred yards. In what is called 'retreat' mining, the roadways are driven sometimes for miles in to the seam, and then coal is worked by cutting back towards the start. Otherwise, the gates are driven out roughly in line with the coal-face. One of the roadways, called the 'main gate', is used to carry all the coal away to the pit bottom. The other roadway, at the opposite side of the face, is called the 'tailgate'. The machine that cuts the coal moves along the face, on top of an armoured conveyor belt. As it cuts, so the coal is loaded on to the conveyor below. Once the cutter-loader has travelled the length of the face, the whole lot, including the conveyor belt, is moved forward ready for the next cut. The roof is kept up by hydraulic supports. Once the cutter has gone by, the collier lowers them and then moves them forward using powerful rams. Once they are in their new position, they are raised until they are tight against the roof once again. The roof of the open space that they have left behind is left to collapse under its own weight.

It sounds straightforward, but of course it's not. There are many things that can interrupt the smooth flow of coal from the face, not least being the unpredictability of the coal measures ahead. Even where the lie of the land is fairly well known, there could be faulting: the seam could split or narrow down drastically. Similarly the response of the roof as the coal is being cut is highly unpredictable, as the blue scars on many colliers' arms and backs bear witness. The blue colour is caused by the coaldust congealing into the scab of a wound.

The face is very hot and very noisy. As the shearer runs its course it sprays the coal with water in an attempt to keep the dust down, but there is still a colossal amount in the air. A good circulation of air is necessary to remove methane, which is present in every measure of coal, and dust and heat. Obviously the faster a machine works on the face, the more heat is produced, the more gas comes out of the coal and the more dust is created. If the levels of dust or gas go beyond certain specified limits, then the face has to stop work. Air is therefore drawn down one of the pit's two shafts, called the downcast shaft, along one of the roadways to the face. The air then crosses the coal-face, back along the other parallel roadway to the pit bottom where it is sucked up the upcast shaft by giant fans. An elaborate system of air crossings and ventilation doors ensures that the circulation works efficiently. Despite all this, it is still very hot.

The height of the face of course varies from pit to pit and area to area. And it is surprising how men seem to get used to even the most cramped conditions. One miner, for example, started work in the Barnsley area in a seam eighteen inches high. He had to work either flat on his back or on his stomach. But when his pit closed, and he went to work in a four foot seam, he was nervous at having so much room above him while he worked. The amount of space for working in is lower than the height of the seam. Machinery and hydraulic props take up some of the height. Miners develop a half-stoop, half-crawl method for getting along the face if it is a very low one. As a result, many suffer from a form of housemaid's knee, made worse by the fact that the straps from the knee-pads cut into the back of the legs.

One of the most difficult and arduous jobs on the coal-face involves hollowing out a chamber in the coal seam to take the cutter-loader and the conveyor when it advances forward ready for the next cut of coal. Because the men are working in front of the face, the ventilation is very restricted and the heat and noise combine to make the environment exceedingly inhospitable. The chamber they hollow out is called the 'heading', and it is supported by steel girders set on hydraulic props. But far better to let the miners themselves tell the story. This was the evidence given by one faceworker to the Wilberforce Inquiry in 1972. His description of the work he does, it is no exaggeration to say, shocked the nation; his name was Jack Collins and he was from the Kent coalfield. He described conditions at the new pit he had moved to two years previously.

I am working at a pit which is much hotter than the previous one. Indeed, the men at the pit where I now work wear no clothes at all when working. This was unusual to me when I went there because I was used to working in short trousers, but eight out of ten men in the headings work with absolutely no clothes on because of the heat and, because of the amount of sweating they do, they have to drink a lot of water. Many, many men at Snowdown Colliery drink eight pints of water a day and the Coal Board has provided them with salt tablets to put in the water to stop them getting whatever they are supposed to get by drinking a lot of water.

This is a way of encouraging the men to work in hot conditions rather than improving the conditions in the pits. What I have said is no exaggeration. It is there for everybody to see at any time. Since the advent of nationalization in the industry, the amount of dust which is in the places of work has to be seen to be believed. Dust suppression methods are used but in many cases they are not effective. I work with a dust respirator to stop the dust from going into my lungs but a number of men do not wear these masks.

At the same time as the coal is being cut and the headings excavated, other men are working to make sure that the roadways keep up with the progress of the face. The roadways obviously need to be much higher than the face and the only way to do this is by tearing down the roof, or 'ripping', as it's called. It is one of the most dangerous and heavy jobs in the pit. If the stone above the coal is particularly hard then it has to be blasted down: holes are bored into the rock using powerful drills, the holes are charged with explosives and then fired by a 'shotfirer'. The sound, in such a confined space, is deafening, and rock is flung through the air like shrapnel. The rippers then resume their work pulling down loose stone from the roof, making sure they move very quickly if unexpected bits fall down. They then assemble the girders, packing and timber that are used to protect the roadway. In the majority of cases where the rock is softer, huge machines with a cutting head mounted on the front of a telescopic boom bore up into the rock: in front of these machines a series of mechanical scoops takes up the debris and moves it backwards out of the way. Once more the noise and dust and heat are tremendous.

The facemen are the highest paid in the pit. They're the élite. But they depend on other underground workers like the haulage men for keeping them in supplies. They also rely on the men, many of them older workers, who do the dangerous job of repairing the roadways away from the face, where the earth has tried to reclaim them. And as mechanization has come to dominate underground life, so they have also come to depend on skilled craftsmen, like the fitters and electricians whose numbers have grown so greatly since nationalization. A mistake by any of the face team or the back-up men could, at the very least, bring production to a halt. The cause could be the failure of a machine or the breakage of the main conveyor belt. The worker may find himself idle for no fault of his own. At worst, mistakes underground can cause loss of life.

One of the great secretaries of the miners' union, Arthur Horner, had this to say: 'One Sunday, somebody left a ventilator door open in the Glynmeal level, and my grandfather, going in at evening to examine the pit, was blown to pieces by an explosion. They collected his remains with a rake, and brought him back home in a sack.' Other members of his family were also crippled by coal: 'My uncle worked in the mines until his back was broken by a fall of roof. Another uncle went nearly blind with nystagmus. I learned very early that there was blood on the coal.'

Although safety has improved considerably since those days, men are still getting killed and badly injured every year. And with mechanization, the types of injuries have changed: men are more liable to lose a finger or a hand. This is the story of one accident that I doubt ever made even the local paper. It is told by David Sim, a faceworker at Highgate Colliery in Yorkshire, writing in *Essays from the Yorkshire Coalfield*, a compilation of work done by miners on a day-release course at Sheffield University. His essay is entitled 'The day I will never forget': he had been cleaning up spillage:

I was just getting to my feet when there was an almighty crash. I was sent sprawling across the armoured conveyor, which luckily was stood still at the time. Coal and stone buried me to above my waist. Men came rushing to my aid, they were tearing at the debris to free me. One asked, 'Are you all right, what happened?' I didn't know if I was all right or what had happened. I was still wondering what the hell had hit me. My first reaction was to put my helmet back on, which had been knocked off my head. Whilst I was collecting my thoughts, the debris around my waist and thighs had been removed, leaving my legs buried below the knees. One of the men went to the back of me. He put his forearms under my armpits and intertwined his fingers across my chest. 'Now then Dave,' he said, 'as I pull, you push with your feet.' He pulled with all the strength he could muster but I couldn't push. 'It's no good, my right leg is trapped, I can't move it,' I explained. 'A couple of us will have to move the biggest lump,' someone suggested. This was promptly done and it revealed a prop laid across my ankle. These props extend to eight feet in height and are very heavy, they must weigh well over one hundred pounds. The prop was lifted and there, turned completely round, was my foot. Gasps of astonishment were emitted by my rescuers when they saw the extent of the damage. Whispered comments were passed around such as, 'Christ that's bad, he might never walk again. He'll be lucky if they don't take his foot off.' None of these comments were doing much to boost my morale. After staring at my foot for what seemed like a decade, my first comment was: 'I've heard of ten to two feet, but three o'clock feet are beyond a bloody joke.'

Sim was off work for six months with a badly fractured foot. There is no union official who cannot tell of such injuries and the subsequent claims for compensation. All are sad, but some are more sad than others. In 1980 at North Gawber pit in Barnsley, the branch secretary, Albert Frost, had to deal with the case of a fifty-nine-year-old man just coming up for retirement after a lifetime in the industry. On the first day back after the pit's annual holiday, a stone fell from the roof and hit him on the head. He fell to the floor but somehow got himself onto a stretcher that had been brought. They carried him out of the pit and into the intensive care ward of the local hospital. His upper and lower jaw had been broken, five ribs had been smashed and both his eyes had been crushed. He told Frost that his wife was in hospital to have cataracts on her eyes removed, and he had told her only the night before, 'Don't worry, I'll look after you when I retire in July.'

In 1950, with on average 691,000 men employed in the industry, there were 476 fatal accidents and nearly 2,000 reportable accidents. In 1979/80, with over 233,000 men employed in the industry, there were thirty deaths and 456 men seriously injured, many of the fatalities or injuries occurring either in front of the powered supports on the face or at the end of the face during ripping or excavation of a heading. But, perhaps surprisingly, most of the fatalities and serious accidents during the seventies have occurred during haulage and transport underground. At Bentley Colliery in November 1978, for example, a paddy-train ran out of control killing seven men and seriously injuring three. In December 1979, three lives were lost when mine-cars ran out of control at the Kinsley drift mine. A spark from a piece of electrical equipment ignited an explosive mixture of firedamp and air in an inadequately ventilated roadway at Golborne Colliery in Lancashire in March 1979. Ten men died, some of them after failing to recover from horrific burns. Many accidents also happen on the surface, less dramatic maybe, but just as serious.

And the toll can go on. This is how Alec Wilkinson, a coal-face worker at Houghton Main Colliery in Yorkshire, described the tragedy at his pit on the morning of 12 June 1975 in *Essays from the Yorkshire Coalfield*. Six men were unaccounted for after a terrific explosion underground. Wilkinson was one of the men who volunteered to go underground and help the rescue team:

As we walked across the pit yard, to the No. 2 shaft, cap lamps and respirators already being collected, we saw one of the missing men, Ken Upperdine, had been found and brought to the surface. He was alive, but only just. His hands and face were very badly burned and he was suffering from numerous broken bones. Ken's family had lived next door to my own all through my childhood. He is a pleasant, homely man and I pray to God that he will be all right. When we did arrive at the shaft side we were told we would be needed for stretcher bearing. That was the job of bringing the injured or dead from the scene of the incident underground and transporting them into one of a fleet of waiting ambulances which were queuing up on the colliery surface.

The rescue teams, who were already down the pit, had established a fresh air base where it was safe to proceed to without using breathing apparatus. As we travelled 'inbye' from the pit bottom, we could not help but notice the thick black dust which had settled over the full length of the paddy road, and we told ourselves that no one could possibly have survived what must undoubtedly have been a living nightmare; but then Ken Upperdine was still alive, so hope was not all gone.

No sooner, though, had we arrived at the fresh air base, when we were struck by the full force of the most horrifying experience of our lives; a dead workmate. At first we did not know who he was, as he lay covered up by a dark blanket and strapped to a stretcher. I remember someone asking who it was and I replied that I didn't want to know. Six of us were then detailed by the doctor to take the dead man out of the pit. As we were waiting for the paddy to take us to the pit bottom, we were informed that the motionless body underneath the blanket was that of Dick Bannister. Dick was one of the nicest men a person could have wished to know; a handsome, strapping young man who would go out of his way to help anyone; but alas, all help for Dick had vanished. He had been found ten yards the wrong side of air doors, ten yards from breathable air, probably ten yards from safety, ten bloody yards.

After placing the stretcher on the paddy, the six of us who had been sent off with Dick could not help but stare at the lifeless bundle. One of my mates was actually physically sick, but what could we do, the job had to be done. When we reached the surface, we lifted our dead workmate into a waiting ambulance, while at the same time being blinded by television camera lights and the flashing of photographers' bulbs. The six of us then returned down the mine and travelled on the paddy-train back to the fresh air base. As we reached the far end, we could see numerous cap lamps in the distance and we knew that someone else had been found. Sure enough, when they reached us, we could see that they were bearing a stretcher with another dead body upon it. My younger brother, along with five colleagues, had been landed with the gruesome job of taking the badly mutilated body of Alvin Lakin, a colliery deputy, out of the pit. Alvin had been a God-fearing man who always carried a small Bible down the mine with him. He was noted for the way in which he read his 'book' when he had any spare time, and even after his body had been removed, the tattered pages of his once-proud possession were still to be found, rustling in the air which had earlier turned foul on him.

We were then told to wait at the fresh air base while the Mines Rescue Teams carried out their search for the three missing men. The night dragged on. Every time a rescue team – who must rank among the bravest on God's earth – emerged through the door which divided safety from danger, expectations of good news died as quickly as they had been born. Then came the news we had all been waiting for. A part time rescue team had found the dead body of Raymond Copperwheat, check number 715. Exactly one hour later, I saw my last rescue team emerge from that gateway to hell. The news that they carried was the kind of news no one likes to hear, but nevertheless has to be heard. Len Baker, an electrician, and Arni Williamson, a deputy, had been found dead. One rescue man said that they looked as though they had just fallen to sleep. Another, a young lad, experiencing his first taste of the real thing, broke down weeping. Who could blame him, we all felt the same way.

That was a disaster at Houghton Main. In 1973 seven miners were killed when an inrush of water from old workings swamped part of Lofthouse Colliery in Yorkshire. In the sixties, South Wales suffered three major disasters. Forty-five men died in an underground explosion at Six Bells Colliery near Abertillery in 1960. Five years later Cambrian Colliery was the scene of a blast that killed thirty-one miners, highlighting once more the problems of inadequate ventilation. And there were more: Seafield Colliery, Fife; Michael Colliery, Fife; Cardowan Colliery, Lanarkshire; Auchengeich Colliery, Lanarkshire; all pits that suffered the horror of a disaster.

Perhaps the worst disaster of them all, though, was at Aberfan. At quarter past nine in the morning of Friday, 21 October 1966, part of one of the huge waste tips that dominated the village began to move. Many thousands of tons of waste were turned to a mud flow by streams below the tip. With incredible speed the local primary school was engulfed, as well as some houses nearby. One hundred and forty four people died, and most of them were little children. South Wales, the whole of Britain, the whole of the world, in fact, reacted with horror. Who could forget the television pictures of coats hung up in the cloakroom never to be claimed? The National Coal Board accepted full responsibility, and began removing and landscaping waste tips.

Disasters rightly concentrate the attention of the public and media alike. The problem is that tragedies on a smaller scale, but tragedies nonetheless, are passed by. Pneumoconiosis, by no means the only health risk miners take, is one such example. It is caused by dust in the air which leads to what the Americans call 'black lung'. Old miners, especially in South Wales, suffer from it; in milder cases they can be seen stopping half-way up the stairs to get their breath back; in bad cases, the men are put on to respirators. Eventually they die. Although it is generally accepted that mechanization causes greater dust, there are strong indications that the prevalence of the disease is being reduced. In 1969, for example, 629 new cases were diagnosed, whereas in 1978 there were 476 new cases reported. Compensation has also been improved with the introduction of a lump sum payment to sufferers. But although there is a statutory limit on the amount of dust allowed in the air, there are fears among many miners that, despite improvements, the limit is still too high, and the more machines are used, the higher the amount of dust produced.

In March 1930, a large colliery in the anthracite area of the South Wales coalfield selected a football team for the championship matches. They were all colliers noted for their strength and skill. The condition of the team thirteen years later showed the impact of disease and injury on the miner. The story was told in Margot Heinemann's book, *Britain's Coal*. And this was the state of the eleven in 1943:

Goal Keeper	Age 37. Buried in 1937 under a fall of roof. Injured spine and fractured pelvis. Alive, but will never be able to walk again.
Right Back	Age 41. Total incapacity due to silicosis.
Left Back	Age 34. Buried by a fall in 1934. Only able to perform light work on surface.
Right Half	Age 42. Partial incapacity due to silicosis.
Centre Half	Age 42. Total incapacity due to silicosis.
Left Half	Age 40. Total incapacity due to silicosis.
Right Wing	Age 40. Total incapacity due to silicosis.
Inside Right	An exceptionally good workman and strong. Always willing to work the wettest places. At the age of 25 he contracted rheumatic fever and died.
Centre Forward	Age 42. Total incapacity due to silicosis.
Inside Left	Age 33. Partial incapacity due to silicosis.
Left Wing	Age 36. Buried by a fall of roof. Injured his spine and will never be able to work underground again.

But what, you may wonder, about those left behind, in particular the wives? The feelings and fears of one woman were expressed most eloquently during the 1974 dispute in a letter to the *Sheffield Star*. She lived in Wath-on-Dearne and preferred to sign herself 'Miner's wife':

Not being brought up in a mining family, I used to wonder why my husband was always tired, but have realized since that miners can sit in a chair and drop to sleep anytime. As well as this, the health hazards are so numerous. Athlete's feet can never be cured when a man has to wear socks thick with coal dust every day. Boils are caused through working in water which my husband says 'burns'. Gloves which are worn now hold coal dust, sweat and cause dermatitis. Very few miners get through their working lives without accidents – my husband had at least four. Many of these leave a blue disfigurement and I have seen my husband ashamed to bathe on holidays because of the marks on his body.

A miner's job even affects the work his wife can do. In my case I have worked most of the years we have been married but tried to work the hours convenient for us both. Is it fair for a man to get up at 4.30 a.m., do a hard manual shift and then come home at 2.30 p.m. to no dinner and no fire on cold winter days?

Under these working conditions it is not surprising that the union has developed in the strongly political way that it has. A powerful union was necessary to secure better working conditions as well as higher wages. Today, the centre of union activity in the pit is the 'union box', an office generally tucked away in some colliery outbuilding. The box can be the scene of some friendly talks about nothing in particular, or the door can burst open revealing two or three strapping colliers swearing about some change in the task they have been set. The rows can be intense. A branch official, usually the secretary, sits down and tries to calm things down by taking names, what happened, when, and where.

Each lodge, or branch, has a committee whose members are elected each year. Every union member can vote in the ballot, which is secret. The branch officers hold the real power, and, generally speaking, they are elected every two years. In practice they are difficult, though not impossible, to remove once they are voted in. Of the four posts of president, secretary, treasurer and delegate, it is the secretary who is the most important.

All of them face grumbles about only being in the job for what they can get for themselves. The secretary and the delegate, in particular, have to travel away from the pit a fair amount on union business, or take a regular shift to ensure that they can carry out their duties. The secretary and the delegate represent the pit at area council meetings where decisions are taken which are binding on the area officials of the union. They can get a rough ride from the men if, when they report back to a pit meeting, the men do not like what has been decided. The secretary is more than just a union official. Certainly he deals with all the nagging disputes, problems and worries of the men he represents. He negotiates with the manager, and at the same time has to keep in close touch with opinion within the pit. That alone is a time-consuming and exposed job. But on top of that he is the focus and the anchor of the whole mining community. He has got to deal with problems involving injured miners or miners' widows. He will be the person who goes visiting pensioners and their dependants. The N.U.M. branch secretary, even after the many changes of recent years, still fulfils a role much akin to that of a priest in medieval England.

To outsiders, mining communities are still objects of legend, mystery and even awe. It is not so much that pit villages are geographically isolated, but rather that the pit, and the type of work done there, dominates lives in a way that few other jobs do. Mining is always uncomfortable and dangerous, and the nature of the work binds men together: at the face, for example, teamwork is essential. This, and the very act of going underground into a world that most outsiders cannot understand or comprehend, adds to the social isolation of mining communities.

The shift system also lessens the chances of contact with people from outside the pit. The so-called day shift begins at six o'clock in the morning, and ends at a quarter to two. As anyone who has ever got up in the morning at five o'clock for five days a week will bear witness, it is not a habit that encourages enthusiasm for work. The afternoon shift, or 'afters', is between two o'clock and nine forty-five in the evening and rules out most social life. And finally there is the night shift which, by definition, cuts people off from the normal flow of events. Many men work one of each of these shifts over a three-week period, and this is particularly exhausting. The end result, though, is a tendency only to meet other mining people.

Again, whilst recognizing that generalization in this sort of field can be dangerous, the social centre of mining communities still tends to be the miners' welfare, or working men's clubs. Miners and their wives tend to meet there, along with men who have retired and remember very different days. Mining communities are additionally united by strong family ties. There are traditions binding fathers and sons to certain pits. An outsider who has never worked in the industry before will be welcomed, but will never have the respect accorded to someone whose family has been in mining for several generations. One branch secretary in South Wales held the position his father held before him and his father's father before that.

And beyond all that there is the shared history of mining: the way in which the victory of 1972 can be seen as retribution for the defeat of 1926. There can be few other groups so knowledgeable or obsessed, with good cause, about their history. Even though the coal-owners lost their power over thirty years ago, memory of their great misdeeds is fresh. Old miners recount their memories of appalling conditions under private enterprise, and their stories fire the minds of many miners today. Only because the history of mining is so bad do the reminders of it still have such importance. And it is far too easy for outsiders to criticize this sense of history as a desire to fight the battles of the past. One branch secretary told of how he delighted in reading branch minutes of a century ago, written out in beautiful copperplate handwriting. One entry concerned the ordering of a new banner: 'There will be Christ upon it, with children all around and cherubs with pink bottoms.' To him, he was sharing a joke with predecessors whose outlook had been so appalling, compared with his own.

To add to the apartness, each coalfield, even each pit, has its own language and culture. Conversations between miners from different areas can often become very heated over some technicality, until they discover that they are calling the same thing by a different name. Such conversations are inevitably incomprehensible to the outsider.

The result is sometimes hostility. Malcolm Pitt, in his excellent book on the Kent coalfield, describes how, when the collieries first opened, notices went up in Deal saying 'Rooms to let – miners need not apply' or 'No miners or dogs allowed'. Another famous headline in a newspaper read 'Miner in fight with man'. The nineteenth-century image of the irresponsible, hard-drinking, foul-mouthed miner lives on, even today. Although the big strikes have made a great deal of difference, the general public are still not certain what to expect from a miner. It was no accident that, during the 1974 strike, the railwaymen asked the miners to wear their helmets when mounting a picket; that was what was expected of miners.

Another outside view which reinforces a lack of understanding comes from the intensely political nature of the union. Yorkshire miners, for example, are always 'militant', and therefore, one assumes, waiting for the revolution around the corner. This ignores the fact that almost all of them belong to the Labour Party and care not one jot for being branded along, maybe, with assorted Trotskyists.

Part of the trouble is that they are seen by many in the Labour movement as 'the vanguard of the proletariat'. One senior Labour ex-cabinet-minister went so far as to say that if barricades were put up to protect Transport House, he would feel safe if he knew the miners were shoulder to shoulder with him. But how much do the rest of the trade union movement and the Labour Party really know of them? At the time of the 1972 and 1974 strikes, the answer was very little. Trade union leader after trade union leader was asked what he thought the miners were up to, and each time the reply was a shrug of the shoulders and the confession that he didn't know: 'They keep themselves to themselves.' An anecdote about Gormley's behaviour at one particular T.U.C. General Council meeting makes the point. He wandered in late, with his hat on, and sat down. He withdrew a crumpled up bit of paper from his top pocket, gave his views and left.

And the other great paradox about miners is this. They will describe at length the horrors and hardship of mining. They will encourage and even plead with their sons to find another job. Yet at the same time there can be no other group that would fight as hard for their traditions, collieries, colleagues and industry.

3. The Struggle for Unity

The demonstration made its way from the N.U.M. offices through the town centre to Locke Park, where, during the afternoon, men and their families were offered such attractions as a competition to find 'Miss Miners' Lamp', tag wrestling and a fashion show organized by the Co-op, and where political speeches vied with the beer tent for drawing the biggest crowd. The excitement was occasioned by the Yorkshire Miners' demonstration and Gala, which in this particular year was held in Barnsley. At no other time is the power, unity and strength of the miners so readily apparent. At the head of the march were two mounted policemen, followed by the officials of the Yorkshire N.U.M. and their guests. Behind them came men from every colliery in Yorkshire, each group led by a band and a banner. Those who, clinging to stereotypes, would expect to see the procession filled with brass bands, would not be disappointed, but increasingly the men are marching to new, more brash musical phenomena: the so-called jazz bands. These owe little to New Orleans and much to the efforts of the union to try to discourage the historically high levels of drinking and foster an atmosphere more fitting for the family. Led by teenage drum-majorettes covered in badges, these bands consist of children in identical smart uniforms playing pop-songs on kazoos to the accompaniment of drums. The music is nasal and has none of the stirring qualities of the old brass bands, but the children enjoy what they're doing. Behind them are the banners, suspended between two poles fixed into tubular steel trolleys equipped with rubber wheels. Five or six men push each contraption along while four men, one on each corner, hold ropes that run to the top of the poles to keep the banners upright in gusts of wind. Behind the banner, at a distance that allows it to be seen at its best, march the pit committee, followed by the men

48

and their families. As they walk through the streets, people wave flags and sticks with strips of coloured paper on the end. Greetings or humorous insults are traded with colleagues or friends standing on the pavements. The sheer numbers of people taking part, and the very act of marching together with men from all over the coalfield, gives an immense feeling of unity and power. The banners themselves are the pride of each pit, almost a religious relic confirming the continuity of history. All are brilliantly coloured. Some stress the struggle for better conditions, a couple show union officials in a graveyard comforting a bereaved family, others great mining leaders from the past. All proclaim the theme of strength through unity. But it was not always so. The unity of the N.U.M. today was hard won from the internecine struggles that only ended formally in 1945. The grey gothic towers of the offices of the miners' union in Barnsley, where the march began, bears witness to a time when district associations held power, and national unity was a dream.

Trade unionism in the mines was born of a struggle unparalleled in any other industry. The bitter relationship between men and coal-owners, which many outside the industry, including other trade unionists, found difficult to understand, came from a history of ruthless strike-breaking and oppression. The first systematic strike by the miners was in the middle of the seventeenth century. It arose out of the custom of the colliery owners of the Tyne and Wear to hire men each autumn for a year, and whilst they did not guarantee them work, the men had to report to the pit whenever asked. As if this wasn't bad enough, in 1765 the owners tried to impose an even more rigorous form of bonding. In a remarkable act, 4,000 miners came out on strike, and stayed out until they won. The miners of Tyne and Wear had shown the powers of combination, but it was a victory before its time.

The Combination Laws of 1799 and 1800 stilled further protest. The laws made it illegal for workmen to join together to demand more pay or better conditions, but, despite their draconian nature, it is certain that some trade unions continued to exist as secret clubs or disguised as friendly societies, and there were still sporadic disputes, most notably in Somerset and Durham. Nonetheless, the repeal of the Combination Laws in 1824 brought forth a flowering of trade unions where none was supposed to have existed.

The scene was now set for the really big battles between embryonic unions and the colliery owners. In 1830, for example, a miner called Thomas Hepburn formed a union in the North East and called a strike over a claim for better conditions. Despite the support of special constables, the local militia and marines from Portsmouth, the owners capitulated. But the miners' victory was shortlived. In 1832, the owners began to evict old employees and bring in new men from outside. There was a great deal of violence, during which a magistrate was dragged from his horse and beaten to death, and, in a separate incident, a miner who was trying to restore order was shot and killed by a special constable. The union was effectively destroyed and Hepburn was forced to walk the roads looking for work.

There was a violent struggle in South Wales too, caused by the system of the 'tommy shop', whereby instead of owners paying their men in cash, they paid them in goods which had to be bought at the company shop. There was a meeting to discuss a strike to end this feudal arrangement, and troops were called in to break it up. But the miners attacked the soldiers, disarmed them, and sent them packing. A week later though, they returned, and hanged the leader of the strike, Dic Penderyn. Unionism was then ruthlessly suppressed by the colliery owners in South Wales, and so strong were these measures that a secret society, calling itself 'Scotch Cattle', developed to fight evictions and black-legging.

The same fate befell the first attempt to form a national mining trade union. The Mining Association of Great Britain, started in 1841, was based on the county unions that had grown up in the northern coalfields in the 1830s. In 1844, it felt strong enough to take on the owners in Northumberland and Durham coalfields over the issue of the annual bond. Every single pit in the two counties went on strike. The mine-owners, led by the Marquis of Londonderry, used every possible method to end the dispute – intimidation, scab labour, evictions and gangs to 'tough up' strikers. In the end the unity of the miners was broken. The Mining Association eventually disappeared during the economic crisis of 1847–8 and its leader, Martin Jude, died in 'very abject circumstances'.

Nevertheless, unionism in the mines survived. At pit level, the focus for trade union activity in this period was the checkweighman. The Coal Mines Regulation Act of 1860 enforced the custom of electing a man to check the tubs of coal when they were weighed to ensure that the colliery company did not cheat the men of some of their money. Around him grew the miners' lodge, and out of these grew broader unions, sometimes based on a district, sometimes on a county. But could these bodies, locally based, form themselves into a strong national union?

In the late 1850s there were attempts to revive the idea of a national union. Foremost in this campaign was a remarkable man called Alexander MacDonald. He had started work in the pit at the age of eight, and yet managed to educate himself in his spare time, so that by his twenty-fifth birthday he had taken up a place at Glasgow University, supporting himself by working down the pit in the holidays. In 1863, he became the first President of the Miners' National Union. Under his guidance, and his eventual election to Parliament, the union pressed for legislative changes to better the lot of the miners. This was, however, a little too sedate for the men who formed a rival body, the Amalgamated Association of Miners. Founded in 1869, its membership was mainly in South Wales and the western counties of England. Its president, Tom Halliday, saw the prime aim as being the establishment of a strike fund to support disputes. In the 1870s these two bodies faced an important test of unity: could they protect the mineworkers against the doctrine of the sliding scale, whereby owners tried to fix wage rates to the price of coal?

In fact the movement split over the issue. Only the Amalgamated Association opposed the sliding scale, and faced the wrath of coal-owners who were determined to enforce it. After a series of humiliating wage cuts, the unity of the men in South Wales was broken. In the late 1870s and into the 1880s the wage cuts, tied to the price of coal, continued. Pit by pit, area by area, groups of miners were picked off one by one for wage reductions. No union organization could withstand it, blacklegging was rife, and the membership of the unions fell dramatically. Lloyd James, the trade unionist and politician, condemned the sliding scale, saying, 'It is throwing the bread of the children into a scramble of competition where everything is decided by the blind and selfish struggle of their employers.' But to oppose the system would need a very strong organization indeed.

Eventually, the poverty and suffering caused by the sliding scale in the 1880s acted as an agent of unity. When in 1888, Ben Pickard, the Yorkshire miners' leader, brought together a number of delegates from various coalfields, they decided to press for a 10 per cent rise. Their action was well-timed: the price of coal was rising again, and they won what they were asking for. This loose federation had proved its effectiveness, so much so that in the following year, in Newport, Monmouthshire, they gave formal recognition to its existence. The Miners' Federation of Great Britain was born.

Its first great trial of strength with the coal-owners came in 1893. The owners announced a wage reduction of 25 per cent, and when it was refused, began a lockout. The Federation were worried in case they had not got the support of the rank and file, but when they balloted the membership their views were clear: 221 agreed to the owners' terms, whilst over 143,000 turned them down. The Federation was united for what was to be a long and bitter struggle. Six weeks into the dispute, there occurred one of the most violent episodes in the history of the miners when soldiers, under the orders of local magistrates, fired into a crowd at Featherstone Colliery in Yorkshire. Two were killed and sixteen injured, but still the lockout continued. Then, gradually, the owners began to give in, and the men seemed stronger than ever. After more than three months, the Prime Minister, W. E. Gladstone, appointed no less a person than the Foreign Secretary, Lord Rosebery, as arbiter. The result was an agreement to return to work at the old rates. In what are now famous words, Rosebery wrote in his diary: 'Dined alone, very tired. But it would have been a good day to die on.' For the Federation it was a great victory.

The Federation now went from strength to strength. In 1899, the South Wales miners joined, to be followed nine years later by Northumberland and Durham. For the first time ever there was national unity. An issue was also growing that would unite the coalfields in one of the greatest strikes in mining history. It arose out of a demand to have a fair wage for working in abnormal places. This was a vitally important issue for every miner because, under a system of piece-rates, a man could find himself working in next to impossible conditions where the rewards were so small that he and his family would be reduced to poverty. Often a man could be put on such work by the supervisor to settle old scores. The answer, said the Federation, was a minimum wage, but were they strong enough to achieve it?

It was the problem of pay for working in abnormal places that lay behind the lockout at Ely Colliery in South Wales in 1910. The dispute led to disturbances throughout the coalfield, though the eyes of the world turned to the violence at one place in particular, Tonypandy. Despite well documented allegations of brutality by the police, the Home Secretary, Winston Churchill, refused an inquiry into their conduct. His decision brought him the hatred of miners for years to come. In the end, the South Wales miners lost their battle, but they had at least ensured that the question of abnormal places and a national minimum wage was now firmly on the agenda.

In February 1912, the Federation called a national strike to achieve a minimum wage. The impact of their decision was enormous, for coal was many times more important to the economy then than it was, say, in 1972. The Government rapidly realized that there was too much at stake to leave a settlement to the miners and the owners. They passed a bill through Parliament that established in each district a joint board of employers and miners who would set a minimum rate. The Federation had really wanted a national minimum rate but they accepted the compromise. It was still an impressive victory.

The Federation began looking for ways to broaden their industrial power. In 1913, they, with the railwaymen and the Transport Workers' Federation, formed what became known as the Triple Alliance, but it was not a success. In April 1921, the miners felt themselves betrayed by their allies who had deserted them at a crucial moment in their struggle against a wage cut. In the middle of the twenties the owners once more ordered reductions in wages, and a Royal Commission, under Sir Herbert Samuel, appointed to look at the problem, could see no short-term alternative either. Thus began the great lockout of 1926. Much has been written about the General Strike, but suffice to say that the consequences of it set back the cause of unionism in the mines by at least two decades, and its effects are still being felt in the N.U.M. today.

The defeat of the miners in 1926 all but destroyed the power of the Federation. The terms of the settlement were humiliating, as was the way in which victory was won. In the last months of the lockout the suffering in every pit village was intense, and in the words of a contemporary account there was 'a sad stillness; an appalling quiet at the colliery head, where winding shafts look idly down at little groups of men and women. No smoke; no song; no laughter; only the occasional rattle of the collector's box.' Nearly 5 million men, women and children were flung upon the charity of other unions and supporters abroad, most notable being the Soviet Union. Newspapers such as the *Nottingham Journal* opened a relief fund to provide sandwiches, soup, rice pudding and prunes for miners' children. Faced with desperate poverty, some men began to mine 'outcrop coal', while a few, then more and more, started to drift back to work. In the end, after attempts at a more just settlement, the Federation capitulated, wages fell rapidly and the hours of work were lengthened.

In the years that followed, the output of coal did not revive, indeed it fell, causing ever increasing unemployment and with it widespread malnutrition. The hardship suffered among miners and their families was particularly acute, because of the numbers out of work and also because coal-mining was often the only occupation available. In July 1928, 'the darkest year of the British Coal Trade' according to the Miners' Federation, one out of every three miners was without work. The Federation launched appeals for help, declaring the mining population to be faced 'with a cataclysm comparable to the destruction wrought by some great earthquake or other giant disturbance of nature'. Even the *Daily Mail*, which during the lockout had been an inveterate critic of the miners, joined in, asking its readers for food and cast-off clothing.

The world economic crisis served only to add to the desperation in the British coal industry. In the summer of 1930 over a quarter of a million miners were out of work, whilst two years later well over 40 per cent of the workforce was unemployed. And so it went on, a bitter experience that was to sear the memories of the miners and the generations that followed. That their Federation was able to do so little was to cause disillusionment and great strife within the organization.

Membership of the Federation fell rapidly after 1926, from about 800,000 to just under 530,000 by 1930. The blame was put on unemployment and low wages, for men thrust out of work could hardly afford to pay subscriptions, and those in work were powerless to stop their pay falling from 19s 8d a day for a qualified miner in 1921, to only 10s 9d in 1927. The emasculated state of the Federation dominated the minds of every delegate at the annual conference of 1927, held in the Prince of Wales Hotel at Southport in surroundings so plush that the miners agreed not to smoke for fear of damaging the 'splendid' carpets. One delegate spoke of the victimization applied by colliery pit owners at pits where union membership was low. Others recounted sad tales of the unemployed, for whom area associations, with few if any funds, could do little by way of providing benefit. The President, Herbert Smith, tried to rouse the delegates to action: 'These opponents of ours,' he said, 'may seek to beat us like iron on the anvil, but we shall be all the harder, all the tougher, and all the more powerful for the process.' Stirring words indeed, but tempered with an edge of realism when, on calling for a concerted drive to achieve 100 per cent membership, he added, 'We shall do this only if we have less bickering and more unselfishness in our ranks.' His warning went unheeded. A call for just such a membership drive led to attacks and insinuations so bitter that at times the proceedings of the conference seemed out of hand. Nothing had been done to convince anyone that the Federation was anything but disunited.

The Federation was also losing members to other unions. In Durham, men were being enticed to join the Electrical Trades Union, and, more seriously, in Lancashire and South Wales the General Workers' Union was recruiting from the ranks of disillusioned miners. The most pernicious threat, though, came from the rise of the rival 'yellow' or non-political unions. By September 1926, the M.P. George Spencer and a number of other officials of the Nottinghamshire Miners' Association (N.M.A.) had realized that in their county more than in any other the lockout was collapsing on a huge scale. They felt that the dispute was continuing nationally only because a few militant areas, such as Lancashire, Yorkshire and South Wales, refused to accept defeat, and they hoped that as Nottinghamshire was so profitable they could gain reasonable terms by settling. It was a belief encouraged by the colliery owners, who were delighted at the possibility of wooing them from the Federation.

Without waiting for a national settlement, George Spencer set up a breakaway organization, the Nottinghamshire and District Miners' Industrial Union, signed a local wages agreement and won the active support of the owners for the new body. In many pits, continued membership of the N.M.A. was enough to secure dismissal, inspectors were threatened if they reported poor conditions, and men who won compensation for injuries in the courts were summarily thrown out of work. Spencer himself was expelled from the Federation after being denounced as a 'blackleg of the worst order', but, undeterred, he launched his campaign into other areas – Durham, Northumberland, South Wales, Staffordshire, Derbyshire and Scotland – setting up a total of 273 branches. The Federation viewed the breakaway with alarm, and despite a secret ballot showing little support for the non-political union, membership of the Nottinghamshire Miners' Association fell by about five-sixths. Over the next decade, wages in Nottinghamshire remained lower than those in other comparable areas, and far from there being more industrial harmony, there was less.

The establishment of the Spencer Union added to the confusion about what the Federation should be doing to rebuild its strength. There were those who, after the experience of 1926, argued that a strike should never again disturb the 'peace of industry', and, along with many in the Trades Union Congress, took refuge in 'Mondism' – so called after its progenitor Sir Alfred Mond, who believed in encouraging a policy of cooperation between management and trade union to increase efficiency, profitability and eventually wages. This, said A. J. Cook, the miners' leader, vitriolically, was 'Mond Moonshine', adding that the proponents of such a view had 'made a desolation and called it peace'. The struggle between the two opposing views in the Federation reached a climax in Scotland, where a split between left and right in the Fife, Kinross and Clackmannan Miners' Association led to the setting up of a rival union. The South Wales Miners' Federation was also rent between left and right, with most of the controversy centring on the figure of Arthur Horner, an outstanding communist speechmaker, writer and organizer. His continued advocacy of militant unionism, when most around him were quiescent, brought down the wrath of the South Wales Federation on himself and his lodge. Both were expelled from the organization, until November 1933.

Such internecine quarrels only reflected national disharmony, and the reports of the executive committee for both 1928 and 1929 ended with pleas for unity. The battles, though, became something of a personal vendetta against the leader of the 1926 lockout, A. J. Cook. In the early 1920s, Cook had been held up as the darling of the left; a tough, energetic and incorruptible fighter for the working class. But in the recriminations following the lockout, some erstwhile supporters began to remark on how the radical views expressed during his barnstorming speeches at open-air meetings were distinctly more moderate when delivered in the more staid atmosphere of a conference. The Federation's President, Herbert Smith, charged him with falsifying the minutes of the executive committee. Most seriously, he was accused of conducting secret negotiations during the 1926 lockout with people close to the owners and the Government without telling the executive committee of the Federation. A committee of inquiry upheld the charge. One official described Cook's actions as 'a piece of deception unprecedented in the history of trades unionism'. In 1931 Cook, one of the greatest ever miners' leaders, died at the age of forty-six. 'When you hear that A.J. has been dining with royalty,' he frequently told meetings, 'then he will have deserted you.' Towards the end of his life he did, on one occasion, dine with the Prince of Wales. On returning to the valleys he was accused by the men of having broken faith with them. It was an accusation that hurt him very deeply.

The struggle between various factions within the Federation represented a still deeper malaise. After 1926, the Federation had lost its most important guarantee of unity: its power to negotiate nationally for all its members. The defeat of 1926 led to the replacement of national agreements with district settlements, returning the power to bargain about pay and conditions to a score of small and weak district associations. The owners in some areas, such as Kent and Somerset, refused to have any dealings with the local associations at all, even after considerable pressure from the Government. Areas were picked off one by one for lower wages, for the owners knew full well that if there was a dispute in one district, coal could still be had in another. Very quickly, a number of miners' associations began to pursue their own parochial interests and ignore national decisions altogether.

Confusion reigned. There were those, mainly on the district executives, who had regained bargaining power and who believed that all efforts were best directed towards finding ways of ameliorating the existing situation. Some in the more profitable areas attacked even the idea of a national wages agreement, arguing that it was bound to lead to the levelling up of wages in the poorer areas by taking from the pay of those in the richer ones. The more radical in the Federation believed, on the other hand, that the only way to fight ever worsening pay and conditions was by forming from all the local associations a strong, single, mineworkers' union, which could fight to achieve the only solution to the underlying problems of the coal industry, nationalization. But there was no broad agreement on this, or any other strategy for the Federation. Full well could Tom Richards, the chairman of a special conference of the M.F.G.B. in early 1931, tell his audience: 'What a horrible condition we are in as a Federation generally.'

And conditions became even worse. No areas were hit as badly as mining communities by the appalling poverty of the thirties. In the Rhondda, for example, among the ruins of old pits and blast furnaces, men, women and children were living in humiliating conditions in housing built a century earlier. There were demonstrations, evictions, attacks by the police and hunger marches. In 1935, there were protests almost every week in the Rhondda: 1,000 women were out one week, 6,000 people the following Sunday, emptying chapels, churches, and bringing all traffic to a standstill. Sometimes the demonstrations ended in 'riotous assembly' and prison sentences. But there was also the kindness, described by Will Paynter in his autobiography, of an anonymous benefactor who treated 500 hunger marchers from South Wales to a fish and chip supper as they passed through Newbury. Without doubt, though, the desperate nature of this period was to give a unity of purpose that would fire the miners' leaders and the men they represented. The problem was to decide when and how to start rebuilding the miners' strength.

In 1932, the power of the Federation was at its lowest ebb. 'We have got the tribal system in operation, with all the little chieftains,' said Noah Ablett, a delegate at that year's annual conference. But with an eye to the future he went on, 'We do not desire to continue institutions that are ossified and fossilized. We don't want the little tribes. We want one union.' How could they do it? The experience of the years after 1926, the destitution, unemployment, internal strife and dwindling membership, all had shown that the Federation needed desperately to reorganize itself to champion the miners' cause. But whilst the Federation had discussed proposals for one strong union in both 1926 and 1927, general indifference and the hostility of many district associations ensured that nothing was done. The difficulties were without doubt enormous, as the report on reorganization to the annual conference of 1932 demonstrated only too clearly. Every district had different subscriptions, membership rules, benefits and organizations, and the link between these separate mining unions was at best tenuous, founded only on a single elected officer and a small national office that was dwarfed in both style and staff by those of the district associations. Quite obviously, welding these disparate groups together would require an act of great will.

In the spring of 1932, one of the shrewdest political minds ever to hold office in the Federation was elected Secretary, a Northumbrian called Ebby Edwards. He realized that it would be almost impossible for a single union to be created out of the Federation in its present weakened state. Instead it would make much more sense to regain unity gradually by pressing for national negotiating machinery for wages, to stop colliery owners conducting guerrilla attacks on individual districts. The reconstruction of the Federation's power would take time, but the executive committee report for 1932 reflected a feeling that at last things were changing for the better: 'If the men in the coalfield realize that organization is the only power they have, then great things are possible, because the power of the whole body of mineworkers, wisely directed, is still one of the greatest forces in national life.' To this end, Edwards secured the unanimous agreement of all the districts to give the executive committee the power to call a strike, or take any action, in pursuance of a national wage.

Persuading some in the Federation that this more cautious approach would reap benefits was not easy. Within three months of coming into office, Edwards was fighting off strident demands for a strike to secure an immediate improvement in conditions. 'You have got to watch you don't lead your men to a stoppage which will not be successful,' he told a special conference of the Federation. These words did not go down well with some delegates, who had to return to the coalfields without so much as a promise of national action to relieve desperate conditions. 'Are we to take it,' said Noah Ablett, 'because it is suggested this Federation cannot strike that we are finished? That we are dead? Have we to be ridden over roughshod?'

For an answer Ablett had to wait for the summer of 1935, when Edwards decided the time was ripe for action. Whilst the ultimate aim was to be the nationalization of the industry, the immediate demand was for a national wage advance of 'two bob a day'. The campaign was not to be rushed, but was to move carefully step by step. Districts were asked to make a levy of 2d a member to provide a special campaign fund. To spread the word, there were meetings up and down the country in mining and non-mining communities, and there were large numbers of leaflets and posters given out, as well as frequent statements and advertisements in the press. At the end of six weeks, there could have been few who weren't thoroughly familiar with the miners' case.

The owners still refused to negotiate. The executive committee of the M.F.G.B. called a special conference and won the power to call a ballot for a strike, the first time they had done so for fifteen years. Three days before the country went to the polls for a general election, the miners held their pithead ballot. Further negotiations came to nothing and so they gave notice that a strike would begin on Monday, 27 January 1936.

Then something quite remarkable happened. Some of the big consumers of coal, led by I.C.I., offered to pay a higher price on condition that the extra money went exclusively towards higher wages for miners. The owners worked out that in the most profitable areas this would lead to a wage rise of one shilling a day, though in other districts it would be less. Although the Federation would have preferred an across-the-board rise, they decided to accept the deal: it was after all the biggest single increase since 1916. The coal-owners also made an important concession by agreeing to set up a Joint Standing Consultative Committee to discuss all national issues, including pay, which affected the mineworkers. A brilliantly orchestrated campaign had, within the space of a few months, given the Federation back its strength and pride. According to the Federation's executive committee, the dispute had shown that the miners would win when the Federation spoke as an authoritative national body and not merely as the mouthpiece of a number of autonomous districts: 'Only national action can be really effective in raising the standards of our men.'

Despite the great victory of the 1935 wages campaign, there was still outstanding a major threat to the unity and strength of the Federation. In the high summer of 1936, two boys at Harworth Colliery in Nottinghamshire were assaulted by a company official. Two weeks later, two men were dismissed for refusing to take 'snap' three-quarters of an hour early. In both cases the owners would not even discuss the matter until the men went back to work, and until what they called 'the ringleaders' had been punished. The dispute soon escalated into a battle to destroy the Spencer Union which allowed such conditions, and to win recognition of the Federation in the Nottinghamshire coalfield. For the miners, it was to be a tough struggle. The chairman of the company that owned Harworth was also chairman of the committee that controlled the local constabulary, and so it was hardly surprising when the village was overrun by policemen. Miners who continued working were given escorts to the pithead, earning them the nickname 'the chain gang'. There were scuffles, allegations of intimidation by pickets, and inevitably arrests, though often for no very good reason. Of the many documented cases of harassment, there is one example of a woman who, when ordered into her house by a policeman, pointed out that her husband was still working down the pit; the constable apologized and left.

By April 1937, the atmosphere at Harworth had become even more tense. The police began to take tougher and tougher measures to stop the mass picketing of the chain gang, and in the end there was a riot during which thirty-four people were arrested. More than half of them were acquitted, bound over, or given very light sentences, but the rest were sent to trial where they were sentenced with a severity that caused great alarm and anger throughout the Labour movement. Meanwhile, a national ballot had shown that seven out of every eight Federation members were in favour of going on strike to achieve recognition in Nottinghamshire. It was clear to all, including the Government, that, as with the two-bob-a-day dispute, here was an issue that could unite the Federation. At a special conference called to debate the events at Harworth, sentiment was so strong that the delegates overturned the recommendations of the executive committee and voted to give notice of a strike. But in fact it never came to that. In the Commons, Baldwin appealed for industrial peace in terms so moving that the executive of the Federation postponed their strike call for fourteen days to allow negotiations. They tried very hard to reach a settlement with the owners, and eventually it was agreed that the two organizations, the Nottinghamshire Miners' Association and the Spencer Union, should amalgamate. It was not a complete victory, but at least the Federation had again proved the necessity for unified national action. Most important, the Federation was whole once more.

Could the miners now achieve a single union, much stronger than the Federation? One national union had been demanded at every annual conference since 1932, but it was not until 1937 that another report was drawn up by a special reorganization committee. Once more there was the rhetoric – 'We must build up powers equal to those against us' – and once more the pragmatism, principally concerned with vested interests; the man who, for example, had given his life to the district association and who was worried about his future in any new body. Significantly, a resolution of the Kent area calling for a 'National Association of Mineworkers' was accepted by the conference with over 325,000 in favour of the idea, but with nearly 262,500 against. Once more the report and the resolution were not followed up. A far greater catalyst was required.

The greatest changes of all were to come with the Second World War. The outbreak of war welded the Federation together as never before, as the district secretaries gave the national leaders the power to deal 'with all the problems that might arise in industry during the war period'. Thus armed, Edwards astonished the mine-owners with a demand for an across-the-board national pay rise. It was a gamble, but if it worked, the Federation would once more win the right of conducting national negotiations. His ruse was successful, and though both sides compromised at a pay rise two-thirds of what the miners had been asking, they had won one other vital concession: for the first time in decades the owners had met with the Federation and agreed a national pay rise.

Even so, some districts, mainly Yorkshire, Scotland and South Wales, voiced their disquiet about a deal reached without the normal, exhaustive district and conference discussion. The tendency towards disintegration and faction became even stronger when agreement was reached on a formula that would adjust wages in line with the cost of living. A number of district associations held up the deal because they were reluctant to surrender some of their powers to federal officials. Edwards was furious, and wrote to every member of the executive committee explaining how the division of opinion had seriously weakened his bargaining position. Clearly, national negotiations by themselves would not be enough to unify the Federation.

But the Second World War also brought nationalization of the industry closer, and that in turn provided the best argument for one strong national union. It was clear, at least to some, that the coal industry was far too important to be left outside the control of government in wartime. For a start, things were in a mess. For the first nine months or so of the war, production was crippled by a shortage of manpower. Many had left to join up or to go into munitions factories where the pay was a lot higher. Then, by the late summer of 1940, the position was reversed, because the bombings by the Germans had so disrupted industry and transport, and the markets for coal in Europe had gone. Miners were actually being made unemployed. A year later and the position had changed yet again. The Government's response only depressed morale even further. Bevin introduced an essential work order to cover the coal industry, which in effect bound men to their pit more closely than at any time since the annual bond. At the same time, there were exhortations to work harder and longer hours, even though all the statistical evidence showed that the labour force was already stretched to the maximum. At some point, something was bound to snap. In the new year of 1942, there were strikes in Yorkshire and elsewhere. But the biggest dispute of all was at Betteshanger Colliery in Kent, where 1,017 men appeared before magistrates at Canterbury for going on strike without giving the notice necessary under wartime regulations. Three of the men, the alleged ringleaders, were sent to prison, whilst all the rest were fined. It did not go unnoticed that the sentences were more harsh and vindictive than those passed a week earlier on food racketeers.

The answer to the problems of the coal industry increasingly appeared to be control by the Government. The miners hoped that that meant nationalization. As early as November 1940, they had pressed both the Labour Party and the T.U.C. to implement their declared policy of the 'socialization' of the industry, but they were told that such a course was 'not feasible in the present crisis'. It was not until the Labour Party's Hugh Dalton took over the Board of Trade in 1942 that the Government took full control of the industry, establishing advisory boards at national and regional level, with a miners' representative on each. Financial control and legal ownership would remain in the hands of the coal-owners, but responsibility for wages and conditions would rest with new permanent machinery. While all this was going on, a board of investigation was working away under Lord Greene, looking for a solution to the manpower problem. Its answer was to establish a guaranteed weekly wage for miners, which Edwards described as the 'greatest single increase in the history of the Federation'. At the annual conference at Blackpool in 1942, Will Lawther, the President, said: 'Miners prefer these practical steps in cash to the tap dancing of the intellectuals over ideological staircases.' Significantly, he drew the delegates' attention to the changes necessary in the union if they were to cope with the new national control of the industry, warning, 'the bow and arrow trade union cannot function with a dive-bomber coal organization'.

The possibility of achieving the great ideal of one union for all mineworkers was now within their grasp. But would parochial interests take precedence over national unity, as they had done in the past? In 1942, a special sub-committee was sent off to prepare a scheme for reorganizing the Federation, and a year later, they submitted their recommendations to the executive committee of the Federation. They ruled out the complete dissolution of the district associations and instead proposed that only their industrial activities be taken over by a national body. All other matters, as well as many delegated powers, would always be 'subject to the overriding authority of the national organization'. To avoid an outbreak of tribalistic jealousies, they recommended leaving the unification of all the different rules of the various district bodies until a year after the formation of the new union. And to calm the anxieties of the district officials who might see no role for themselves in the new organization, they proposed that all existing full-time officials and staffs should be maintained. These ideas were accepted by the miners' annual conference, but were then sent to the districts for amendment: this was the most hazardous process of all.

In August 1944, the miners met to make or break the proposals for one union. Ironically, the conference was held in the birthplace of Spencerism, Nottingham. There were very many amendments. South Wales was successful in adding to the rules that no one should work in the industry if he was not a member of the union. Durham added a new object for the union, namely 'to seek the establishment of public ownership and control of the mining industry'. South Wales carried another resolution pledging the union to the 'complete abolition of capitalism'. The scheme nearly foundered on a proposal to add the negotiation of a national wages agreement as an object, but a speech by Sam Watson, the Durham miners' leader, brought agreement: if they didn't have a national wages agreement, he argued, they would have one union in name only and district organizations in practice.

The debate then began to hot up, as the districts were asked to vote for more and more restrictions on their power. Should the National Executive have the power to organize in an area where an association had broken away because it disagreed with national policy? Should the National Executive have the right to recommend the amalgamation of district associations? How much should the weekly contribution to the new union be? Discussion on all these topics threatened to unleash a backlash of parochialism that would wreck the chances of achieving a new union. In the event, they didn't. The district bodies were left with enough power to ensure their acceptance of a strong national union. Was it a compromise that should not have been made? Yorkshire certainly felt that the new union was not strong enough, and that it was still to a large extent a balkanized organization. But the truth of the matter was that compromise was the price for achieving unity.

The last conference of the Miners' Federation of Great Britain then broke up. Arrangements were made for a national ballot of all the members to see whether they would accept the rules endorsed by the Nottingham conference. When the National Executive Committee met on 16 November in Cambridge, as their old premises in London had been blasted by a V1 bomb, the Secretary reported the result of the ballot. The establishment of the new union had been accepted by roughly 10 to 1. What would have seemed an impossibility a decade before had now been accomplished, and district rivalries and interests had been subsumed to the greater good and unity of all miners. On 1 January 1945, the National Union of Mineworkers was given life.

4. The Miners and the Government

'The fate of Shinwell and the Government is in our hands,' said one speaker at the N.U.M.'s annual conference in 1945. 'Without coal the economy will fall, and if the economy falls so will Labour.' His words echoed an awareness throughout the union of the desperate importance of coal to Britain and to the programme of reconstruction of the economy after the war. The election of the first majority Labour Government was a watershed in British Labour history. The acceptance of recession that had characterized the two decades before the war was replaced by a commitment to full employment. Organized labour found itself more closely involved in government than ever before. If trade unions generally found themselves in a favoured position, then of none was this more true than the miners. They were a powerful force in industry, in the Labour Party, and in the Labour Cabinet. They were, in Gaitskell's words, the 'fighter pilots of the 1946 Battle of Britain'.

At their first meeting with Emanuel Shinwell, the Minister of Fuel and Power, the National Executive Committee were asked to do all they could to increase coal production by 8 million tons in the winter of 1945. Within a fortnight they returned with a plan. They established production officers in every area who, with help from the Ministry, were to ensure that the N.U.M. pledge to produce as much coal as possible was carried out. At that and every subsequent meeting with the Government, officers of the union stressed the serious shortage of men in the pits. More coal, they argued, meant more men: The Government recognized the problem and appointed a Director of Recruitment, a Mr Noel Newsome, who as the 'Man in the Street' had broadcast widely to resistance groups during the war. Newsome toured each coalfield in turn, using posters, pamphlets, films, exhibitions and trips down pits to boost recruitment. The Government also put the union under a lot of pressure to accept foreigners, mainly Poles, to work in the pits.

The miners saw both these unorthodox schemes as merely window-dressing, doomed to failure. In their view, the Government refused to face up to the fact that too many youngsters and ex-servicemen were finding better pay, conditions and a shorter working week elsewhere, and the only way to attract them was by making the job more appealing. To this end, they suggested a package of measures known as the 'Miners' Charter'. What better way to win recruits, they maintained, than to guarantee a seven-hour day, a five-day week, and two weeks' paid holiday a year? There were fears that implementing these proposals would lead to less coal being mined. But the union countered that they would instead reduce absenteeism, secure the better servicing and repair of equipment, and ensure an atmosphere of greater cooperation and effort on behalf of the rank and file. The justice of the claim was eloquently put by William Lawther, the union's President: 'When Britain wanted Spitfires and tanks to defeat Hitler nothing was allowed to stand in the way of getting them . . . As Britain now wants coal it must be prepared to adopt similar measures . . . whatever is given to attract manpower to the mines will be understood. Whatever is given to the miners as their just reward will be understood.'

Shinwell, however, was preoccupied with setting up the Coal Board, and despite extensive meetings between the Government and the union in his first year of office, he took practically no action on these and many other issues contained in the charter. Small wonder, then, that on the day he was due to make a speech at the 1946 conference of the N.U.M., the newspapers wrote that the stairs would be soaped for him. The miners felt that their restraint and undoubted achievement in producing more coal with fewer men, over the previous twelve months, deserved greater immediate reward.

Shinwell's delay was to cost him dear. He knew that the position over manpower was serious, telling the House of Commons, 'It contains an element of industrial disaster,' but was unwilling to accept the N.U.M.'s solution. Throughout 1946, the number of men employed in the industry continued to fall, and although the amount of coal mined actually rose, the increase nowhere near met the scale of demand. Attlee, Morrison and the electricity authorities became very worried, especially as the rapid rise in demand for electricity showed no sign of abating. Shinwell alone remained optimistic, maintaining in a speech that everyone was expecting a fuel crisis except the Minister of Fuel and Power.

During the autumn things got worse. Recommendations from Shinwell's officials for measures to restrict the use of fuel were sent to the Cabinet with a note expressing Shinwell's own reservations. But on 3 January 1947, he rather belatedly warned his colleagues of the possibility of the breakdown of supply, and shortly afterwards asked for priority for the transport of coal on the railways. On 30 January, a blizzard began. A few days later, he stood up in the Commons on a Friday morning to announce a shut-down of industry. The news came as a bombshell after the rather hopeful tales that he had been telling all week. The following Sunday, Arthur Horner, the Secretary of the N.U.M., was summoned to an urgent meeting with Shinwell, his private secretary, Hugh Gaitskell and Harold Wilson. Now, in a moment of deep crisis, the support of a communist barely six months in office was desperately sought by the Government. They told him that unless London's power stations had coal by the following Wednesday, the city might have to be evacuated. There was little Horner could do, as the miners were already producing more coal than ever, but he promised to use all his influence with the lightermen and tugmen to move coal brought by sea as soon as possible.

In the event the crisis lasted nearly a month, and the damage that had been done was enormous, with possibly £200 million of exports being lost, nearly 2 million people unemployed at the peak, and power cuts on a scale that were not to be seen again until 1972. Most important, and as Dalton noted in his diary, there was a feeling that the crisis had 'broken the morale of us all', providing as it did a rallying cry for the Conservatives, who coined the slogan 'Shiver with Shinwell and starve with Strachey'. What of Shinwell himself? Clearly, he was not responsible for the worst winter of the century making the transport of coal impossible. But he had ignored both the low level of stocks of coal and the miners' advice on tackling the urgent problem of manpower. His mistake was to expect the miners to achieve what they had told him was beyond their existing capabilities. The result was to provide ammunition for those critical of the miners, the industry and the Government.

The struggle for more coal now took on an intensity hitherto unequalled, for Britain had been to the brink, and in the words of Emanuel Shinwell, 'such an experience was more than enough for one century'. In the first three months of 1947, the miners met the Prime Minister twice. Attlee told them that he wanted at least 200 million tons of coal that year, and more if possible so that they could start exporting again. Many of the recommendations of the miners, ignored up to then, were now put into practice. Mining equipment, for example, was given top priority, extra food rations were granted to collieries, and amidst great rejoicing, it was agreed that the miners would start to work a five-day instead of a six-day week. The Cabinet, though, still remained a little suspicious of them, and in an attempt to reduce absenteeism, made the sixth day's pay conditional on working a full five days. The result was much as the miners had said: the output of coal was maintained, absenteeism was reduced and the number of men joining the industry began to rise.

In the high summer of 1947 the Government once more faced serious economic problems. This time the cause was a run on sterling, the so-called convertibility crisis, of such a magnitude that the Government was forced to introduce a programme of austerities. Now, the Government argued, there was a direct relationship between exports of coal and imports of food. At the end of July, the big three of the miners' union, Lawther, Bowman and Horner, met Attlee, Shinwell, Cripps and Bevin at 10 Downing Street. Bevin asked whether the miners would work six days and be paid for seven. Not unnaturally the miners expressed their reluctance but suggested instead that they might work a sixth day for extra pay. Bevin saw this as being less than cooperative and became very angry. 'You have got a damned cheek,' he exploded, 'you've got your five-day week on a basis that's not unreasonable, and now you're offering to sell us the sixth day at overtime rates.' In the end the Government once more won the support they needed. The miners abandoned their newly won shorter working week and worked either an extra six and a half hours on Saturday or an extra half hour a day during the week.

For the next three years, the considerable power of the union was firmly thrust behind the Government. The risk increasingly run by the leadership was unpopularity, even open disaffection, amongst the rank and file. Within the Government, the miners were now dealing with a new man, Hugh Gaitskell, who had replaced Shinwell as Minister of Fuel and Power. Gaitskell never won the affection felt towards Shinwell, even though he had spent his politically formative years working in a mining community. Nevertheless he achieved great respect for his administrative abilities, producing, for example, coal targets that were both intelligible and realistic. He realized very clearly that he had to win the confidence of the miners if they were to produce the coal that, in his words, every country demanded of Britain in negotiations. He toured the country addressing large meetings, finding even the communist leadership in Scotland surprisingly friendly.

The union, meanwhile, had taken their response to the Government's appeals for more coal a stage further: they appointed Jim Bowman as their own 'Director of Manpower'. His first campaign was to try to win acceptance of the European voluntary workers, men from Poland and Italy, who, the Government insisted, would make an important contribution towards meeting the shortage of manpower. The press and the Opposition made much capital out of the resistance of many lodges towards their employment, but the reality was that the numbers involved were so small as to make little difference to output, and the delays in sending them down pits were as much to do with the time it took the Government to train them and teach them English, as they were to do with any hostility from union lodges. But that, of course, was not very good press copy. Jim Bowman recognized the need for good public relations and urged the acceptance of European voluntary workers as a gesture towards the national economy. He also suggested a number of specific, practical proposals to boost recruitment, but the Government, to say the least, was not very responsive.

At the annual conference in the summer of 1948, great stress was laid on winning more coal for export. Bevin, the Foreign Secretary, was given a very warm reception and devoted his speech to the need to exchange coal for food. Horner reached new and dizzy heights in extolling the virtues of coal when he declared that it was better than dollars. Throughout the following autumn and winter the N.U.M. and the Coal Board met the Minister at regular intervals, and at the miners' instigation set up a joint production committee to look into such things as the better use of men, supplies of equipment and more regular working.

All these efforts certainly won more coal. The target for 1947 was missed only by a whisker, 'a milestone', said Gaitskell. In 1948, production rose again, this time to nearly 210 million tons, and productivity rose quite dramatically. The target, however, was missed, and by a larger margin than in the previous year. 1949 saw production of deep-mined coal rise by over 3 per cent, but still the demand was for more. The Government urged the union to do everything in its power to get collieries to work harder, despite the fact that the agreement to work an extra day a week had twice been renewed, each time for a further year. The real reason why production was not increasing as rapidly as was hoped had little to do with absenteeism, the favourite *bête noire* of the press and Government, but instead was the result once more of a rapid and serious decline in the number of men employed in the industry. This was soon to develop into a major crisis.

Apart from the struggle for more coal, wage restraint was seen as vital to the economic success of the country, the Coal Board and the Labour Government. The policy divided the union even at the outset, though when the National Executive Committee decided to back the Trades Union Congress's conditional support for a wage freeze in March 1948, the membership acquiesced at least for the first year. The following March the policy was once more confirmed by the National Executive Committee, much to the relief of Sir William Lawther, who had been knighted in that year's New Year's Honours List and, sensing rank-and-file hostility, had made sure the agreement was not put to a pithead ballot. At the annual conference, though, he was forced to defend what he had done. In an address that foreshadowed the blood-letting to come, he argued that wage restraint was a small price to pay for all the benefits brought by the Attlee administration, and he warned against unofficial strikes that were the work of the Communist Party, an organization that he believed was equal to the Tories as an enemy of the Labour Government. The rancour building up in the union was, however, too great for his words to soothe, and the conference, acting in a manner that Lawther denounced as 'criminal', rejected his advice and unanimously demanded an increase for lower-paid workers.

Throughout the autumn the resentment between the two sides grew, culminating in a strike in Scotland that enveloped seventeen pits employing 5,000 men, who argued that their last pay award in 1947 had been eroded by inflation, while other men in other industries had won cost of living awards despite the wages policy. Lawther himself was shaken when he visited Scotland and realized the strength of the feelings. The same arguments rent the December meeting of the National Executive Committee, and only after a complete day spent closeted away did the right wing manage to win the support of the majority for continued wage restraint. Delegates to a special conference endorsed the decision and then it was put to the coalfields for approval. The Government and the T.U.C. waited anxiously for the result, as it was the only test by any union of shop-floor opinion on the issue. One by one the results came in: Yorkshire, Lancashire, Scotland, South Wales and Nottinghamshire all showed widespread disillusionment with restraint at a time of inflation and, overturning the decision of their leaders, voted 'No'. By chance, Sir William Lawther stood in as chairman of the next meeting of national trades union executives on 12 January 1950. Ironically, one of the greatest champions of wage restraint had to cast the miners' vote against the furtherance of the policy. The support of the Government by wage restraint came to an end.

Wage restraint had made it very difficult to attract men into the industry, a difficult enough task at the best of times. Manpower employed in the mines fell dramatically, as men worked for wages on which it was almost impossible to maintain physical fitness. By the autumn of 1950 the number at work was the lowest for fifty years, and stocks of coal, as the winter drew on, were alarmingly scant, leading to fears of a repetition of the crisis of 1947. The Government were slow to react and seemed oddly bewildered, but eventually decided to risk unpopularity with the miners by allowing the import of coal and by resurrecting the old chestnut of the use of foreign labour, this time Italians. Despite this, the response of the miners to appeals for more coal was so good that the Minister, Philip Noel-Baker, declared: 'There are no more valiant or patriotic Britons than the miners.' Lord Hyndley, the Coal Board chairman, sent a congratulatory message to all pits saying, 'The battle for coal is on – you can win it.' A few days into the new year, the union's National Executive Committee met the Prime Minister at 10 Downing Street for just over an hour and a half. As tended to happen at times of crisis, the miners secured most of what they were asking for. Within a fortnight, they won great improvements in pay and an agreement on the establishment of a pension scheme. For their part, the union undertook to reduce absenteeism and strikes, to continue working on Saturdays, and to press for pits to accept foreign labour wherever possible. All the miners in the country were sent 'personal' letters from the Prime Minister emphasizing the importance of their continued support and concluding, 'The Nation looks to you: I am sure you will not fail the Nation.'

But no efforts could stop the power cuts to industry that were introduced at the beginning of February. They brought stinging criticism from the Opposition, principally from Brendan Bracken who, in the Commons, recalled a remark of Aneurin Bevan's that only an organizing genius could produce a shortage of coal, and triumphantly concluded that now the Government had found one. Geoffrey Lloyd, who had been a Conservative Minister of Mines during the war, joined the fray and blamed the Government for failing to take action to build up stocks and manpower until it was too late to avoid widespread disruption and panic among shipping companies and railways. But by the end of February, an extra quarter of a million tons was being mined each week and by

May Day, the Government's targets had been overtaken despite reduced manpower and increased absenteeism due to illness. The union also spent a great deal of time and effort that spring, trying to win acceptance of Italian workers in the pits. They were partially successful, and on 21 May, after a visit from Alf Robens who was sent by the Minister of Power, the first batch left Milan for Britain by train. Those last months of the Labour Government brought signs of a fresh policy on energy, the establishment of a Fuel Efficiency Committee, showing Noel-Baker's realization that the country should adapt itself to a shortage by finding better ways of using coal. In October, however, Britain was plunged once more into an election, and the result saw the miners fearful lest they lost all that they had gained from six years of Labour government.

For despite the conflict and sharp differences of opinion, the miners had gained a new world from those six years. Quite apart from the substantial benefit of nationalization, there were also better facilities at collieries, such as free pithead baths and the granting of a week's annual holiday, aid to help the sufferers of pneumoconiosis, improved safety regulations and a fund to help the dependants of victims of fatal accidents. Miners could additionally grow old in the knowledge that there would be a pension scheme to care for them. Above all else, the miners had been put at what they believed to be their rightful place high in the national earnings league. Full well could Philip Noel-Baker, as Minister of Fuel and Power, quote the remarks of a miner who had started his life working in a twelve-inch seam: 'When I think of my young days,' he said, 'my boy and my girl are growing up like princes and princesses.'

The portents were not good for the miners' relationship with the new Tory Government. A few months before the General Election of 1951, Arthur Horner declared that the policies of the Conservatives, if elected to government, 'would inevitably result in industrial resistance by the miners'. Churchill savaged the speech, arguing that such a threat imperilled British democracy and insulted the will of the people. These recriminations did not augur well for the future, and continued during the election itself. The N.U.M. in their election manifesto, for example, made clear that history was not forgotten: 'The Tory Government of which Churchill was a member,' it proclaimed, 'stood by and saw our people starved and hounded, forced to work longer hours for less wages, subjected to the vicious means test, and yet now they have the temerity to suggest that their policies will improve the position of the industry and those employed in it.' The specific policy that aroused so much ire was the commitment of the Conservative Party towards some form of decentralization of power in the industry, either to groups of collieries or to individual pits, as a way of winning more coal. Their belief, nurtured by a long-time critic of the Coal Board, the Tory M.P. Colonel Lancaster, was that the industry was swamped by bureaucracy which made life impossible for the men doing the work at pit level. To the miners, this was nothing short of a betrayal of nationalization, a way of introducing capitalism by stealth, and an ingenious method of curtailing the national power of the union by setting each pit in competition, making broader industrial action almost impossible.

In fact, after the election, the leadership of the union struggled hard to ensure that strikes would not be used to influence the Government. Sir William Lawther spoke of the 'great evil' of using industrial power for political objectives, a policy that could 'only lead to national suicide', whilst the Vice-President, W. Ernest Jones, warned of actions that could 'pull down the temple and not remove the arch-priests'. More than that, they managed to swing the union behind the idea that Saturday working should be continued, and not ended as a snub to the government. They had the eloquent support of Arthur Horner, who argued that to refuse to work the extra time would lead only to blame for wrecking the economy and would cause some 3 million people to become unemployed for every 10 million tons of coal that their action would lose. Of course, Horner remained strident in his condemnation of the Tory Government, whereas Sir William Lawther caused apoplexy in the union when he went to Sir Winston Churchill's birthday party.

But there was still a great deal of deep-seated hostility. A Conservative M.P., Mr Victor Raikes, provoked an enormous row when he gave voice to his theory that the objections to Italians working in the pits were due to their immense sex-appeal to the miners' wives and daughters. More seriously, the new Government's economy cuts spurred on some pits in Wales to refuse to work on Saturdays for a time in protest, and their first budget, while causing some tough speaking at a special conference called to discuss it, led one pit actually to go on strike.

This ideological conflict with the Government gained strength in the mid 1950s. The sharp increase in purchase tax, among other measures announced in the Conservatives' supplementary budget in the autumn of 1955, prompted the union to demand a new pay rise. The union's President, Ernest Jones, wondered why they should show wage restraint when, in his words, 'the national economy has gone out of control'. The speeches at the annual conference of 1956 showed many delegates fearful of a return to the thirties, especially after men had been laid off in the car industry. There were protests at the increase in bank rate and the cutting of building subsidies by local councils, and demands that the Government make substantial increases in pensions and national insurance benefits because they were not keeping pace with the cost of living. At the following year's conference, the demands were even stronger. Will Paynter, soon to become the Secretary of the union, won great support when he declared: 'If this Tory Government is going to pursue this anti working-class policy, then I say we will be justified as an organized Labour and trades union movement in using the maximum power we have in our control to remove them from office.' The next year, the whole system of arbitrating wage awards, one of the great successes of the coal industry, was threatened after 'obvious political interferences' had led to the rejection of one of their pay demands.

But apart from the ideological battle, a struggle shared with the whole Labour movement, were there any other sources of conflict arising with the Government? Ostensibly, they appeared conciliatory. During the debate on the King's speech, the Tory Minister of Fuel and Power, Geoffrey Lloyd, told the Commons: 'Once you have accepted a nationalized industry you cannot sit around looking at it with neutral or semi-hostile eyes, much less mess around with it.' But whereas the controversial plans for reorganizing the industry were quietly forgotten, for the time being at least, the Government still interfered with the Coal

Board in a way which the miners' union found insidious and intolerable.

The Coal Board enjoyed an illusion of complete freedom. By statute they were supposed only to make enough money to pay their way on an average of good years and bad. But the Government used a 'gentleman's agreement' unique in the power industry, to keep the price of coal below the level of the free market so that Britain enjoyed the cheapest coal in Europe. This could have worked to the N.C.B.'s advantage if the Government had made some allowance for the fact that the coal industry, by selling its product more cheaply than it would have liked, was in effect subsidizing the use of coal in the rest of British industry. But the Government made no concession whatsoever, indeed they made matters worse. Of the ten price rises the Coal Board asked for, four were granted for less than they needed, one was turned down, and five were accepted but with such delays that planning was made near-impossible. One price rise was held up until after the General Election of 1955, as the Government increasingly realized the sensitivity of the inflation rate to the price of coal. As the Coal Board remarked in its annual report for 1956: 'The Board has not always been in a position to raise prices to cover costs as they might have otherwise done.'

But the malicious effects of Government interference did not end there. The low price for coal encouraged demands for more and more. So great were these pressures that Enoch Powell warned the House of Commons that the Government was assisting in subsidizing the inefficient use of coal in a way that was earning Britain the title 'The champion coal wasters of Europe'. The Coal Board simply could not keep up with the demand, and the Government felt they had little option but to continue to import coal. However, the Government also insisted that the Coal Board met the difference between buying the coal on the world market and the selling price at home, which was much lower. The cost was enormous, some £10 million a year, and, as the miners pointed out, this put a burden on the Coal Board that no other fuel industry had to bear. The miners' union continually expressed their resentment at this, and pointed to other serious handicaps, such as the interest payments on the loan needed to buy out the colliery companies when the industry was nationalized, all of which, they argued, made the Coal Board's performance look a lot worse than it was. But this was seen as special pleading, and the image of the inefficient coal industry was perpetuated.

The way in which the coal industry was exploited in the early and mid fifties makes what happened later all the more poignant. Within the space of three years, the consumption of coal fell by no less than 33 million tons, leading to the loss of 120,000 jobs. The changes experienced between the autumn of 1956 and the end of 1959 were enormous, especially in the many mining communities where the pit had traditionally provided the only occupation. The N.U.M. set out their policies in two documents, one published in 1958 and the other a year later. They maintained that the Government's tight credit policy was dampening down demand for coal, and they called for vigorous economic expansion. The main target of their concern was, however, oil. 'In our opinion, it is clear that imported oil is being given a priority over coal because of the political and economic power wielded by the oil interests.' In 1955, the Government had agreed to the conversion of seven power stations to oil because of the continuing shortage of coal. The union now asked them to postpone converting four more, and to end the tax rebate given to fuel oil. Above all else, the union wanted a coordinated national fuel policy, along the lines suggested some years earlier by the Ridley Committee, and prophetically, they warned of the danger of relying on a fuel source gleaned from some of the most politically unstable parts of the world.

The Government appeared unmoved. In April 1957, the Paymaster-General, Reginald Maudling, told the Commons that one third of the increased demand for power by 1965 would be met by coal, and he added, 'Looking beyond that our basic energy source is and will remain coal.' The next year the Parliamentary Secretary at the Ministry of Power, Sir Ian Horobin, saw no need for any panic measures, arguing that people did not change to oil for fun, but because it must be the most economical fuel. He believed there was hope for a smaller but more efficient coal industry, fulfilling a vital part in the country's economy. The exact size of the contribution of coal was, however, left unclear, to be determined by free-for-all competition between the various sources of power. Alf Robens summed up the Opposition's attitude when he said that if the consumer was to have freedom of choice then the Coal Board should be made really competitive, instead of fighting with one hand behind its back. The agreement with the Government on pricing meant that the oil companies could undercut coal at any time.

1959 was one of the most critical years in the history of the industry. In his first major speech as Secretary of the union, Will Paynter declared: 'I would accuse this Government of an act of betrayal, not only of the miners but also of the National Coal Board.' Later, at the annual conference, attended incidentally by Harold Wilson, he argued that the Government had continually interfered with the Coal Board but had now, suddenly, turned somersault, 'leaving the industry to carry the whole brunt and burden of the economic crisis'. The feeling of betrayal was echoed by Alf Robens when he warned the House of Commons that unless the Government changed their policy, the industry would be engulfed in a tide of revolt, with wholesale unemployment and deserted villages. By the autumn, though, there were signs that the union was resigning itself to a contraction of the industry. When the leadership met the Minister in November, they stressed that they were fighting against unemployment and social misery and asked for financial help for the Coal Board, much as had been given to industries experiencing similar problems in Britain and Europe. The Minister, said the N.U.M. report on the meeting, gave no real hope of change.

Distrust of the motives of the Government grew even greater the following year when the union announced that it had learnt of 'fairly authenticated' plans to decentralize the industry. The plans were outlined in a document prepared by the Government and passed on privately to Will Paynter by the Chairman of the Coal Board, Jim Bowman. The idea was to vest real power in the divisional boards, whilst a national committee would simply coordinate some of their activities. The object was to make it easier to channel money into profitable coalfields at the expense of the unprofitable. Bowman knew Paynter would make the document public, and hoped that that would kill it dead. The outcry was enormous. 'Such measures,' said the union, 'would resuscitate the anarchy and trade competition between districts, weaken the position of coal in competition with fuel oil and lead to the ruin of the industry,' adding that the proposals would be fought using every legitimate means. Despite denials and reassurances in the House of Commons, the issue of decentralization dominated the annual conference of 1960. Paynter told the delegates that the Conservatives were trying to break the nationalized industry, first by competition from oil, then by making the Commons annually responsible for how much money should be made available to the Coal Board, and finally by decentralizing the whole operation. The idea was not heard of again.

As the closures continued in the early sixties, the Government still denied the industry the overall support that it needed, and in fact, by their White Paper on the financial and economic obligations of nationalized industries, tried to inject a greater element of profit-making into the Coal Board. But the decision of the Chancellor of the Exchequer, Selwyn Lloyd, in his budget of 1961, to tax fuel oil at the rate of an extra 2d a gallon was of great help. While the new Minister of Power, Richard Wood, rejected the idea that the N.C.B. was suffering under unfair financial burdens, he did ensure that measures were taken to alleviate unemployment. And while the Gas Council, against pleas from the N.U.M., were allowed to import methane from the Sahara, the Steel Company of Wales was forbidden to import coking coal from the United States, which they claimed was much cheaper. The union also won agreement to reduce the conversion of power stations to oil, and in 1963 the Minister announced construction of two coal-fired power stations, one on the River Trent, and the other at Fiddlers Ferry in Lancashire. It must be said that Wood was given a fairly rough time as Minister, facing back-bench revolts over the appointment of Alf Robens as Chairman of the Coal Board, and over a bill to provide funds to meet the industry's deficit. He was also embroiled in a major row in connection with the wage freeze imposed in 1961, when he gave the impression that he had warned the Coal Board not to defy the pay pause. The concessions he won were therefore by no means easy to achieve, but throughout his time as Minister,

Richard Wood showed himself sympathetic to the problems caused by the run-down of the industry. As far as the miners were concerned, though, there was still no coordinated fuel policy and neither was there the financial reconstruction of the Coal Board that both Lord Robens and the N.U.M. agreed was so badly needed. For the achievement of those aims, the union looked to a new Government.

At the Labour Party conference in 1960, Harold Wilson concluded the debate on fuel policy by appealing to the Party to stand by the miners, as the 'mineworkers have always stood at our side even in the darkest days'. That September, the Labour Party issued a statement on energy policy produced by a team led by Wilson. In the light of what was to happen when Labour was returned to office, the document was of great importance. It expressed concern that the run-down in the pits was leading to too many men leaving too fast, causing problems of unemployment and hardship, and sharply criticized, for reasons of security and the protection of the balance of payments, the Government's 'complacent reliance' on oil. Shrewdly, it explained that a mine, unlike a factory, cannot be closed for a year or two, and then reopened when circumstances change. The remedy was clear: 'Without a specific target the N.C.B. will not be able to plan sensibly their investment and production programmes, nor will the crisis of confidence that those working in the industry are now experiencing be overcome.' There were many more such assurances. In the run-up to the election of 1964, George Brown wrote a letter to the N.U.M. guaranteeing output of 200 million tons a year, at least in the short run, and the election manifesto confirmed the promise. The N.U.M. had high hopes of the victory of Labour.

The very first meeting with the new Minister of Power left the N.U.M. deeply concerned. Fred Lee, a left-winger, despite all the election pledges avoided any commitment to a definite size for the industry, preferring instead to emphasize the role of coal in providing the 'base load' within an overall fuel policy. The union held hasty meetings with the miners' parliamentary group, and went to see George Brown, then Minister for Economic Affairs, who re-emphasized his commitment to the promises made during the election, and indeed in the manifesto itself. Two days later Fred Lee told the House of Commons: 'The Government accepts for the present the case for trying to maintain the position of coal . . . at around its recent level of 190–200 million tons.' The union found his words 'encouraging', while realizing that they were not a complete reaffirmation of Labour Party policy.

The N.U.M. continued to stress their great concern at the drop in the consumption of coal. In April, the Government announced some short-term measures to help boost the demand for coal by some 4–7 million tons, by winning agreement from the electricity authorities and the Gas Council to use more coal, and by giving preferential treatment to coal for the heating of public buildings. In July, the Minister announced measures to reconstruct the Coal Board's finances by writing off £415 million of the debt owed to the Exchequer, an amount which Lee saw as a gift, but which the Coal Board and the union viewed as merely going some way towards meeting the cost of the burdens that governments had consistently placed on the industry. Nevertheless, when Fred Lee addressed the union's annual conference that year, some pride was taken in the fact that it was the first time they had heard a speech from a Labour Minister of Power for fourteen years. And Lee told them: 'There is no occasion for alarm or despondency.'

But even as he spoke, the executive committee were desperately assessing other, more controversial Government decisions. The National Plan set a target for coal production of 170–180 million tons by 1970, a figure supported by the White Paper on fuel policy. Even more worrying, a special fund was to be created to speed the closure of uneconomic pits, assisting redeployment within the industry and resettlement in others. The Government also insisted that every pit would be placed in one of three categories so that all would know their future prospects. The 'C' grade contained about 150 pits that failed to cover even their running costs and were therefore 'a bigger menace to industry than anything else'. These 'dead-weight' collieries, employing around 120,000 men, had to be eliminated speedily in two or three years rather than five, to leave a 'healthy core' of economic pits, mainly in Yorkshire and the East Midlands.

In Will Paynter's view, the policy of accelerating pit closures must have created a sense of jubilation among the oil barons, and he warned the Government against pursuing policies which would undermine the 'faith and loyalty of the great mining communities'. Over the winter, the leaders of the N.U.M. met the Minister of Power many times both formally and informally, and on two occasions he attended meetings of the executive committee. Lee explained that he felt unable to take any further steps to protect coal short of 'totalitarian measures'. He believed that a tax on other fuels would damage our trade position by adding to the costs borne by our industries, and that the men leaving pits would be better employed in more efficient ones, or in other sections of the economy where there was a shortage of labour. Various members of the executive committee expressed their dismay that the closures were being rushed through in two years. They told the Minister it was an act of complacency and a betrayal.

The talks achieved little, so, at a special conference, the union spelt out their policy. They asked the Government not only to underwrite a sales target for the industry to produce the kind of confidence needed to stop men leaving the pits, but also to provide further short-term financial help for the industry to pay for all the social costs of the pit closure programme, and to encourage the gas and electricity authorities to use more coal. The N.U.M. tried once again meeting ministers, the Prime Minister, organizing a national demonstration, but it was clear the Government was immovable.

Between 1965–6 and 1968–9, the Coal Board closed over 200 collieries. Put another way, one pit closed almost every week for four years, and this under a Labour Government. From the early days of 1967, hints began emerging of the shape of the Government's new fuel policy, and any hopes the N.U.M. might have had of a new, better, deal were quickly dashed. In the spring, the new Minister of Power, Richard Marsh, called the heads and top officials of the nationalized fuel industries to a secret meeting at Selsdon Park. The first study documents for discussion showed the production of coal down to 80 million tons by 1980, and by his own account, Lord Robens had to fight hard to save the coal industry from emasculation. In mid summer, the Prime Minister, Harold Wilson, prepared the ground for the shock of the White

Paper by announcing a temporary stop to pit closures that would last for one month, until the end of September. Paynter described the manoeuvre as nothing but window dressing, 'a shabby political pantomime'. Later, as delegates to the Labour Party's conference met at Scarborough, Wilson met the miners and told them that sixteen collieries, due to be closed in the following three months, would be given a reprieve until the end of the year at least. The N.U.M. was already feeling that the loyalty of its membership was being strained to the utmost, and the meeting with the Prime Minister was, according to Paynter, an angry one. The union knew that the move only postponed inevitable closures, and that it would lead, as indeed it did, to the highest number of closures ever made in one year.

Five days before the Government eventually published its White Paper in mid November, Lord Robens held a meeting at Hobart House to which he invited Paynter and Ford of the N.U.M., and the chairmen of the Regional Development and Economic Planning Councils, who would be responsible for helping to find jobs for unemployed miners. Robens gave them the Coal Board's forecast for output and manpower based on the Government's predictions, showing that by 1980, employment in the pits would be reduced to only 65,000. As Robens must have known, any promises of confidentiality were worthless after such news. Wilson described the disclosures as 'sensational and inaccurate', some N.U.M. lodges in Durham, Lancashire and Nottinghamshire voted to stop paying the political levy to the Labour Party, and the Kent area of the N.U.M. told David Ennals, then a junior minister, to prepare to resign if they called upon him to do so. When the White Paper was published, it proclaimed the Government's basic objective to be cheap energy and argued that the expansion of nuclear power and natural gas could not be held back to help coal without a 'misallocation of manpower and capital to the detriment of the economy as a whole'. The all-important projection for coal output was for 120 million tons by 1975. The miners' M.P.s were furious, and just over a week after the document was published, the Prime Minister yielded to pressure and withdrew a motion approving the White Paper. But the damage had been done: the document remained in being as a basis for planning, and the Government had incidentally avoided the strong parliamentary pressures for a full Commons debate.

After the row over the White Paper, the Government offered some additional help to the coal industry to relieve hardship. The Coal Industry Act of 1967 provided for special assistance to men who were over fifty-five years of age and who were being made redundant. And to the extent that the gas and electricity authorities used coal in preference to other fuels which would have been cheaper, the cost would be borne by the Government up to a maximum of £45 million. But then the Government embarked upon a decision that was to do even more harm to the prospects of the industry and the morale of the men in it.

For a number of years there had been a proposal to build a power station at Seaton Carew near Hartlepool, in the middle of the Durham coalfield. The Durham miners had always been among the staunchest supporters of the Labour Party, and in recent times they had seen the number of pits in their area reduced by about half. In the pits that remained, the Coal Board had spent a great deal of money on modernization and securing greater efficiency. It was, to both the N.U.M. and the N.C.B., hardly conceivable that a new power station could be anything but coal-fired. The Central Electricity Generating Board thought otherwise, and in March 1967 finally decided to ask for authority to build a nuclear-powered station. The miners were incensed, and told the Prime Minister so at a secret meeting during the Durham Miners' Gala. The Chancellor of the Exchequer, Jim Callaghan, the Minister of Labour, Ray Gunter, and Lord Robens were also present and when the three representatives of the miners' union, Paynter, Ford and Alf Hesler, finally left, all seemed convinced that the force of their case was fully accepted. The Coal Board offered coal that was as cheap as the estimates they had been given for nuclear power, and challenged the electricity authorities and the Ministry to have an independent inquiry to see which was really the cheapest. The parliamentary pressures on the Government to accept the case for coal were enormous, and eventually, on 21 August 1968, the Government announced their decision. The House of Commons was in recess for the summer and the new Minister of Power, Roy Mason, made up his mind after just over six weeks in office. As an ex-miner, Mason was well aware of the traumas that the industry had been through and of the importance of the decision to the union that sponsored him. He chose nuclear power.

5. A New Era

Before dawn on New Year's Day 1947, a huge crowd assembled at the pithead of Deep Duffryn–Mountain Ash Colliery in South Wales. Some of the men were coming on shift, others were just finishing. Hundreds of miners' lamps could be seen twinkling in the cold. There was not a sound as they heard speeches from their local M.P., union officials and management. But as the royal blue flag of the National Coal Board was hoisted over the pithead, there was a loud and long cheer. A plaque was unveiled that read:

'This colliery is now owned and managed by the National Coal Board on behalf of the people.'

Such scenes were repeated at pits throughout the country, often to the accompaniment of pit buzzers and brass bands. The oldest employee and the most junior pit-boy were usually chosen to raise the new flag, and there followed demonstrations, parades, teas and entertainments. The ceremony at the Coal Board's headquarters in London was short. Declaring, 'We are now at the beginning of a new era,' Emanuel Shinwell, the Minister of Fuel and Power, gave a bound copy of the Nationalization Act to the Chairman of the Coal Board, Lord Hyndley. The Prime Minister, Clement Attlee, likened the Board to 'a fine team going in to bat on a distinctly sticky wicket', adding that he thought they would score a great many sixes.

'The whole country is watching this huge experiment,' said the general manager of one of the N.C.B.'s new areas at another ceremony that day. 'I am sure you all realize your tremendous responsibilities. You can put this country on its feet, or you can put it on the floor.' Nationalization, union leaders and management agreed, demanded new attitudes, new relationships, new responsibilities – in short, cooperation rather than conflict. But in the summer of the first year of the N.C.B.'s existence, a strike occurred at Grimethorpe Colliery in Yorkshire which threw all these aims into doubt. According to one union leader, the strike was 'one of the most bitter I have seen in the whole of my life'. The strikers made a caricature of the N.U.M. President, William Lawther, showing him with a halter around his neck, because he had suggested that the strike was damaging nationalization. The Divisional Chairman, Major-General Noel Holmes, had effectively locked the men out, and when told that someone had threatened to punch his nose if he left the security of his office, he walked around Grimethorpe village challenging anyone to touch him. Eccentricities apart, the strike showed that the problems of nationalization were to be far greater than even the most pessimistic speeches had allowed.

The bill to establish public ownership and control of the coal industry had been produced in a tremendous hurry. The report by Sir Charles Reid had produced such a damning indictment of private enterprise that it was clear to almost everyone, except the coal-owners, that nationalization had to be introduced quickly if the country was to have coal. But the structure of the industry had to be right: too much experiment would cost coal and damage the reputation of nationalization.

Shinwell, who drew up the bill, ignored the more radical ideas of workers' control that had been a part of the miners' demands for nationalization in the early years of the century. In 1912, for example, the historic pamphlet 'The Miners' Next Step' had called for a united industrial organization based on the cardinal principle that every man would be required both to join and observe its decisions: 'This would mean real democracy in real life making for real manhood and womanhood.' Bills put before Parliament in 1919, and again in 1923, 1924 and 1925, also stressed a managerial role for the miners, envisaging the industry being run by a mining council consisting of a president and twenty members, ten of whom would be appointed by the union. But all these ideas of workers' control, which had dominated thinking in the Labour movement as well as the miners' union up to the late twenties, were turned down in favour of the beliefs of Herbert Morrison, who, in putting London Transport under public control, had set up a public corporation with none of the democratic features so long hoped for by the miners. Instead there was a belief in the technocrat who could rule for greater efficiency. These were the ideals that were dominating thinking in the Labour movement by the 1940s, and these were the ideals that permeated the new National Coal Board. They prompted the following assessment: 'This is not socialism; it is state capitalism. There is not too much participation by the mineworkers in the affairs of the industry; there is far too little.' The words were those of Harold Macmillan.

The bill to nationalize the coal industry was given a first reading in the House of Commons on 19 December 1945. At its third reading, the M.P. Jim Griffiths recalled singing a mixture of 'Cwm Rhondda' and 'The Red Flag' in the Labour lobby. As he went through, someone said to him, 'Jim, this must be a proud night for your miners,' and he replied, 'Yes, but I've one regret: I wish there could have been a clause to make it retrospective to 1919.'

The National Coal Board was entrusted to nine men. Lord Hyndley, the Chairman, had been managing director of the Powell-Duffryn group of mines, and J. C. Gridley, who was put in charge of marketing, had also been a director of the company. Another former coal-owner on the board was Sir Charles Reid, the author of the famous report, who shared responsibility for production with Mr T. E. B. Young. Outsiders were represented by Sir Charles Ellis, Professor of Physics at King's College, London, who was given charge of the scientific department, and Mr L. H. H. Lowe, a chartered accountant with experience in government, who was made the member for finance. Sir Arthur Street, a distinguished civil servant who was appointed deputy chairman, developed a very friendly relationship with Arthur Horner of the N.U.M., and often used to drive him home, sit by the fire, talk and drink a pint of beer. Ebby Edwards, one of the great leaders of the union, took charge of labour relations, and Lord Citrine, who for long had been General Secretary of the T.U.C., was given responsibility for manpower and welfare. Edwards, comparing himself with Citrine, once remarked on how glad he was not to have accepted a knighthood: 'I went round

Europe with Walter Citrine,' he said, 'and you should have seen how much he was charged when people found out he was a "Sir".'

The tasks facing these men were enormous, and as soon as the composition of the Board was announced in July 1946, they began their work. Lord Hyndley and his small staff were given two rooms at the Ministry of Power, while other members of the Board either used the offices they occupied before joining, or had none at all. To solve the problem of office accommodation in the regions, they bought large mansion houses, an action that was later to generate a great deal of public criticism. Lord Hyndley toured the country meeting representatives of the coal-owners and the mineworkers, carrying out the interviews for the men who would command the new industry in the private sitting-room of whatever hotel he was in. An apocryphal tale recounted by one of the staff concerns a man who spent ten minutes being interviewed by Hyndley, before being thrown into utter confusion when asked: 'Are you coming over to us?' It turned out the man worked in the fruit trade and had walked into the wrong room.

Hyndley and his Board had to work fast. Shinwell insisted that they took over the industry as quickly as possible, because he felt that neither the miners nor the colliery owners would exert themselves greatly in the twilight of private enterprise. Hyndley started with nothing, and from that had to build an organization which, on 1 January 1947, would be able to pull together and control over 800 companies. They divided the country up into nine divisions which recognized the broad geographical boundaries of the coalfields, and put a chairman and board in charge of each. Beneath them were the basic commercial units, the areas as they were called, fifty of them each consisting of anything between six and sixty-six collieries. The Board adopted the military 'line and staff' system of organization, the only precedent they had for large-scale state control, whereby there was a direct line of responsibility and command from the chairman to the pit, each official along the way having a staff or department to assist him. This organization, entirely the child of Hyndley and his team, was charged by statute to 'supply coal of a quality, size and price and in quantities as may seem to them best calculated to further the public interest in all respects'. The question was where to start.

The state of the industry was appalling. For example, almost a fifth of the coal was cut by hand, and 21,000 pit ponies were still employed to haul tubs underground. Many of the collieries were old, nearing exhaustion and suffering from a consistent lack of investment. Hardly any techniques were used to suppress dust, the standards of training were far below those of other European countries, and there was little scientific research. There were not enough youngsters in the industry, there was far too much absenteeism and injury, and a relationship between employer and employee that was generally sour. Added to this formidable list of problems facing the Coal Board was an insatiable demand for coal. The task was gargantuan, and the Board's response never failed to produce criticism.

Less than two years after vesting day, Sir Charles Reid, the author of the report that had exposed the weakness of the coal industry under private ownership, announced his resignation. It was not a quiet affair. After months of disagreement he declared: 'I have resigned from the N.C.B. because I have no confidence either in it or in the organization it has set up.' He made public a letter he had sent to Shinwell some months earlier in which he had written:

I do not believe the present cumbersome and uninspired organization will produce for the country the coal it needs for home and export purposes; and at a satisfactory price; it cannot deal with the indiscipline so rampant in the mines today; it cannot keep an effective check on production costs; nor will it, in my judgement, accomplish the vital technical reorganization of the collieries on which the Government has decided and which the country expects to see carried out. Moreover it cannot give confident and effective leadership to management or men.

Reid maintained that the Coal Board should have been producing an extra 30 million tons a year with the men and machinery they already had. Instead, they were destroying individual responsibility and initiative by concentrating decision-making on the national and divisional boards, where many of the members had little or no experience of mining, and where departments were built up with little regard for cost or efficiency. The N.U.M. too was criticized for failing to appreciate the sincere desire of the

Coal Board to raise the status of the miner, and to gain the confidence of the leaders and the rank and file.

Commenting on Reid's resignation, Arthur Horner said that the Board were 'well rid of the reactionary'. The *Colliery Guardian*, an independent publication, ominously warned that the upper echelons of the Coal Board had so 'exasperated men of action on the lower rungs that many of them have thrown their hands in; and now the revolt has spread to the heads, and discontent is rampant in the ranks'. Were these criticisms merely the birth pangs of a new industry or were they symptoms of a deeper malaise?

The weaknesses of the industry were all too apparent. In its first decade, the Coal Board ran at a loss of £20 million. This record was not as bad as its critics implied because most of the losses were concentrated in 1947, when problems were inevitable, and 1955, when political interference with the price of coal was at its height. Furthermore, the heavy burden of interest payments on the Board's finances made the balance sheet look a lot worse than it was. In fact, if they were set aside, there was only one year in which the industry actually ran at a loss. Despite the controversy caused at the time about every rise in the price of coal, in fact the Government kept prices below their commercial level. Throughout this period, the Board were also spending a great deal of money on modernization, slowly at first, but reaching £100 million a year by 1955.

The Board redesigned the underground layout of many pits, developed powered supports and improved conditions generally. The fact that by 1957 about 90 per cent of all coal was got by machine was another considerable achievement. At the end of the first decade, Jim Bowman, the former N.U.M. Vice-President who by then was Chairman of the Coal Board, claimed that the best coalfields in Europe could not compare with the best in Britain. 'New life has been put into an old body,' he wrote, 'though the industry is still weak and full of problems.'

Another target for critics was the way that the amount of coal mined each year ceased to rise after 1951, and productivity stagnated. The Board's policies were said to have collapsed and failed. In 1950, a document called 'A Plan for Coal' set out a programme for reducing costs, increasing output and improving productivity so that 240 million tons would be mined each year in the period from 1961 to 1965. The criticisms intensified when, five years later, a new plan called 'Investing in Coal' lowered the target to a more realistic level. Should the Board have been able to produce more coal, and were they, as *The Times* suggested, perpetuating known inefficiencies?

They had, without doubt, been over-optimistic and had underestimated the huge task before them. They were greatly shocked to discover that putting extra men into the pits did not necessarily increase production. It was not a matter of the miners working less hard, but rather that the changes needed in the industry cost coal and, of course, money. The decision to give the miners two weeks' annual holiday for the first time in their history lost the Board 4 million tons a year. The Ministry of Fuel and Power determined that a further 10 million tons were lost annually because 21,000 men were involved in development work, rather than in meeting current demands. Above all there was the problem, long recognized by mining engineers, that each lump of coal was more costly and more difficult to mine than the last, because seams became thinner, distances longer, shafts deeper and so on. This meant that every twelve months the N.C.B. had to replace 4–5 million tons simply to stay where they were. Put bluntly by the Board's economic adviser, E. F. Schumacher, the number of completed new schemes 'could not match the loss of capacity due to obsolescence,' especially when it took an average of ten years to complete the sinking of a new pit, and eight years to carry out schemes of large-scale reconstruction.

But production statistics were not the only criteria for judging the success of the first decade of public ownership. Nationalization was also the realization of a dream, a whole new form of industrial organization never before attempted on such a large scale. The Lord President of the Council in the Attlee Government, Herbert Morrison, hoped to see management and men developing a 'higher social outlook'. 'It is a revolution of the spirit we need,' he maintained, 'good cheer and comradeship instead of depression and negation.' His appeal, endorsed by both sides of the industry, was particularly emphasized by the General Secretary, Arthur Horner. He told the 1947 annual conference:

A new consciousness must be created, a new morality, a new understanding of our true interests which will present irresponsible minorities with such a wall of opposition on working-class grounds as will discourage and make impossible success in their endeavours to interfere with production.

The days of protest were over. The Executive Committee pledged themselves to 'do everything possible to promote and maintain a spirit of self discipline . . . and a readiness to carry out all reasonable orders given by management'. Officials would now spend large amounts of time in administration and on committees helping to make the industry a success.

Nonetheless, the N.U.M. was careful to maintain its independence of management. This was vital, said the T.U.C. in 1944, 'not only for the maintenance and improvement of the standards and conditions of the workpeople, but also because of the power of independent criticism the unions can exert'. The N.U.M. therefore chose not to have formal representation on the Board. Instead the N.U.M. preferred to see that the labour department in particular was staffed largely with their own ex-members. Very many regional officers took up jobs with the N.C.B., even though the union's rules forbade them to keep up their membership. But their loyalties were stretched two ways: managers were inclined to suspect them as troublemakers and union sympathizers, whereas the men could see them as 'turncoats'. Horner himself believed that nationalization could not end conflict: 'They buy labour, and we sell it, and of course we sell it dear. That conflict is still there and we must try to handle it sensibly, not in the old way, but in an intelligent way.'

But the search for this 'new way' had to overcome the bequest of a history in which conflict had been inevitable. So as early as the summer of 1947, for example, a delegate at the annual conference spoke of the 'terrible tendency throughout the country to paint the face of the coal-owners over the face of the Coal Board'. Two years later a survey by Margaret Cole for the Fabian Society found the great majority of mineworkers disillusioned with 'too many of the old brigade' and 'too many major-generals' sitting on the Board. In fact the number of ex-coal-owners on the Board was remarkably small, though Attlee admitted that too many military types had found their way into the organization. South Wales, for example, was put in charge of an army man who had a mountain named after him in Malaysia. The rear-admiral who controlled Kent established an office overlooking the sea in Dover, so that he could continue to watch ships. He remarked to a colliery manager, 'I don't know anything about mining, but they're awfully nice chaps.' In South Wales there was the added difficulty of what was seen as a takeover of all the important jobs in the coalfield by ex-employees of the Powell-Duffryn company. But the real problem was the many officials and managers throughout the N.C.B. whose attitudes were felt to be unchanged since the days of their employment under private enterprise. At pit level especially, men would often see the same managers carrying out the same jobs as before vesting day. Full well could they wonder what had changed. Once the Coal Board began to prosecute men on unofficial strike, the similarities with the old days were underlined at the expense of the differences. Jim Bowman, N.U.M. Vice-President in the first years of nationalization, warned that the 'goodwill that has been built up so laboriously since vesting day is being replaced with cynicism'. And Will Paynter commented that after a decade of public ownership 'a bad set of employers has been replaced by a better set, but a relationship of master and servant still exists'.

Quite apart from the question of the staffing of the Board, there was also great concern over its organization. Surprisingly, perhaps, many mineworkers agreed with the *Daily Express* view of the N.C.B. as an overstaffed, overfat bureaucracy. There were more resolutions at conferences on this subject than almost any other. The joke became that at one pit a job was advertised at £20 a week as Inspector of Canaries. Officials, according to Margaret Cole's survey, were seen as a 'ubiquitous kind of spiv . . . when they visit a pit, which is seldom, it is like a football team turning out'. Managers too complained that they were required to write too many reports and were not given enough discretion on matters affecting pay and conditions.

W. Ernest Jones, who in the late 1950s was President of the union, pointed out on many occasions that many of the new white-collar employees were to provide research, planning and medical facilities that the industry had previously lacked. But he also concurred that the 'spirit that caused our men to sing at the pit top on vesting day' was being swamped by a top-heavy bureaucracy. Following the resignation of Sir Charles Reid, the N.C.B. appointed an inquiry under Sir Robert Burrows to look into organization. He reported that generally things were working well, but the doubts continued. At last the N.C.B. sought the advice of men with experience of large-scale undertakings. In early 1958, a team headed by Alexander (later Lord) Fleck, the chairman of I.C.I., began work.

Generally speaking, it was the kind words of Lord Fleck that received most attention. He recognized that the Board had faced 'difficulties unparalleled in any other industry', and saw no serious defect in the main structure of the organization. 'Much of the criticism of the Board,' he asserted, 'has been ill-informed.' But what tended to escape attention was his concern about the quality of management in the industry. The men at the top, for example, had changed around so frequently that only one member remained from the original Board. Far from there being too little decentralization of power, Fleck found the Board unwilling to ensure that their decisions were carried out, as often they were not. Many area managers failed to measure up to their job. Those who were ex-mining engineers were far happier solving technical problems than working as administrators, and so spent a great deal of time interfering in the day-to-day running of the pits. This casual approach to management was reflected in industrial relations, where Fleck recommended the establishment of a new department to deal with the ever more complex problems. The Board wholly accepted Fleck's recommendations. The union were more critical. They noted that the result of the inquiry had been to increase the number of non-producers in the N.C.B.'s employ by one quarter, to 50,000.

The general disillusionment with the men who were running the industry and the organization they had created made it difficult to generate the 'new responsibility' so earnestly desired by Horner, the leadership of the union and the Coal Board itself. But they met with some considerable successes. Most notable was the union's acceptance of a national system for the conciliation and arbitration of wage demands. Effectively they had surrendered the right to strike. Any matter affecting pay or conditions was dealt with by a body called the Joint National Negotiating Committee, consisting of fourteen members of the N.U.M. and every member of the National Coal Board. If they failed to agree, then a referee, the National Reference Tribunal, gave a decision that was binding on both sides. The Board saw the scheme as a way of ending the bitterness that had dominated the previous relationship between the employers and the employed: 'By meeting the just claims the Board hoped to infuse a new spirit into management and men, new partners in a public service.' Horner gave his support, believing that it would achieve 'the maximum results for our own forces with the least possible damage to them'.

The union leadership used all the influence they could muster to ensure restraint in wage negotiations. 'If we asked for the moon,' Horner was fond of saying, 'we could get it.' 'Instead,' he concluded, 'we have shown the highest sense of social responsibility of any organization in this country.' And indeed they had. Admittedly, their support for the conciliation scheme looked a bit shaky on the occasions when their wage demands were turned down. One such event, in 1952, prompted Horner to declare that they faced the worst crisis since 1926. There were also sectional problems, especially with the craftsmen, who barely concealed their ill feelings as their differentials became eroded by the union's efforts to raise the wages of the lower-paid. Nevertheless, the union could have mercilessly exploited the shortage of labour in the industry to win more money. But they didn't. Why? An altruistic desire to cooperate with the Coal Board was only part of the reason. Most important was the fact that the union was effectively split. The day-wage earners were subject to negotiations which were bound by compulsory arbitration. Their rates were also depressed by the overtime they were encouraged to do on Saturdays. Low basic wages were masked by long hours at overtime rates that made the take-home higher than it would otherwise have been. The result was that between 1947 and 1955, the day-wage men won six increases in the national minimum rates. This didn't give them great riches: for by the end of the first decade of nationalization, the wages of hourly-paid workers in the mining industry had done no more than keep pace with the rate of inflation.

Not so the pieceworkers. Despite many, many speeches and resolutions calling for an end to the inequities of piecework, the pieceworkers remained beyond the control of the national union when it came to pay bargaining. They were the élite – the colliers, cuttermen, rippers, borers, packers and power loaders – all with jobs underground, mostly at the coal-face. The main part of their wages was calculated either from a list giving 'prices' for each individual task, or according to the tonnage of coal that was cut. Some of the contracts operating in the sixties were drawn up after the General Strike. Each group tended to conduct its own wage negotiations with the pit management, sometimes quite independently of the local union officials. Their strong bargaining position as the front-line troops of the industry was further enhanced by the Coal Board's policy of only breaking even financially, thus relieving some of the pressures on individual pits to be as efficient as they might have been. By continuing to bargain at pit level, the pieceworkers did much better than those whose negotiations were carried out nationally. In the first ten years of nationalization, pieceworkers' earnings pushed the miners to the top of the wages table. Their average pay for a shift doubled, whereas prices went up by under two-thirds.

Piecework also caused strikes. Before the Second World War, the number of working days lost through stoppages in coal-mining equalled the number lost throughout the whole of the rest of British industry. In the first ten years of nationalization, the industry, with less than 4 per cent of the country's labour force, accounted for about one-third of all days lost because of strikes. It was a reduction, but the real change came in the type of strike that was dominant. After the war, the number of separate disputes multiplied, to a greater number than they had ever been, involving fewer men and on average lasting a shorter length of time. Every single one of them was unofficial.

Most of the strikes lasted a day. They also occurred at the very first stage of an elaborate pit conciliation procedure worked out between the Coal Board and the N.U.M. The most common cause was a disagreement about wages. A study of two pits in Lancashire in the early sixties showed that the faceworkers were the most strike-prone because they knew their skills were in short supply, and their wages tended to vary a lot. The longwall method of mining also encouraged the development of negotiation by team or occupational group. Disputes were therefore often handled at a very early level by lay representatives, ignoring the branch officials of the union almost completely. Allied to this was a common belief that the union was concerned with higher policy, often to the neglect, it was alleged, of pit problems.

The tendency to strike also varied from area to area. In the first years of nationalization, Yorkshire, Scotland and South Wales accounted for upwards of three-quarters of the total tonnage lost through disputes. But when looking for causes, it is important to be wary of generalizations. The communist leadership in both South Wales and Scotland played an important part, but so too did the level of wages in those coalfields, which were substantially lower than those in England. In Wales, dusty conditions caused the highest rate of pneumoconiosis in the country; and in Lanarkshire conflict was caused by religious rivalry between Catholics and Protestants. (For those seeking political plots behind strikes, it is also worth pointing out that throughout the fifties Yorkshire, with its high strike record, had a right-wing leadership.)

It is hardly surprising that coal-mining suffered so badly from disputes. For a start the Coal Board went to great trouble to record every stoppage, of whatever duration. No other industry was so honest, meticulous or maybe even so naïve. For the highly localized nature of mining, the tight introspective communities insulated to a degree from outside opinion, caused tensions. So too did the nature of the job. W. H. Sales, a member of the Coal Board in the fifties, summed it up by saying: 'We must realize how difficult it is to make a man enthuse about throwing twelve or more tons of coal a distance of seven feet or so in about six hours of working time, often in dust-laden, warm, humid atmospheres and in cramped positions, and keep this up daily for forty years of more.'

The inability to solve the strike problem locally through an agreed conciliation procedure was matched by strenuous attempts at amelioration by the union's leaders. Lawther continually harangued the men who 'had not recognized their responsibilities', and who by going on strike had committed a 'crime against our own people'. At the outset, they signed an agreement with the Board pledging the union 'to prevent unconstitutional stoppages' and prohibiting the giving of financial or moral support to people engaged in such actions. Much time was spent in discussing ways of reducing the number of strikes, and in the late fifties the N.U.M. even agreed to a joint investigation into their causes. To have done much more would have been to overestimate very seriously the power of the national union. To have taken disciplinary action against recalcitrant strikers, as some outside the industry suggested, would have been to rupture the bond between the union's officials and its members. As Horner rather gloomily concluded: 'Old habits of thinking went on. Men's minds did not change. Most of them knew that there had been no fundamental change in society.'

The truth of his remarks was shown in another way. The persistence of absenteeism was also seen as a negation of the 'new morality'. The real degree of absenteeism in the mines was almost always exaggerated and often sensationalized. Up to 1955, the absence rate was expressed as a percentage of the shifts that management thought it was 'possible' for a man to work. Put another way, if a manager thought a man could work only four shifts a week, and he did so, his absence rate was zero. But if, and this often happened, the manager decided he could work for six shifts a week, and he only worked five, his absence rate was over 16 per cent even though his attendance was higher. In addition, between a half and two-thirds of all absence was 'involuntary', caused by such things as bereavements or medical visits. Of the rest, the so-called 'voluntary absenteeism', much was caused by the very nature of the job. A man late for a shift, for example, could not get down the pit because coal was being wound, so might as well turn around and stay at home.

Even accepting all these explanations, the National Coal Board and the leadership of the N.U.M. were well aware that better attendance would have produced more coal and a less hostile press. This was especially so between 1954 and 1961, when there was a steady increase in the percentage of men absent from work. Their efforts to solve the problem, though, began in 1947, when a bonus of one day's pay was offered if a full week's work was done. It did not have much impact on absence and annoyed men who had missed a shift through no fault of their own. After four years, the pressure to end the scheme became so strong that the union leadership had to acquiesce. There was also an attempt to make the consultative committees at each pit responsible for policing attendance. Recalcitrant offenders were reported to them, and, in theory, after a strong warning they could recommend dismissal. The main problem was that the consultative committees spent more and more time dealing with absentees, and less and less on other matters of equal if not more significance. The N.U.M. and the N.C.B. even tried to establish joint attendance committees to interview, warn and eventually discipline offenders, but to the embarrassment of the National Executive Committee, the areas of the union overwhelmingly rejected the proposal.

In the late fifties, the N.U.M. cooperated with joint investigations into various pits where the problem seemed endemic. They also agreed to a study of the causes of absenteeism by Dr R. B. Buzzard of the Medical Research Council. His report was a controversial one. He felt that miners tended to strike a balance between earning money and having time off. The use of incentives or deterrents to improve attendance would have no lasting impact. The best strategy would be to make the work less arduous and to select men more carefully. Buzzard's conclusions ran contrary to the whole approach of the Coal Board and their supporters in the upper echelons of the N.U.M. His report was kept unpublished for five years.

The problem of absenteeism imperilled the good workings of the industry's consultation system. This, along with the conciliation agreement, was to have provided the 'new way' that Horner had hoped for in 1947. Great store was set by a network of consultative committees throughout the Coal Board, which, it was believed, would induce a relationship between the manager and the managed that would convert the industry into a socialized one.

In 1944 the T.U.C. had insisted that the 'right of the workpeople to a voice in the conduct of a public industry . . . must find a formal place in its organization and operation'. The Nationalization Act specified that the Board must direct their policy to securing not only the safety, health and welfare of their employees, but also the benefit of their practical knowledge and experience. The colliery consultative committee, the basic unit, was chaired by the colliery manager and was primarily composed of three management appointees and six representatives of the mineworkers, two of whom stood for re-election each year. The N.U.M. cautiously regarded these committees as 'not necessarily controversial, rather do we regard them as providing an opportunity for pooling ideas of all sections of the industry'. But just as the conciliation procedure was successful on an industry-wide basis, but overwhelmed at pit level by strikes and local pay deals, so too the consultative arrangements were to prove most successful nationally.

In fact the contacts through the Coal Industry Consultative Council were so good that the N.U.M.'s President, W. E. Jones, felt impelled to declare that 'the impact on the Board's general plans arising out of joint discussions that took place at the meetings cannot be overestimated'. For example, they commissioned a joint report into steps to reduce wastage including better housing, improving amenities and better chances of promotion. Discussions of the national consultative council helped to smooth the way for the introduction of European Voluntary Workers and Hungarians into the pits. Production problems, absenteeism and disputes all came under review and joint investigation. The fact that the miners' demand for reorganization and mechanization was carried through so effectively had a lot to do with the effective consultation system at national level. 'The views and feelings of the Union,' said Jones, 'are sought by the Board at every stage as the many and varied problems have to be met and overcome.'

At pit level the consultation system had a rough start. The survey of miners' attitudes two years after vesting day showed the typical attitude to be: 'I have yet to hear of a pit consultative committee that is anything else but a wrangling ground about reasons for lost output.' The problem was that they had no real power. The Board insisted on discipline and centralized decision-making, and strictly forbade the release of any financial information to colliery committees, except where the pit was going to close. Even when the pit manager was enthusiastic, the stringent statutory responsibilities vested in him made him reluctant to share power. More often than not, however, managers and officials regarded the committees as an additional and wearisome chore. The bad relations sometimes generated during pay negotiations would spill over into the consultative committee meetings. The committees acted mainly as a channel of communication from the managers to the pit, and only occasionally were they consulted before a decision was made. Too often the committees were seen to be instruments of discipline, especially where absenteeism was concerned. The end result was that it was very difficult to generate much enthusiasm for their deliberations among the rank and file. In Philip Noel-Baker's words: 'Consultation was no wonder drug.'

What was the record of the Board at the end of the first decade of nationalization? Great progress had undoubtedly been made in terms of securing production, increasing mechanization, rebuilding pits and opening new ones. The conditions of work of the average miner had also changed beyond belief: there were better wages, free pithead baths, new canteens, improved housing, good compensation for injury, a pension scheme, and many other facilities unrealizable under private enterprise. The Board itself was beginning to weld the independent traditions of individual pits into a unified organization. But as Bevin said: 'Nationalization cannot give you heaven, but it gives you the means by which you can straighten things out.' Conflict was still there. There were still strikes, still absenteeism, still a feeling of a split between the boss and the worker. There was disillusionment. Shinwell was the first to complain that, whereas he had had the utmost cooperation from the union's hierarchy, he had had little from the men further down. For the Coal Board's part, W. H. Sales believed that 'the fund of goodwill, of determination to succeed, of idealism and of hope which the Act of Nationalization created, is being drawn upon steadily year by year, and is not being adequately replaced'. Ebby Edwards, despairing of ever reducing unofficial strikes, concluded, 'If goodwill can be bought, the N.C.B. has paid for it.' For the miners, state capitalism with however genial a counten-ance did not accord with the ideal of nationalization proclaimed during the savagery of the twenties.

6. A Dream Gone Sour

From the perspectives of the 1980s, and an acute awareness of the limitations of energy supplies, what happened to the Coal Board in the sixties appears at most disgraceful and at least short-sighted. Pits were closed and their coal, one of our great national assets, lost for ever. Successive governments ignored the example of the shortage of oil that followed the Suez Canal crisis of 1956, and allowed oil companies to dominate the British economy. They said it was in response to inexorable commercial pressures, but in reality the competition, as far as the Coal Board was concerned, was not even fair. Whole mining communities were destroyed, the industry was changed beyond recognition, and the miners were left disillusioned with the Coal Board, the Labour Government and even, to an extent, their own leaders. From the events of the sixties sprang the militancy of the seventies.

There was little sign in 1957 that either the Coal Board or the N.U.M. knew what was about to hit them. The union were worried about the decline in coal consumption, but saw it mainly as the result of the Government's deflationary policies, while the Coal Board believed that any setback would only be temporary. The following year there was less room for optimism as the demand for coal continued to fall and both sides of the industry began to twitch. The Coal Board started to consider ways of reducing output, and their first decision was to end Saturday working. They did so without consulting the union, and as by this time the average miner had come to depend on the extra money from such work, the result was 'anxiety not known since nation-alization'. So strong were the feelings of delegates to the annual conference of 1958 that Sam Watson, the Durham miners' leader, felt compelled to warn that to talk the language of 1926 in 1958 'was a negation of intelligence'.

Within a short space of time more drastic measures were needed to meet the crisis, and so, for the first time in its history, the Coal Board began to close pits before their reserves were completely exhausted. After a decade of expansion, the shock to the miners cannot be overstated. The Coal Board announced that in 1959 they intended closing thirty-six pits, twenty of which would be in Scotland. A total of about 12,000 men would be affected. The union was stunned, and there were strong pressures to resist the closures actively. In early January 1959, a group of some 200 Welsh miners protested outside the union's headquarters while the executive committee met to discuss pit closures. At the end of the month, the South Wales miners arranged a march through the West End of London, finishing with a lobby of Parliament. But most of the men were delayed by fog, and arrived two hours too late. The march was brief and was confined to the fog-bound silence of Eaton Square, a whimper of a protest. In February, a crowd of several hundred Scottish miners gathered with their pipe band to lobby and sing outside the Conway Hall in London, where the union was holding a special conference to test opinion on the closures. The Minister of Power and the Coal Board were targets for parody and abuse. So too was their own President. Inside the hall, the delegates agreed on the need for a national fuel policy to make full use of indigenous sources of energy which represented no cost to the balance of payments. And in words that foretold the events of 1973, the President, W. E. Jones, warned: 'Only two years ago those of us who ran motor cars were not able to draw up at a petrol pump to get petrol unless we had unit coupons in our pockets to secure it, because there was a political controversy about a transport way for oil from the Middle East. The Middle East is an unstable area of the world, and we believe we cannot afford to link up our fuel and power policy and our economy to that extent with oil.'

That summer, the Coal Board's Chairman, James Bowman, bemoaned the state of the industry. They had built up stocks of coal to try to keep as many pits open as they could, but the cost of doing so was 'debilitating psychologically as well as financially', and as demand continued to fall, they could see no option but to amend their forecasts. In August, Bowman and the Board told the N.U.M. of the 'Revised Plan for Coal', which set a target of between 200 and 215 million tons a year by 1965. To bring output into line with this, they would close between 205 and 240 collieries, mostly in Northumberland, Cumberland, Durham and the North West, and only about half the closures would be because reserves were exhausted. It was a depressing scenario at a time when the industry should have been reaping the benefits of all the hard work and planning of the previous decade. And for the future, they included the following warning to governments:

Coal reserves must in the Board's view be husbanded notwithstanding the development of other sources of energy. Moreover, in all the established coalfields, around almost every colliery, there are houses and shops and schools – whole communities – whose reason for existence is the local colliery. All collieries must eventually die, but the decision to end the life of one of them prematurely must not be taken without regard to the effect on the community and the social assets dependent on or associated with it.

Their words went unheeded.

At first the union blamed the Coal Board for making the crisis a lot worse by 'giving away export markets' and not arguing strongly enough for restrictions on the imports of oil. They also believed, with justification, that the Coal Board were producing too much of the wrong kind of coal, and too little of the type that would sell. A special conference in 1959 formulated the union's line of attack. Open-cast mining should be stopped, and the distribution of coal should be improved by merging it into the rest of the nationalized industry instead of leaving sales in the hands of none-too-enterprising private firms. There should be restrictions on the use of oil, a halt to the conversion of coal-power stations to oil, and a thorough examination of the true cost of the nuclear programme. Repeatedly, they stressed the danger to the economy of an over-reliance on oil imported from politically unstable parts of the world. And in a document published to put their case to the country, they argued:

The crux of the union's attitude is the urgent need to take steps to secure from the Government an assured place for the coal industry in the British economy. This means securing from the Government a firm estimate of what part the coal industry is to play in meeting the country's future energy requirements, rather than haphazardly trying to estimate the course of future demand for coal in free competition with other fuels.

In the union's view it would be economic lunacy to let coal run down too far. Oil is a product of areas throughout the world, many of which are politically unstable. A political crisis could quickly be transformed into fuel scarcity.

Unlike the National Coal Board, the oil companies have no moral responsibility to the United Kingdom. We consider this to be a matter deserving a political decision by the Government that will guarantee fuel supplies.

In the meantime, faced with the grave social consequences of the Board's policies, the union decided it was 'essential to give the Board the maximum cooperation to ensure that there was the least possible hardship to the men concerned', while insisting that no pit would close until alternative employment was found.

The changeover to oil showed no signs of relenting. Imports of fuel oil increased by over a third between 1957 and 1959, and in only the first nine months of 1960 they rose by another 50 per cent. The result was even more pit closures. In the three years to 1960, 120,000 jobs were lost, mainly in isolated communities which could provide little, if any, alternative employment. In 1960, another forty-four pits were closed, with a loss of 51,000 jobs. What was equally depressing was that year by year the industry was actually in better and better shape. All the benefits from the programme of mechanization and reconstruction that had been carried out since vesting day, at great expense to the Board, the miners and the nation, were now coming to fruition. It was a cruel irony: by the early 1960s an annual coal output of some 200 million tons could be produced, mainly from efficient reconstructed collieries or brand new ones. About half the coal was also coming from fully mechanized faces, and the result was rapid rises in productivity. The industry should have been a great national asset in its finest hour. Instead, it was in fear for its very existence. Such was the industry bequeathed by Sir James Bowman to his successor as chairman – Alfred, later Lord, Robens.

Robens's appointment was as controversial as his reign. For a start he was a senior member of Labour's shadow Cabinet, and had been asked to take up the job by the Conservative Prime Minister, Harold Macmillan. To add fat to the fire, news of his appointment leaked out before Hugh Gaitskell, then leader of the Labour Party, had been told. Managers within the Coal Board criticized the Government for not promoting someone from inside the industry, and the N.U.M. were concerned that Robens was supposed to put a human face on the Conservatives' plans for decentralizing the N.C.B.

When Robens joined the Coal Board as Chairman-designate in October 1960, he decided, in his own words, to 'grasp the nettle'. He confirmed that he wanted to build the industry around producing 200 million tons a year, and of course Jim Bowman had left him the wherewithal to do so. But he also warned the miners that no one owed them a living, and that the only route to a better life was by concentrating output on the best pits in the most productive coalfields. 'This is the only way we can maintain the industry at its present size in the face of fierce competition from oil,' he told the miners' conference in 1962. 'This is not an era of coal at any price – that ended in 1957 – we are in the era of hard selling based on price, quality and service, and in this situation the fundamental need is to be able to produce the right product at the right price.' He also made it clear that the Board would act commercially and not tolerate any interference from the Government. If the Minister wanted to give the Board a directive then it would have to be a statutory one, and published in the annual report, so that everyone could see the difference between commercial decisions and purely political ones.

Robens intensified the sales drive already begun under his predecessor. His approach was a highly personal one – using a picture of himself in advertisements, for example, so that all could see that the 'gaffer was prepared to get stuck in'. Power stations were providing the one growing market for coal, but under Robens's direction, the Board put up a massive resistance to the rundown of its use in other areas too. With the N.U.M.'s cooperation, they tried to convince local authorities that they should use coal for their new houses or offices. Sam Bullough, the N.U.M.'s Yorkshire area president, refused a drink in his local pub after it converted to oil. New methods were introduced for distributing coal more cheaply, and the 'merry-go-round system' was developed whereby trains could unload coal at power stations without stopping. When the steel industry wanted to import cheaper foreign coking coal in the early sixties, Robens convinced the Government that it was ridiculous to allow private companies to play the market when a great deal of public capital had been invested, at their request, to ensure a supply of indigenous fuel.

Above all, Robens gave the industry personality. He was a natural publicist, and at first spent a lot of time rebuilding the morale of the industry. He attacked the 'Jeremiahs' who were constantly decrying coal: 'If you cry "stinking fish" about your own industry, do not be surprised if the consumer says, "Perhaps it does smell after all." ' Robens travelled extensively from pit to pit getting to know the men and preaching his doctrine of vigorous competition. Whenever he met anger or resentment, he confronted it head-on. His working-class origins and his reputation in the Labour Party helped him to gain a hearing, appealing to the 'innate good sense of the miners', sometimes over the heads of their area and branch officials. A lot of this rapport, though, was to be shattered in the events that occurred towards the end of his time at Hobart House.

From the perspective of 1962, it looked as if the Coal Board's policies might have worked. In 1961, productivity had risen by 8 per cent and the industry made a profit. Robens had additionally won from the Government a tax on fuel oil of 2d a gallon which helped in the battle against oil. The Board's finances looked relatively strong, and between 1962 and 1964 they continued to show a small surplus. But it was a false dawn. Giant oil tankers and brand new refineries meant that the cost of oil could be reduced on a scale that coal could never hope to match. Oil companies could also offer special discounts to break into a market, or use a higher price charged to some customers, to pay for the lower price charged to others. By statute, the Coal Board could not adopt similar tactics. As Robens put it: 'We were fighting with one hand tied behind our back.' And the worst was yet to come.

By the mid sixties, the competition from oil had become even more intense. The Labour Government instituted a review of fuel policy which, when published in 1975, presented the predicament facing the Government. Should they support the industry to save imports and preserve the large investment that had been made in the coal industry? Was it possible for them to predict a time when oil might suddenly become more expensive than coal? Or should Britain instead move towards a more diversified energy policy based on the cheapest sources of fuel, with aid being given to the coal industry to make it even slimmer and even more competitive? The Government decided that they would set a target for the industry but would not underwrite coal's performance. There could be no subsidy and no featherbedding: coal would have to compete. And to do so, the coal industry was forced to close pits faster than at any time previously.

The new, accelerated contraction of the industry only added to the problems caused by the closures that were already taking place. In 1960, there were 698 collieries in Great Britain. By 1965 there were 534, and by 1970 there were only 299. Of more than 600,000 men employed by the Coal Board in 1960, about half had left by the end of the decade. Has any major industry ever contracted on such a massive scale in such a short space of time?

The closures made the N.C.B. seem just like any other employer. Great bitterness was created by the apparently off-hand way in which the Coal Board closed the first round of pits in 1959 without any chance for negotiation. The decisions appeared to have been made in London, far away from the pits, by men who mouthed condolences but whose sincerity was open to grave doubts. Above all, their decisions seemed quite arbitrary. Often, for example, the local N.U.M. lodge would respond to appeals for greater effort to save a pit by cooperating with measures to increase efficiency. Occasionally, the local union men would lay their reputations on the line and win agreement to a six-month test period. Imagine the bewilderment, then, when after substantial improvements in productivity the pits still closed.

The most dramatic closures in the early sixties were those of two new pits in Scotland, Glenochil and Rothes, which it had been thought would provide secure employment into the future. The Coal Board closed Glenochil even though the union argued that it could be used to maintain supplies to a power station near by. In the case of Rothes, the N.U.M. submitted a detailed plan to save the pit, maintaining that they would rather see older pits close than one with first-class modern facilities. But the decision of what was profitable and what was not was left, as in every case, with the Coal Board. After more discussions, Rothes pit was closed.

Other examples are legion. A delegate from a North East pit told the Labour Party conference in 1966, 'Some three years ago at the cost of £1 million a new shaft was sunk, and yet today that pit is closed.' Time and time again, the men and their union representatives expressed their dismay at the closure of pits for short-term economic reasons when there was still coal left in them. It appeared scandalous to lose pits that today would be economically and financially sound, because oil enjoyed a temporary price advantage. And it is extremely unlikely that coal measures lost then will ever be opened up again. For one thing tunnels would have collapsed, making it a dangerous and highly costly undertaking. Other reasons were given by Will Paynter, the N.U.M.'s secretary at that time, when he recalled the fate of one anthracite pit in South Wales where the Coal Board effectively sterilized 60 million tons of coal because they needed the men to boost employment in other pits: 'Most of that coal will be lost for ever because of the build-up of water, gas and so on. And the worst of it is, future generations may need that coal.'

Often it appeared that the Coal Board were deliberately abusing their power to decide which pits were profitable. Remarks such as 'If they want to close a pit they'll find a reason' were common. The closure of Wharncliffe Woodmoor 'A', for example, prompted one such accusation. The pit was the last remaining in the Borough of Barnsley, in South Yorkshire, and still had substantial reserves of coal. The depths of disillusion with the Board were shown by a speech made by the pit's delegate, Peter Tait:

When a pit is earmarked for closure, then the Board has its own methods of ensuring that in spite of everything we do or say, close it will. We have listened time and time again to reports of new belting that never arrived, machines taken down the pit which had to come out again faulty, about levels where cleaning up and repair work are neglected over long periods. The reserves aren't exhausted, but rather the N.C.B. have decided to close certain seams gradually for their own reasons.

But what happened to the men when a pit closed? Details varied from pit to pit and area to area, but there was a basic well-worn routine. Each man at the colliery was given an interview where he would state his preferences for his new pit. The management and the union representatives would then sit down and try to work things out. On the Saturday morning before starting at their new place of work, the men were taken by special transport to familiarize themselves with their surroundings, meet the managers and trade union officials, and have tea and sand-wiches in the canteen.

In the coalfields which were particularly badly hit by the closures, like Scotland and the North East, there was also the 'pick your pit scheme', designed to tempt men to move to different coalfields altogether. Once the closure was announced, each man was sent a letter 'about your personal future' from Lord Robens. With his picture in the corner, and new houses and a modern pit in the background, he wrote: 'There will be no high pressure salesmanship, no attempt to push you into a decision. All we want to do is to give you the facts about jobs and prospects for a secure job in mining.' One of five 'pick your pit' mobile vans moved into any colliery that was closing. The employment officers arranged visits for miners and their families to new locations in the central coalfields. Money allowances were paid to help the men transfer, and elaborate arrangements were made to welcome them at the new pit. But the great incentive appears to have been better housing.

Despite the allowances, transferring to a new pit often meant a loss of income, sometimes quite a substantial one. The best jobs were already occupied by men who had been at the colliery for a long time, and the redundancy scheme for those over fifty-five, begun after 1967, by no means solved this problem. Miners also found themselves having to travel considerable distances to work, which not only cost them money, but also meant less time at home. The change was a dramatic one, as often the walk to work was replaced by a bus journey, usually at an awkward time of day and for distances of sometimes twenty or thirty miles. It was difficult for the men to be very happy with the idea of change.

In addition, unrest was caused by the Redundancy Payments Act which was supposed to compensate men for the loss of jobs and make it easier for them to move. In fact, the Act, according to Lord Robens, reduced the flow of transferring miners to a trickle, and increased conflict between the N.C.B. and the workers. The Coal Board wanted to minimize redundancy payments by proving that they had offered work elsewhere, whereas the men, tempted by the lump sum payment, saw less advantage in moving, especially when they were offered new jobs miles away. The decision as to whether money should be paid in such circumstances was the responsibility of a tribunal, which, forced into making a highly subjective decision about whether a job fifteen miles away was a 'reasonable offer of alternative employment', often appeared arbitrary and capricious.

All this might have been more acceptable if the process had been once-and-for-all. But it wasn't. There were miners who, over ten years or so, were transferred from one pit to another five times. There were some who had moved even more than that. They left the comradeship and familiarity of their own pit for a promise of job security for life elsewhere. Then that pit too would be threatened and closed and the men would have to move on, each time more dispirited and chary of the Coal Board's promises. They were, in the words of Mick McGahey, 'industrial gypsies', breeding sullen resentment that would one day explode in anger.

The closures also brought the end of some of the closed pit communities. Men with Scottish accents could be heard in the clubs of the Kent or Yorkshire coalfields. Pits with long local traditions now became 'cosmopolitan pits', employing men from other collieries with other ideas about how things should be done. At North Gawber pit in Yorkshire, for example, they had to work hard to assimilate men from Monckton Colliery. They refused to allow them all to work on the same shift, so that cliques would not develop. But they also had to woo the Monckton men away from the round shovels that they used underground, and convince them that with the narrower seam, shovels with little shafts were better. It may seem a trifling point, but to a man of maybe fifty-five, used to one style of work all his life, the change was traumatic.

The real losers, though, were the old, the disabled and the sick. For the young man with craft skills it was possible to see a future outside coal mining, albeit on less pay. But for the older men, there was nothing beyond the pit. The problem became even more acute when the economic growth generated in the first years of the Labour Government began to slacken off and unemployment began to rise. The redundant mineworkers' pension scheme encouraged men over fifty-five to leave the industry and, in effect, become unemployed. The sick and the disabled, who by tradition had been given light work on the surface of their pit, found it impossible to get jobs elsewhere. After 1965 they were given redundancy pay, which they generally used to make up their social security benefits to something approaching their previous income. But it was a wasting asset, and once finished, severe hardship ensued.

And what were these men who stayed behind left with? Whole mining communities in Scotland, South Wales, Durham and the Bristol area were obliterated. For example, in the Rhondda Fawr, once the greatest coal-producing valley in the world, there is today only one pit where once there was one at least every mile. Railway lines were torn up, pit buildings bulldozed away, and waste tips flattened and grassed. The miners' welfare halls, which in the fifties and earlier were the most tangible sign of the miners' belief in socialism, are today, more often than not, bingo palaces or carpet warehouses. The social cohesion provided by the N.U.M. lodge and its officers disappeared. In areas of emigration, little replaced it.

What, the miners were entitled to ask, had gone wrong? How had the firm commitments to the coal industry been ignored with such devastating results? Will Paynter, the N.U.M. secretary, vividly remembers the shock of his first meeting with George Brown, in November 1964: 'It was clear then that they were going to put industry and power stations on to fuel oil and nuclear.' The idea of a fuel policy that would maintain coal production at 200 million tons a year was forgotten. And the reason was the belief that coal had become obsolete.

By the time Richard Marsh introduced the White Paper on 'Fuel Policy' in 1967, the Government was stressing that the country was moving from being a two-fuel economy, based on coal and oil, to a four-fuel one, with the addition of gas from the North Sea and nuclear power. In the case of oil, it might have been expected that the Six Day War would have created worries about the reliability of supplies. But the White Paper showed no sign of concern, stating that 'it was right to base fuel policy on the expectation that regular supplies will continue to be available'. Furthermore, the White Paper declared that 'it seems likely that oil will remain competitive with coal and that pressure to force up crude prices will be held in check by the danger of the loss of markets'. In other words, six years before the price rises decreed with such force by O.P.E.C., the Government were basing their policy on a permanent future of cheap oil, and for that reason were closing pits which could never be reopened.

By the late 1960s, there was yet another competitor: natural gas. The first discovery was made in the North Sea in September 1965, and it soon provoked exciting forecasts about a great new source of abundant energy from 'High Speed Gas', as it then became. The Government accepted the claims of the Gas Council, and Richard Marsh, as Minister of Power, was particularly enthusiastic. The effect on coal was two-fold. The Board was saddled with pits which they had sunk or maintained solely to provide coal for gas-making. Of necessity in the coal industry, decisions had been made perhaps a decade earlier to ensure that supplies would be there, but as there was no contract between the Gas Council and the Board, no compensation was paid for fuel they no longer wanted. The other effect was that by 1970, gas had taken a market of something like 25 million tons away from coal.

The other great challenge came from nuclear power, which threatened the main growth market for coal as a generator of electricity. The Central Electricity Generating Board appeared firmly wedded to nuclear energy, for both its alleged cheapness and its export potential. When, in 1965, the C.E.G.B. decided to base the second generation of nuclear power stations solely on advanced gas-cooled reactors, the Minister of Power, Fred Lee, called it 'the greatest breakthrough of all time'. Constantly, ministers were told that in the end nuclear power would produce cheaper electricity at about half the capital cost. The claims that were made for these reactors, based incidentally on a small prototype built at Windscale, led to an even greater attack on coal. As events turned out in the case of the advanced gas-cooled reactor, the attacks were unnecessary. The Coal Board continually called for an independent inquiry into the comparative costs of producing electricity by coal and by nuclear means, as they believed that the comparisons that were made were arbitrary and unfair. Time and time again Robens claimed that the capital cost of building nuclear power stations was much higher than the cost of building coal-fired stations. He also maintained that the electricity produced from coal was much cheaper: the costings for nuclear, upon which the Government were basing all their statements, only looked better because of a sleight of hand by the C.E.G.B. and civil servants. They took no account of the very expensive research and development costs for nuclear energy borne by the taxpayer, and they extended the life-span of a nuclear power station from twenty to twenty-five years, making the capital costs look cheaper. Robens also put forward what he called the 'total sum' approach to decisions on energy, whereby if the Government wanted to put large amounts of money into nuclear power development, they should also include in the estimated cost to the nation the cost of running down coal.

The N.C.B.'s suspicions and anger were further aroused by the Government's refusal to disclose the true comparative costs of coal and nuclear power. Roy Mason, when he was Minister of Power, said that to do so would have destroyed the morale of the miners. Yet at the same time Robens quotes the Chairman of the Atomic Energy Authority, Lord Penney, who in the late sixties claimed that the first programme of nuclear reactors had not been a success 'partly due to the fact that coal-fired stations had proved more economic'. Robens also draws great significance from the fact that when coal was allowed to compete in the open for an aluminium smelter, Alcan, the company concerned, chose coal.

He concludes that by 1970, electricity could have come from coal 'more cheaply and at about half the capital cost' of nuclear power.

The competition to coal was therefore strong, though in the case of nuclear power, unproven. But the tragedy facing coal was that far from making the industry better able to compete, the closures made it even weaker. The N.U.M. opposed the accelerated rundown of the pits not only because jobs were being lost, but also because they argued that the insecurity was threatening even the profitable areas. The shortage of men, caused by the fact that many of them could see no long-term future in the industry, meant that many erstwhile economic pits were often working well below their optimum capacity, and therefore at a loss. Even after the financial reconstruction of the industry, the profits of a smaller and smaller number of collieries were having to bear the increasing burden of closing uneconomic pits. The special funds that the Government had allocated to hasten the closures they had demanded still required the N.C.B. to contribute half the amount. How could the industry be competitive, the N.U.M. argued, and still bear such financial burdens? Ironically, the nub of what they were arguing was actually contained in the controversial White Paper of 1967: 'In certain circumstances, the money cost of a particular resource may not be an accurate measure of its real cost to the nation. For example, if the displacement of miners adds to unemployment in the short term, manpower at marginal collieries may be regarded as costing less in national terms than the wages actually paid.' Why weren't these arguments acted upon?

The Government and its civil servants were understandably concerned to maintain the cheapest possible sources of energy. And there was a belief, though not shared by all, that the coal industry and all its many problems were best got rid of. To a greater or lesser degree each Labour Minister of Power shared these ideas. Fred Lee, for example, was a left-winger with no mining background, and there was a feeling that although his heart was in the right place, he was under the influence of his civil servants. His successor, Richard Marsh, committed some of the worst excesses against the coal industry, causing great battles with mining M.P.s in the Commons, yet he genuinely believed that without the closures coal would have no future at all. Roy Mason had a much harder task, because as an ex-miner more was expected of him, yet he too showed no desire to halt the run-down of the industry. And even if they had decided to try to do more to maintain the market for coal, say through a subsidy, would the Cabinet have approved it? The answer appears to be no.

Coal had gone out of style. All the arguments of the N.U.M. and the N.C.B. could get nowhere. In his autobiography, Robens recalls trying to persuade Jim Callaghan of the need for maintaining a healthy indigenous fuel policy, and the reply was: 'Well, Alf, I'm afraid I couldn't find an official in the whole of the Treasury who would accept your argument.' The way in which coal was viewed by the civil service was further illustrated by Robens's evidence before the Commons Select Committee on nationalized industries in 1966. He described how the Treasury refused to accept the Coal Board's arguments without even meeting them. He also deplored the 'arm-twisting' that went on:

It takes place in the meetings you have and in discussions. 'Surely you could close more pits? For example, why don't you close this pit?', and you go on and on until in the end you are having to explain about the pits you know so well and the people you are talking to have never seen. You get to the stage when you say, 'Well, we'll have another look at it.' If the capital reconstruction you want is dependent upon that, or it is implied, then you have to go back and make a judgement as to whether you will start all over again on your capital reconstruction ideas or whether you will say, 'Well, let's see if we can satisfy the ministry by these extra closures.'

The role of Lord Robens in this period is a very controversial one. He was very critical of the Labour Government, and the members of that Government are in turn very critical of him. According to those close to him, Robens certainly felt that many of the ministers he was dealing with were lesser men than he, and that coloured all their relationships. On the other hand, one senior member of the Labour Cabinet, who has known Robens a long time, described him as a 'good P.R. man, essentially two-faced: he would blame the contraction of the industry on the Government when talking with the union, but really it was he who acquiesced all along'. There is still a great deal of resentment and hostility in the union for Robens and what he stood for. In a sense, his personality invited it. But there is also a belief that because he stressed the need for a competitive industry 'pulling itself up by its bootstraps', he was in a much weaker position to stand up to the Government and say, 'Protect us.' He could only fight to protect the industry from the worst excesses of competition, and win concessions from the Government to help it contract. Will Paynter, who himself had many fierce arguments with the Labour Government, gave me this assessment of Robens's behaviour: 'A lot of people in the union attack the Coal Board. I don't attack the Coal Board, I attack the Government. It was the fuel policy both of the Tories and of the Labour Government that determined the background in which the Coal Board had to operate. Robens was carrying out Government policy and in his public utterances he had very often to justify it. He used to fume a lot, but he was essentially subordinate.'

In the light of all the controversy between the miners, Coal Board, and Labour Government, it is astonishing that throughout this period of massive upheaval there was not one single national strike over pit closures. In fact, I can only find a couple of local ones. Compared with any other industry, it is a remarkable record. R. H. S. Crossman remarked on the way that the miners felt bound to 'support the Government in an action that really meant the destruction of the mining industry'. Why did the miners who, in the first decade of nationalization, had shown themselves to be strike-prone, accept without a challenge the most dramatic change their industry was to undergo?

For a start, the national union was dominated by the right wing. The union's President, Sid Ford, shared Robens's vision of a slimmer, more competitive industry. 'If we are to obtain the reforms and improvements to which we believe our members are entitled,' he said, 'the industry will have to sell its product, and this will have to be done in the face of keen competition, especially from oil.' He believed that struggle with the Board was therefore 'pathetically outmoded' and 'not a little wearisome', and described one demonstration against the closures as nothing more than 'a circus'. It is no overstatement to say that there was bitterness, even hatred, between Ford and the progressive elements on the National Executive Committee. The fact that he had risen to power through C.O.S.A., the clerical section of the union, was used to demonstrate that he had little feel for pit life. At one N.E.C. meeting, Dai Francis, an old-style miners' leader from South Wales, harangued Ford for acquiescing in the death of so many mining communities in the valleys. 'I'm sorry to get so emotional,' said Francis, 'but none of us would be here without a little emotion.' Ford's face, by all accounts, didn't move. Ford, who was later knighted, held a majority on the largely right-wing-dominated national executive. The progressive elements on the N.E.C., like Paynter himself, were inhibited from criticizing decisions reached by the majority, and to have done so would have gone against the union's rules. So the greatest challenge to this cooperative and acquiescent attitude of the national union came, in the early sixties, from elsewhere.

In fact it came from a document called 'A Plan for Miners'. Written by a number of academics and miners' leaders, it was formulated to bring about a 'fundamental revision' of the policy of the N.U.M. It showed how the miners, in the years from 1957 to 1963, had agreed to changes that would normally have been expected to occur over a generation. The mechanization of faces, for example, had transformed the traditional nature of jobs, and along with the reconstruction of collieries had accounted for more of the fall in manpower than the decline in the sales of coal. The document declared that there should be a steady advance in real wages and conditions to match the increases in productivity. It pointed out that the Board's trading surplus per ton of coal had risen by 165 per cent between April 1956 and April 1963, whereas weekly earnings were exactly the same in real terms, and the wages of surface workers had in fact fallen by 10 per cent. It expressed concern too that the incidence of deaths and injury had risen as fast as the increase in productivity.

But Sidney Ford attacked the plan swiftly and severely. He argued that the author's assertion, that the operating profits of the industry were being masked by large sums of money being deducted for depreciation, was designed solely to create doubt, suspicion and deep resentment in the minds of the great mass of membership. 'People who foster the idea,' he concluded, 'that there are two sides in this industry with separate and conflicting interests not only do a great disservice to those who rely upon this industry for their livelihood, but their attitude serves to project a distorted image of nationalization.'

But the existence of a right-wing executive, and a President whose views coincided with those of Lord Robens, does not go far enough in explaining why there was not a greater challenge to the pit closures. The question is even more pertinent after 1964, when it was clear that the political campaign the N.U.M. had laid so much store by was not going to reap rewards. Part of the reason was that the tradition of support for the Labour Government weighed very heavily on every decision. Another explanation lies in the fact that to get a national agreement on what closures to fight would have been impossible: in a sense the Federation still ruled. Some areas were more badly affected than others, and it was widely believed, and still is, that a common fight against closures would only be possible if it were linked to a battle about wages. And as there was as yet no all-embracing wages system for the whole industry, no conflict would take place.

Could the real seats of power in the union, the areas, have taken action? For a start, any strike would have had to be unofficial, as official strikes could only be approved by the National Executive Committee and they were clearly not going to do that. But even the left-wing area committees held back, because they saw that to strike over a closure would be divisive. Men in one pit would turn round and say, 'I'm not striking for you, because you didn't strike when my pit closed,' or words to that effect. It would have been an impossible task for the executive committees to back one colliery and not another, so they did neither.

There is another explanation of the acquiescence of the miners in the sixties: they voted with their feet. Throughout the period the N.C.B. found it easy to lose men but very difficult to employ them. Younger miners, especially, decided that there was no future for coal in an oil-based economy. They could see that their pits were often old and inefficient. Mechanization had also increased accident rates and cases of pneumoconiosis. They were constantly told by Robens and others that the future of coal was very much in the balance, and they could see the effects of the closures on men, morale, and culture. Up to 1968, it was possible to leave the industry and find work elsewhere, as the Government were creating jobs in precisely those areas where pits were closing. Rather than protest, they fulfilled the hopes that their fathers had always had of them and left the industry. But after 1968, unemployment narrowed the escape route. It was no longer possible to find work elsewhere, so men were stuck in an industry where wages had fallen relative to the rate being paid for cleaner, less arduous jobs outside. The dream of nationalization had indeed gone sour, and the new mixture was explosive.

7. The Union and the Ascendancy of the Right

Until the late 1960s the N.U.M. was not strong enough to carry out a national strike and win. The right wing dominated the union, from national level right down to the areas. Only Scotland, South Wales and Kent were run by left-wing executives. These areas were each still very much a law unto themselves. They had a lot of money, power, and property and were still registered as independent trade unions. There were none of the contacts, official or unofficial, between areas that were to prove so potent a force during the strikes of the seventies. The tactics for a successful strike also needed to be learnt and honed during the unofficial stoppages of the fifties and the sixties. Yet another precondition for militancy across every coalfield was missing. As long as some men were paid by piece-rate and others by the day, as long as some negotiated at pit level and others nationally, there could be no unity within the union behind the only issue that could guarantee the necessary rank and file support: wages. The history of the N.U.M. after the war was a struggle to overcome those handicaps. It was a struggle for unity.

Will Lawther, the President of the N.U.M. until the mid-fifties, was a man of the right. He was born in the mining village of Choppington in Northumberland, and first went down a pit when he was twelve. He 'emigrated' to the Durham coalfield where, at the age of eighteen, he was elected miners' delegate. Like so many trade unionists of his generation, he continued his education at night school, and then at the Central Labour College in London, before doing what he called his 'two stretches', the first inside Durham gaol for two months after the 1926 lockout, and the second as an M.P. for two years until the landslide of the 1931 election. He made a remarkable come-back after his defeat, and by 1934 was Vice-President of the national Miners' Federation, and elected to the General Council of the T.U.C.

Up until the middle of the 1940s, Lawther had held left-wing political views. He often spoke of the letter he had received from his brother just before he was killed in Spain: part of it read: 'I want you as the eldest of us all, who has taught us that freedom alone matters, and without it life is nothing, to use every minute of your time and every ounce of your strength to destroy fascism.' Lawther moved a resolution just after the war proposing the affiliation of the Communist Party to the Labour Party, and wrote, 'We have no difference with our communist colleagues. I find them as good trade unionists as most and better than many.'

It was a surprise, then, when his views changed violently. His conversion was wrought by the Cold War. The high hopes held by the Labour movement in 1945 that a socialist Britain could live in peace and sympathy with the Soviet Union were destroyed for many people, including Lawther, within four years. The coup in Czechoslovakia marked the consolidation of the Iron Curtain around Europe. 1948 saw the airlift to break the Soviet blockade of Berlin, and the following year, N.A.T.O. was formed. The rift caused within the Labour movement by the response to these developments of Ernest Bevin, as Foreign Secretary, was mirrored within the miners' union. Lawther was given the additional benefit of a meeting with the American General Marshall, the progenitor of Marshall Aid, who sent an aeroplane specially to pick him up for the talks. That, and an uncritical desire to protect the Labour Government which bordered on the fanatical, made him totally change his political perspective. Lawther now described the influence of communists in the union and politics generally as representing 'the negation of democratic standards that are operating in Britain'.

On his own, Lawther would not have been the potent force he undoubtedly was. His real political muscle in the union came from the backing and cooperation of Sam Watson, the Durham miners' leader. Watson was a shrewd man, a skilful operator, who, in the words of Lord Robens, ran a kind of 'wholesome Tammany Hall'. He became rabidly anti-communist, yet even his rivals, like Abe Moffat, held him in respect. Moffat wrote of him: 'He was more astute and more capable than any of the right-wing miners' officials or other members of the executive.' Watson's seat on the Labour Party's executive was also a powerful one, and he used all his influence to back Hugh Gaitskell at the time of some of the bitterest internecine rows. He and Lawther between them held the union firmly behind the Labour Government, until the rank and file got in the way.

The effectiveness of this partnership at work could be seen at the 1950 annual conference, one of the most bitter on record. Lawther opened the proceedings by rounding on the 'destructive influence' which, by its persistent misrepresentation and disparagement, had cost the Labour Government a comfortable majority at that year's general election, and expressed his outrage that some miners had voted for Communist Party candidates. The next day there was uproar when, while introducing an unsuspecting fraternal delegate from Belgium, Lawther attacked the comments on his speech made in the *Daily Worker*. They were guilty, he proclaimed, of printing a 'filthy lie'. Men stood and shouted as he continued, 'If anyone can swallow that, then the whale swallowing Jonah was a simple thing.' But the biggest row of all concerned a motion ostensibly reaffirming support for the Labour Government. Will Paynter questioned whether the Labour Government had achieved socialism, 'as some complacently believed'. Sam Watson stormed to the platform, furious at the very suggestion of complacency. Arguing that any qualification of support for the Government meant following the policy of the Communist Party, he declared, 'We reject the theory of totalitarianism and dictatorship.'

The man who was the target for many of these public attacks was Arthur Horner. Horner, a member of the Communist Party, took over the job as General Secretary of the union when Ebby Edwards left to join the Coal Board. Horner and Lawther were the first of what has become a tradition in the N.U.M., a left-wing General Secretary coexisting with a right-wing President. Horner was brought up in Merthyr Tydfil and was a baptist preacher at the age of fifteen. He was elected checkweigher at Mardy Colliery in 1919 even though at the time he was on hunger strike in Cardiff gaol for refusing conscription. Mardy was nicknamed 'Little Moscow', and was for a time expelled from the South Wales Miners' Federation for refusing to support an official candidate in an election and supporting Horner instead. After 1926, Horner became President and principal spokesman for the miners' minority movement, which was dominated by the Communist Party and dedicated to the formation of one miners' union and the nationalization of the industry. Horner's subsequent jobs as agent and then President of the South Wales Miners' Federation were devoted to ending the existence of company unions and once more achieving unity within the coalfield. In 1945, at the request of Emanuel Shinwell, he worked at the Ministry of Fuel and Power as the National Coal Production Officer and was responsible for drawing up the Miners' Charter.

In his first years as General Secretary, Horner was aware of growing differences between himself and the Labour Party, and thereby between himself and the majority of the National Executive Committee. He believed that in the realms of foreign policy they were making serious mistakes in building up armaments for the Cold War, and in opposing liberation movements in Kenya and Malaya. Most of all, he was strongly opposed to the wage freeze. But neither he nor any of the other left-wing members of the National Executive Committee could publicly speak their mind, because of a rule that everyone should support majority decisions once they had been taken. With an executive dominated by the right, Horner was effectively gagged.

There were also some vicious attempts to weaken his position. In the autumn of 1948, Horner, who was visiting France, made a speech in favour of a miners' strike which was taking place at the time. Lawther attacked him for supporting a stoppage that was 'politically motivated', and threatened the continuation of Marshall Aid to France. On his return, Horner added fuel to the fire by claiming that Lawther was trying to discredit him and replace him as General Secretary. A committee of inquiry, chaired by Sam Watson, was set up. The eventual report was rushed out before the sole left-wing member of the committee had a chance to see it. Its content showed a fairly transparent attempt to belittle both the character and the position of Horner. The British and French Communist Parties, it concluded, 'are far more concerned with creating the greatest possible amount of confusion and chaos with a view to sabotaging the efforts of the governments of Western Europe towards recovery than they are with the condition of French mineworkers'. As Horner later told friends, the accusations hurt him very deeply. There were other attempts to undermine his power. Horner's nomination as an N.U.M. delegate to the T.U.C.'s General Council, for example, was rejected year after year in favour of a representative of the Quarrymen's Union of North Wales. The quarrymen's delegate represented only 7,000 members.

In the first years of nationalization, there were few challenges to the authority of Lawther and the National Executive Committee. But what revolts there were, were spontaneous and from the rank and file. The defeat on wages policy was one such successful challenge. A strike in the Yorkshire coalfield in the first year of nationalization was another. In fact, the strike was doubly important, not only because it questioned the new relationship that was supposed to have been established between the N.C.B. and the N.U.M., the 'new era' that Lawther and Watson were keen to promote, but also because it was a revolt against national negotiations and the power of the central union.

The Grimethorpe stint strike was the first major dispute of the nationalized industry. The cause was the five-day week agreement, which abolished Saturday working, but set out to maintain output at its previous level by rearranging work-loads during the rest of the week. The strike started on 11 August when 200 faceworkers in the Meltonfield Seam at Grimethorpe Colliery near Barnsley, South Yorkshire, refused to accept a two-foot increase in the length of their stint. They were annoyed that although the extra work had been agreed in discussions between the Coal Board and the N.U.M., no one had consulted them. If anyone had, they would have been told that the men were already working as hard as they could on their knees in a 3′ 9″ seam, and that far from going home once they had finished their stint, which was the custom in the area, they often worked overtime voluntarily to make sure they completed their allocated task. The men argued that the increased stint would mean that older workers would have to work harder or retire from facework. As a result, the entire workforce of Grimethorpe Colliery, some 2,600 men, came out on strike.

For fifteen days, Grimethorpe stood more or less alone. The President of the Yorkshire miners, Joseph Hall, tried to persuade the men to return to work, but after a three-hour meeting only two men voted to support him. A few days later, the afternoon shift of the neighbouring Ferrymoor pit decided to strike in sympathy, and the following day South Kirkby joined in too. But generally speaking the dispute attracted little attention. The summer was hot, there had been no rain for weeks, and some of the miners on strike went off fruit-picking in East Anglia. The relative calm was soon shattered.

On the Monday morning a fortnight after the strike had begun, the N.C.B. threw open the pit to see who would turn up to work. The atmosphere was tense, as the word had gone round that the N.C.B. intended to prosecute anyone who did not turn up for work. Not one striker walked through the gates. The next day, Major-General Sir Noel Holmes, the Chairman of the North Eastern Division of the Coal Board, announced that in his view the strikers had terminated their contracts. The men's interpretation was that they had been given the sack. Their view was shared by other collieries, who now judged the issue important enough to warrant support. Pit ponies were brought to the surface to graze, a sign that the dispute was going to be a long one.

Within two days, ten pits were out on strike and the dispute had spread into the Doncaster and Rotherham areas. There was a concerted propaganda assault on the coalfield by national and area officials. The General Secretary of the Yorkshire area, W. E. Jones, appealed to the men to choose between the new consultation and conciliation procedures and unilateral action, or, as he put it, between 'industrial democracy and anarchy'. Arthur Horner, the national General Secretary, held a meeting at a club room in Cudworth, with 500 men packed into the hall and about 300 more waiting outside. He was given an attentive reception, but his advice was turned down by a large majority. The same fate befell the long and emotional appeal by the Minister of Power, Emanuel Shinwell, who flew in specially to address a meeting. 'We have got to save the country,' he said, 'and the only people who can save it are the mineworkers. If you do it – glory be to God for the mineworkers.' But real venom was directed by some at Will Lawther. He told reporters at the T.U.C. that the N.C.B. should prosecute the strikers 'even if there are 50,000 or 100,000 of them'. On the wall at the entrance to Grimethorpe pit someone painted a gallows and the slogan 'Burn Will Lawther'.

On 1 September, Holmes promised that if the men returned to work there would be no victimization. But the strike continued to spread. By 4 September, thirty-eight pits were completely shut, and a further ten partially so. The strike was also beginning to make an impact on local industry. Shinwell warned that thousands of Yorkshire firms had only a week's supply of coal left. The Sheffield Gas Company asked for voluntary cuts in the use of gas to avert compulsory measures. The English Steel Corporation shut down part of its plant, and a lot of other industrial processes dependent on gas were closed down too.

The National Executive Committee of the N.U.M. met in emergency session and determined that the disputes procedure had to be obeyed. At a cinema in Cudworth, Joseph Hall, the Yorkshire miners' President, made what he called 'the appeal of my life' to an audience of 1,500 strikers. They ignored his plea, and he left on a pre-arranged trip to the United States. Shinwell called together the N.U.M. and the N.C.B. to talks at the Ministry. After five hours, they decided to set up a fact-finding committee of three members of the Yorkshire area of the N.U.M. Once more the men decided to continue their strike. A spokesman for the strikers said that if only the Coal Board recognized their mistake and agreed that it was impossible for an older man to shift twenty-three feet of coal in a day, they would willingly go back to work. The opinion coming out of Coal Board headquarters was that the men would have gone back if it had not been the week of the Doncaster races.

The loss of coal began to look even more serious. Arthur Horner warned that the shortage of coal caused by the strike could bring down the Government. At Grimethorpe the hardship caused by the strike was beginning to show, as families began selling odds and ends from their homes to try to get money to buy food for the weekend. On 9 September, fifteen Yorkshire miners'

M.P.s toured the strike villages with officials of the N.U.M., once more seeking an end to the stoppage. This time some pits were won over. The rest waited for the result of another meeting at Grimethorpe Colliery.

Before it was due to take place, the Board issued what appeared to be a conciliatory statement setting out their position. They emphasized that the agreed procedures for settling disputes had to be adhered to, as to treat with the strikers would call into question the authority of the union to bargain on behalf of its members. But since the men felt that the possibilities had not been properly assessed previously, the N.C.B. and the N.U.M. had agreed to send in the fact-finding team once the men had returned to work. The next day the men voted almost unanimously to end the strike. They started work again the following Monday convinced that they had won.

The apparent success of the strike led to an upsurge of interest in local bargaining as opposed to national deals, and so set the trend for the wage increases that pieceworkers were to win for themselves in the fifties. It was also clear that there had been a serious breakdown in communication between the rank and file of the union and the officials, especially at national level. The men finally went back not because of any appeals by Lawther, Shinwell or even Horner: they eventually went back because the leaders of the strike told them to. Their achievement was to have shown the necessity of having men on the spot deal with their own problems. They had also demonstrated to themselves that unofficial action would bring ministers and national officials scurrying to the coalfield.

The frustrations of the rank and file were inevitable. The N.C.B. maintained the coal-owners' policy of ruling the union by dividing it. The union, on the other hand, fought hard for increases in the national minima for the day-wage men, but each time their ability to take strong action in support of their demands was curtailed by their voluntary acceptance of compulsory arbitration. This self-denying ordinance was all the more remarkable at a time when the Government was deliberately holding down the price of coal. Each time a wage demand was referred to the arbiters, the National Reference Tribunal, an assessment was given in terms of what the industry could afford, yet it was obvious to those on the left of the executive that the industry could afford a lot more if they were free to set whatever price they wanted. It was hardly surprising that a growing body of opinion began to argue that the miners were in effect subsidizing, through lower wages, the cheap coal enjoyed by other nationalized industries and private enterprise. This position became increasingly identified on the national executive with Will Paynter. He, and those who thought like him, argued that there should be increases in wages for the lower-paid men to match the rises in the cost of living, and as evidence, they pointed to the steady drain of men leaving the pits for better-paid jobs with safer and more amenable working conditions.

It was clear that all the superb negotiating skills of Arthur Horner, and they were very considerable, could not achieve what the miners wanted. Surprisingly, he never tried to end the system of compulsory arbitration, probably because he knew that at that time there would not have been a majority in favour on the National Executive Committee. But he did oppose Saturday working, commenting just before he retired that it was 'savage and monstrous' that the measures taken under national duress were becoming permanent. His position was supported by the left on the national executive, who had fought Saturday working throughout the fifties. They believed that the boost to earnings from overtime was used against them by the N.C.B. to depress the basic rates of pay. They also felt that the union should distance itself from the Coal Board, and cease the cooperation which, they argued, was too close to be healthy. These views, though, were not accepted by the majority on the national executive, and the frustrations they represented had to find other outlets.

The most natural outlet was the unofficial strike. It was also the most dangerous for the cohesion and stability of the union. The Grimethorpe strike had shown the importance that the union attached to sticking to the rules and the agreed conciliation procedure. The reason was the fear that if the N.C.B. spent so much as a minute in talks with unofficial strikers, the position of the elected officials of the union would be weakened. In this respect, the most serious threat came from unofficial committees formed by dissident groups who felt that their particular problems and grievances were not being dealt with by the union. For the N.U.M. to allow such groups a hint of recognition or legitimacy would, it was argued, have provoked other groups into similar actions. Unity would be lost.

This was especially so with the craftsmen and other skilled men. After nationalization, for example, the colliery winders felt that they were not being adequately represented and wanted to regain their former status and pay. They formed a breakaway organization called the National Union of Colliery Winding Enginemen and asked the N.C.B. for recognition. A special court of inquiry was set up, which turned down their request. Meanwhile, the N.U.M. won a wage award for the winders and threatened that if any of them went out on strike, they would be replaced with N.U.M. men. But the result was yet another breakaway, this time by a group based in Yorkshire calling themselves the Colliery Winders' Federation of Great Britain. After a series of unofficial strikes which got them nowhere, they decided to sue for peace and ask the N.U.M. to allow them to return on the condition that they had their own administrative unit within the union. The N.U.M., fearing balkanization, said no. Eventually, the Federation rejoined, but in 1952 went on strike again against the Yorkshire leadership. In fact, disputes between the union hierarchy and the winding enginemen continued well into the sixties, a seemingly never-ending running sore demonstrating the underlying fragility of the union.

In South Wales, too, an unofficial body challenged the elected officials of the union. Will Paynter, in a dramatic address to the South Wales miners' conference in 1951, his first as President, said that he could not recall a time when there had been so much internal upset in the union. 'The right of the minority to seek to change policy is not challenged,' he maintained, 'provided the change is sought by constitutional methods. Our strength in gaining redress to grievances whether industrial or political is represented by our organizational unity.' Paynter's concern was over an unofficial movement consisting of men from forty or so pits, who met regularly to coordinate policy at the Shakespeare

Hotel in Neath. One strike called by the 'Shakespeare' at a pit in the Aberdare Valley showed the difficulty of dealing with such action. Paynter was able, through his negotiations with the N.C.B., to secure all the demands of the men on strike, though he was not able to say as much in public. At a pit meeting, he told the men that if they returned to work he would stake his reputation on them having everything they were asking for before the first shift was over. Anyone who knew anything about negotiations knew that the deal was in his pocket. The lodge chairman knew too, but still he refused to call off the strike until he had reported back to the Shakespeare Hotel. Paynter commented: 'I could see no justification for this in a coalfield whose executive consistently pursued left-wing policies. It was a stupid position really and was creating two leaderships.' Unofficial action appeared again in 1955 and 1956, led by pieceworkers. Paynter believed that the situation had become so serious in some pits that any semblance of unity was destroyed: 'Elected leadership is ignored, as are the interests of the general body of workmen. Union organization and policy count for nothing, the selfish interests of a few being regarded as paramount.'

If Paynter found himself unable to justify an unofficial movement in South Wales, he had no such reservations about Yorkshire. Yorkshire was ruled by an entrenched right-wing leadership which resisted or ignored pressures from below. The battles in Yorkshire had the added piquancy that the area represented a powerful jewel in the crown of any tendency, whether of the left or of the right, that sought dominance of the National Union of Mineworkers. When the political character of Yorkshire changed in the last years of the sixties, so too did the political character of the N.U.M. The strikes there in 1955 and 1961 are therefore doubly important.

The first four months of 1955 had seen well over 200 strikes in Yorkshire alone, all of them primarily about pay. Since nationalization, there had been no revisions of the price lists for tasks done under piecework. Instead, in an effort to keep costs down at a time when coal was greatly underpriced, the divisional board had met demands for more pay by paying greater amounts in allowances. But by 1955, the allowances were making up so great a part of the weekly wages of the pieceworkers that all elements of incentive had almost gone. Furthermore, the allowances depended very much on the whim and discretion of the pit manager, which led to frequent arguments with the men. It was understandable that pressure should build up for this system to change, especially when miners in South Yorkshire could see that their rates were very much lower than those being won in adjoining pits which happened to be in different divisions of the Coal Board.

But the union insisted that all claims for revising the price lists should be dealt with under the agreed conciliation procedure, pit by pit. The problem was that the system could not cope with the pressure of demands. A pit had to wait a long time to have its case dealt with, and once one pit went on strike to try to jump the queue, others had to go too. The response of the N.U.M.'s Yorkshire area officials was to agree with the Coal Board to an experimental scheme at eight pits, to see whether better piece-rates and lower allowances would secure more coal with fewer disputes. It seemed to work. But neither the Yorkshire area of the N.U.M. nor the Coal Board appeared to be in much of a hurry to reduce the growing discontent and apply the scheme across the length and breadth of the coalfield.

On 20 April, the men who loaded coal onto the conveyor belts, or the fillers as they were called, went on strike at Markham Main Colliery after an attempt was made, apparently on the orders of the manager, to cut the allowances paid to them. A few days later there was a meeting of the Doncaster panel, a committee consisting of all the branch secretaries in the Doncaster area who gathered to discuss common problems. They gave the Coal Board an ultimatum: agree to changes in piece-rates within a week or face a strike. They expressed their anger at the way pit managers had often treated their claims, and warned: 'We feel that the Board have not been serious enough about this question, though they know what difficulty we have had in restraining the men. We have had many strikes over these price list complaints. The men are tired of waiting outside the colliery offices to see the manager or some other official over a question of proper payment for work done.'

On 2 May, in response to an appeal from the Doncaster panel, 26,500 men from eleven pits in the Doncaster area went out on strike in support of the fillers at Markham Main. Alwyn Machen, the President of the Yorkshire area of the N.U.M., went to Markham to talk to the men. He asked the miners to go back to work until the 'eight pit scheme' could be given a further trial, and suggested that the district should hold a ballot to see how much genuine support there was for the strike. Despite his arguments, the men of Markham Main voted by a show of hands to continue with their action. In fact the dispute began to spread, not so much because of any deep political plot, but instead rather like a bush fire, the spark of revolt from one colliery firing the next. By the following day the strike had spread to twenty-two collieries, affecting 44,600 men. The next morning thirty-three pits had stopped, and by the afternoon the total had risen to fifty. The resentments and frustrations of years were coming to the surface.

The area officials of the union tried to exert their authority over the men. They summoned the Doncaster panel, and delegates from every other pit in Yorkshire, to a meeting in Barnsley. The union's national President, Ernest Jones, and the General Secretary, Arthur Horner, both attended, demonstrating the national importance of the strike. Outside the offices, a picket from the Doncaster area was set up to remind the meeting of their obligations. But by 93 votes to 14 the delegates decided to recommend a return to work. Their advice was rejected.

The support of the Coal Board was now vital in maintaining the shaky position of the area officials. The following day, they spent a whole morning and afternoon in private talks with the N.C.B. at Sheffield. The Coal Board denounced the strike as an attempt 'to use power rather than reason to solve pit disputes', and declared their support for the 'magnificent work' the area officials were doing in trying to get the men back to work. They expressed their willingness to discuss the implementation of the 'eight pit scheme' and any other grievances through the union's elected officials at each pit. Most important of all, they strengthened the union's hand by confirming that they would not in any way treat with the men until they returned to work.

This legalistic approach to the strike was shared by a specially convened meeting of the union's National Executive Committee. They too recommended a return to work, stressing that 'the continuation of the strike can serve no other purpose than to prevent the men in Yorkshire from achieving the just and proper payments which they have been seeking for so long'. The President, Ernest Jones, was emphatic that negotiations would start at a pit as soon as the men had passed through the gates. Union branches all over the coalfield met to discuss the N.E.C.'s recommendation, and fifteen pits voted to end the stoppage.

The situation the next morning was confused. Overnight, pickets had gone out from Markham Main Colliery to try to change the minds of the men who had voted to return. Some pits ignored their protestations, other new ones joined in. Among the strikers there was a belief that the dispute was a 'strike to end all strikes'; after years of bitterness and frustration they now saw the possibility of solving the problems that individual action had been unable to tackle. The Board would have to surrender to the extent of opening negotiations with them before they would return. As one strike leader put it: 'We would all go back if they would only speak to us for ten minutes.'

Meanwhile, the area officials of the union campaigned throughout the coalfield, stressing what had been achieved by the pits which had started working again. They called another delegate meeting, and after a full day's discussion won from them an assurance that they would use every endeavour to end the strike. The fact that the leader of the strikers at Markham Main was a communist, Jock Kane, was used to good effect. The resolution published after the meeting emphasized the 'deep concern and condemnation' of 'the subversive activities employed by disloyal persons attempting to dissuade pits from resuming work'. The strike began to crumble, though the Doncaster panel remained firm. Eventually they were shown a letter sent from the divisional board of the N.C.B. to their area managers, which conceded many of the claims they had made. The following week was also the Whitsuntide Bull, when men would hope to make higher-than-normal wages before the holiday. So the panel, too, voted for a return to work so that discussions could take place.

The strikers had won a good deal of what they had wanted. Admittedly, they had not won separate talks with the Coal Board outside official union channels. But in the months that followed, almost every price list was revised. Even more remarkably, the Doncaster pits had shown an impressive degree of solidarity: they had gone on strike together and they had ended the strike together. They had also learnt new ways to make their action more effective and how to get their point of view put over to the press. In this latter respect, their handling of publicity was by all accounts better than that of both the union and the Coal Board. But above all they had learnt that effective action to further their hopes and aspirations could be achieved despite the apparent impassiveness of union officialdom.

The big strike of 1961 in Yorkshire showed the official leadership of the union in that area again under attack. The threat came once more from the Doncaster panel. The strike was caused by piece-rates. The levels of earnings and the amount of work the men had to do to get them varied considerably between pits. There were men on mechanized faces who were working less hard than the men who worked the coal by hand, and yet were earning far more. There were also fears that the fall in the demand for coal would lead to a cut in some of the many allowances that were used to make up the pay packet. The Doncaster panel decided to press for a guaranteed minimum rate of 65s a shift as well as a 10 per cent increase on the existing price lists.

Surprisingly, though, the strike started not in the Doncaster area but at the Water Haigh colliery around Castleford. Initially their action won the support of eight pits in West Yorkshire as well as one more in the South. But when the claim of the Doncaster panel was turned down, they too joined in. A spokesman said that the negotiations between the area executive and the Coal Board were going ahead too slowly and their promises were too vague: 'The Coal Board seems to have frightened our union executive, and they in turn are trying to frighten us.'

There then followed a bitter struggle for control of the coalfield. By 1 March over half the pits in Yorkshire were affected, with forty-seven collieries completely closed and fourteen partially so. Nearly 43,000 men had joined the strike. The Yorkshire area council of the N.U.M., which was attended by delegates from the 107 pits in the coalfield, met twice, and twice ordered the men back to work. Each time they were ignored. Mr Fred Collindridge, the area's General Secretary, said that he thought the position was the most serious since 1926: unofficial elements were using 'half truths' to create 'disorder and anarchy throughout the coalfield'. He saw the strike as an attempt by the Communist Party to seize control of Yorkshire and to help the election of Jock Kane, leader of the Doncaster panel, to the vacant position of area Vice-President. Collindridge's position was enormously strengthened by the intervention of Lord Robens, who, in publicly reaffirming that the Coal Board would deal only with the officials of the union, declared that he would not give way to 'force or to anarchy or to blackmail'. The M.P. for Barnsley, Roy Mason, also warned that the Communist Party had set the Yorkshire area as a target to win control over the union and its position in the Labour movement.

The strikers spread the stoppage through the use of flying pickets. The tactic was not new; in the last century miners' leaders in Yorkshire sent out men on foot to spread the word of a strike. By 1947, the strikers at Grimethorpe had progressed into using bicycles, motorcycles and borrowed lorries for the same purpose, and during the 1955 stoppage they used taxis. In 1961, though, the pickets had the use of their own cars. They toured pits, handing out leaflets as the men went on shift, urging them to join the strike. Some even ventured into Lancashire, where they received a frosty reception from the area Secretary, Joe Gormley. For a few days the strike took off and seemed out of the hands of even the unofficial leadership.

Then the generally rather uninspired men who led the Yorkshire area had a flash of inspiration. They sent a letter out to every single miner urging them to ignore the 'irresponsible wreckers' and return to work. The brilliance of their action was that it bypassed the union's branches and the Doncaster panel, and appealed directly to the men on strike. It was a tactic worthy of Lord Robens. The next day, 2 March, was a critical one, with about 60,000 men off work. But during the afternoon the first cracks appeared, as 100 men at Manvers Main Colliery voted to return to the pit for the afternoon shift. Immediately after the vote a loudspeaker van toured the area, with 'Manvers is back' chalked upon it. Pickets were sent to try to make them change their minds, but the men stood behind their officials. Bullough, Collindridge and Schofield, the area officials, were now riding high. They threatened to take disciplinary action against Jock Kane, the leader of the unofficial strike, for allegedly holding private meetings outside the auspices of the union in the weeks leading up to the strike. They then organized a meeting of all the panels in the coalfield, carefully excluding Doncaster. Collindridge, of course, denied that the Doncaster panel had been deliberately left out: 'Any approach from Doncaster would have received the greatest consideration,' he said. But when the delegates to the meeting agreed to get their men back to work as soon as possible, the strategy was clear: Doncaster had been isolated. On 5 March the men at Water Haigh Colliery, where the dispute had started, voted to go back, and gradually more joined in. The strike eventually ended with the defeat of the Doncaster panel on 13 March.

The official leadership had won not only by superior tactics, but also because they had been given the strongest support by the Coal Board, who refused to talk to the strikers. They were also able to play up the 'red peril', as the leader of the strike, Jock Kane, an impressive orator and organizer unlike either Bullough or Collindridge, was also a member of the Communist Party. But although it had ended in defeat, the strike had shown up the great organizational strength of the Doncaster panel, in marked contrast to the relationship existing between the pits and their area officials. They had also learnt new tactics. The high wage pits of South Yorkshire might have been defeated in 1961. But from 1969 onwards, they won their revenge.

But that was all still very much in the future. In the meantime, there had been changes in the top leadership of the N.U.M. Sir William Lawther retired, and Ernest Jones from Yorkshire became President in 1955, beating Abe Moffat, the Scottish communist. Jones, like Lawther, was rabidly anti-communist, and the Soviet invasion of Hungary provided a chance for him to indulge in some attacks. After Arthur Horner had declared his continued membership of the Communist Party, Jones issued a statement saying that he expected that miners everywhere would 'invite their secretary to review his position and take his handcuffs off'. Abe Moffat too came under attack from many of his branches for his support of the invasion, and in South Wales, two lodges called for the removal from office of Will Paynter. In an attack that hurt him deeply, a local Conservative M.P., David Llewellyn, wrote an open letter to the *Empire News* saying that because Paynter had supported the Soviet Union, his hands were dripping with the blood of Hungary. He could not reply to the allegations, and he later found out that his sons had been given a very rough time at school.

Hungary also magnified the problems of accepting foreign labour into the mines. This old chestnut was revived once more by the Government, the N.C.B. and the right wing of the union's executive, as a response to an acute loss of manpower from the pits in the mid fifties. Hungarian refugees added yet another potential area of recruitment. Once more there was opposition in the coalfields, not least because men who had worked at a pit all their lives were worried about who would leave first if there were any redundancies. The issue of foreign workers, though, distracted attention from other changes that were needed.

It was argued, for example, that the best way to win more recruits to the pits was by offering more pay and better conditions, especially for youngsters. One step towards that could have been the implementation in full of the new Miners' Charter. The new charter called for the restoration of the seven-hour day, and the introduction of a forty-hour week for surface-workers. It also asked for a good sick-pay scheme, three weeks' annual holiday with pay, and an end to the bonus shift that was paid if a full week's work had been done. In 1957, after considerable pressure from the rank and file, the union won the removal of the bonus shift. In 1960, the number of hours worked was also reduced to 7¼ hours a day. But pay continued to be a problem, especially when the overtime money, which men had got used to and depended on, was removed by the Coal Board when they unilaterally ended Saturday working.

In 1959, Arthur Horner retired and Will Paynter became

Secretary of the N.U.M. Like Horner, Paynter came from South Wales, and like Horner, he was a communist. His political and industrial education had been the appalling and humiliating poverty of the thirties, which had brought untold hardship to thousands of families. He had also taken part in the other epic struggle of the decade by joining the International Brigade in Spain. From 1936 onwards he was on the executive of the South Wales Miners' Federation, and in 1951 was elected its President. He was a very powerful orator with a great feel for language. His critics and his admirers all agree that he was a man of great integrity.

He took over the job in a particularly difficult period. Since then, he has often wondered whether he was wise in standing for election. The closures had already started in South Wales with seven pits closing in one day, and he had organized demonstrations and threatened stay-down strikes, as a protest. But he knew that as Secretary of the N.U.M. he would be a prisoner of the executive which was still dominated by the right-wingers. Throughout the sixties he did indeed find it difficult working with the executive, but he was always able to put his point of view and win respect for it, though he did not win the votes. As with Horner, and other left-wingers for that matter, he had the problem of having to support in public the decisions taken by the majority on the executive, even though he might well have violently disagreed with them.

From 1960 onwards, Paynter had to work with another right-wing President, the man he had defeated in the contest for Secretary, Sid Ford. In fact Alwyn Machen had been elected President after Jones, but he had died of cancer before he could take up the job. Ford was elected in the subsequent battle against Abe Moffat's brother, Alex. It was a very narrow victory, with only 10,000 votes between them on the fifth count. The vote of the non-miners, C.O.S.A., the clerical section of the union of which Ford had been General Secretary, tipped the scales in his favour. Ford had started life as the administrative officer at the N.U.M. headquarters, and so for the first time in their history the British miners found themselves with a man who had never worked in the pits at their head.

As President, Ford did not take much part in debates at the meetings of the executive committee. If he did make any contribution it would be very short, and he would have it written out beforehand. With his predecessor, Paynter used to meet the day before executive meetings and run through the agenda, but with Ford there was no such contact. Ford preferred instead to lobby the night before, making the odd telephone call to secure the votes that he knew he had anyway.

Despite the executive, Paynter managed to achieve some important reforms with their support. One of the most vital was to give back to the union the right to bargain with the Coal Board in complete freedom. Paynter's desire to end the system of compulsory arbitration was based on his experience as a negotiator. He knew that every time the union discussed wages and conditions with the Coal Board, the Board were well aware that in the last resort they had the union over a barrel. They could refer any matter to the National Reference Tribunal, a body that made decisions in the light of the financial position of the industry. There had been growing pressure at conferences for an end to compulsory arbitration, so that the rank and file could be consulted about what action should be taken to further a wage demand. There were also fears about interference by the Government to influence the decision of the arbiters: as Lord Porter used to say, 'Of course we are not influenced by any Government people, but we do read newspapers and they reflect national policy.' Horner had never been very keen to change the rules, but Paynter saw that in an era when the coal industry's future looked uncertain, it was vital to make arbitration voluntary. Jim Bowman, the Chairman of the Coal Board and himself an ex-trade-unionist, saw the problem and agreed. The union was now free to strike.

The next great reform was to abolish piecework and unify the coalfields behind the issue of wages. For years, it had been the clarion call of the miners' union. The issue which would unify all was wages. The lesson of the strikes of 1947, 1955 and 1961 was that with the right issue, a degree of solidarity could be achieved between pits of isolated and independent tradition. But to achieve concerted national action over wages there had to be a common system of payment. Bargaining by a pit, or by groups within a pit, would not unnaturally prompt the better-off to fight shy of calls for a strike to help the poorer members of the union. A common payment system, on the other hand, would mean that whatever coalfield a miner worked in, whatever job he held, all would have the same basis of pay. The eventual achievement of just such a system was the most important factor in providing the unity that made the strikes of 1972 and 1974 both possible and a success.

Nationalization made it natural for the union to expect 'equal pay for equal work'. The first clause of the Miners' Charter of 1946 called for the 'general application of the day-wage system' and by inference, the abolition of piece-rates. Piecework caused conflict within pits and between them, and also led to risk-taking and 'blood on the coal'. But the creation of one wage system for the whole country raised huge problems. Wage rates varied considerably, according to the policies of the companies before nationalization, the type of coal produced, the geology of the area and so on. And there was also the difficulty of assessing benefits such as cheap housing and concessionary coal, which some miners got and others did not. The annual conference of 1946 pointed additionally to an ambivalence amongst the rank and file: they could see the advantages of a unified wage but only if everyone was brought up to the level of the best-paid miner.

Even with such convincing arguments, it took eight years of negotiation before the first national day-wage system was introduced in April 1955. Thousands of different names of jobs had been whittled down to just thirteen occupational grades by job evaluation, and the outcome was a national wage scale for craftsmen and day-wage workers both on the surface and underground. Of course these men were already paid by the shift, and not by the piece, which in theory should have made matters much easier to settle. In fact, the new wage system produced some anomalies which it took some time to sort out. Some areas received very small increases or none at all, while the less well-off areas caught up. Nottinghamshire was one high wage area that had to hold back, prompting one delegate to an annual conference to remark that 'our day workers' loyalty to the organization was tested to the limit'. The resentments grew when the Coal Board refused any increase in the day-wage rate between 1958 and 1960.

The N.U.M. and the N.C.B. then looked at ways of ending piecework. Between 1955 and 1958, the industrial relations department of the Coal Board tried to work out a scheme, but to no avail. After 1958 the problems of a declining industry became more compelling for both the Coal Board and the N.U.M. Will Paynter in particular recalled that 'the clamour was for the extension of piecework and not its abolition'.

In the mid sixties, Paynter once more pushed for the abolition of piecework. He met a lot of opposition. At the 1965 annual conference, he attacked the 'humbug and hypocrisy' within the union which 'pushed up a whole network of vested interests'. He conceded that the union's members were being asked to undergo great changes involving loss of pay in some cases, but maintained that new techniques and mechanization were tending to equalize the amount of effort that went into each job. The leadership had to face the 'challenge of our time and to accept that we may have to do some unpopular things', but the alternative was the 'continuation of anarchy, drift and the creep that has been traditional inside this industry'. He believed that too often in the past, the union and its areas had approached matters of common concern 'not from the standpoint of what is best for the men generally on a national basis in this industry, but how does this or that proposal relate to their own sectional interests, their sectional outlook and their sectional traditions?'. He left the conference in no doubt that they were being asked to pay for a unity never before achieved in the union.

But to win acceptance from delegates to a conference was only half the battle. There was a lot of rank and file resentment and opposition when the details of the new wages structure, the National Power Loading Agreement, became known. It could hardly have been otherwise. Men in higher-paid jobs were in some cases being asked to take wage cuts if they moved to a new face which was covered by the new agreement. In Kent, for example, there was initial hostility from men who had been earning the best shift rates in the country, but who faced a cut in wages of sometimes between £5 and £10 a week. It was as well that no one at that time realized that the new rates of pay under the National Power Loading Agreement (N.P.L.A.), would in no way keep pace with rises in the cost of living, and would lead to cuts in their real wages of about 17 per cent.

That the agreement was eventually ratified, owes everything to the loyalty of the rank and file to their leaders, and in particular, Will Paynter. At the special conference of the union in April 1966, called to make or break the agreement, Paynter expounded his vision: 'This union has been built up on certain principles of solidarity and unity. An injury to one is an injury to all and it is necessary, even in our wage negotiations and in our advance to national wage agreements, that we embrace these principles in our actions as well as in the speeches that we make.' The agreement would mean that 'by the end of 1971 we will have realized on the basis of substantially enhanced rates irrespective of geography, irrespective of pit or area viability, a uniform rate for men doing identical jobs in the industry'. It would remove 'from the area of wage bargaining, the horse-dealing that has been characteristic of the past, horse-dealing that never results in justice or equity, but results in something better for those who happen, by accident, to be employed in pits or areas that may be more profitable than others'. However, the National Power Loading Agreement only received the assent of the conference by a narrow majority, by 269 votes to 226. Nevertheless, it was an achievement that should not be underestimated, as there can be few other industries, if any at all, where the workers have voluntarily agreed to a wages freeze or even cuts in wages, to help their lower-paid colleagues.

In retrospect it is difficult to see why Robens was so keen to abolish piecework, as the main consequence was to make the union stronger. But he had pushed hard for it, against the opposition of all the production men in the Coal Board. Ironically, the reason seems to have been a belief that piece-rates were, in his own words, 'the principal source of industrial strife'. The rise in productivity caused by the deal and by the introduction of the new power-loading machines would also have cost the Board quite a lot of money if payment had still been under the piecework system.

For the N.U.M., though, the National Executive Committee became important and powerful as never before. This of course brought its problems. Many local officials became very frustrated because all disputes were by definition of national concern, and so had to be referred up the line. Often, this process appeared to take an age, and all sorts of aggravations and frustrations built up. A. R. Griffin, the industrial relations officer of the Coal Board's North Nottinghamshire area, wrote: 'The branch secretaries have largely lost their old function as negotiators, and nothing has been put in its place. Left with a purely negative role, they can hardly be blamed for a negative approach.'

The new technology also changed the lives of miners. Mechanization had made the job underground relatively easier, but had also destroyed most of the collier's skills and pride in his craft. The N.P.L.A. brought to an end the system whereby semiautonomous groups of men underground had a great deal of control over their pace of work, and needed very little supervision. For the first time, collieries became like factories, with coal being cut on every shift of every day. The result was a situation more favourable to militancy.

By the end of the sixties, the miners were unified on the issue of wages. They were frustrated by the closures and angry with the Government which had caused them. A growing body of opinion saw the only salvation through unified, militant action. If the union's officials would not agree, they had already proved by the Yorkshire strikes that they could do very well without them. All that was needed was the right issue, and the right leadership. Both were coming.

8. The October Revolutions

1969 was probably the most important year in the post-war history of the N.U.M. It was the year that provoked what some in the union called the 'October revolution', when the frustrations of a decade and more boiled over in a strike the like of which had not been seen since 1926. Said one strike leader: 'The miners are not going to be brainwashed any longer. They are after good wages, good conditions and shorter hours, and they are going to get them whatever happens.' Up to then the Coal Board had argued that any strike would bring the industry to its knees. But by 1969 things had got so bad that such threats no longer held any credibility or fear. The miners were prepared to call the Coal Board's bluff.

Morale in the industry was lower than ever before. A series of meetings with the Minister of Power, and two with the Prime Minister himself, had got the union nowhere. There was under-standing aplenty, but little action. The Government confirmed that three-quarters of the C.E.G.B.'s generating capacity would be coal-fired by 1975. But they would not give any guarantee that the capacity would actually be used round-the-clock to secure a reliable demand for coal. Equally worrying was the Government's reluctance to order any new coal-fired power stations. Not one had been commissioned since 1966, and in the meantime they had ordered three nuclear plants. As regards other fuels, the position of coal looked similarly perilous. North Sea oil and gas were being used to replace other indigenous fuels. Far better, argued the N.U.M., that they should be used as substitutes for imported oil so that Britain could become self-sufficient in energy. But these arguments were ignored, and the future continued to look insecure. So much so that when in April the new Secretary of the N.U.M., Lawrence Daly, went before the House of

Commons Select Committee on Nationalized Industries to plead the case for coal, he told them that the Government's inaction was having a 'catastrophic effect on morale within the industry'.

This low morale caused grave financial problems. Erstwhile profitable collieries were working at unprofitable levels. Even some of the best pits in the central English coalfields were losing production because they couldn't attract men to an industry that was believed to have no future. The problem was further intensified as the cost of the closures was increasingly being borne by fewer and fewer active collieries, and outstanding debts and interest payments became heavier and heavier. The result was to complete a vicious spiral of an even less profitable industry in which even fewer men saw a future. The N.U.M.'s desire for the Government to help break this spiral by providing a suitable climate of confidence went unheeded.

By 1969, the decline in the number of jobs in the industry was matched by an equal decline in the chances of getting a job outside. In the twelve months to March 1969, fifty-five pits had been closed and over 55,000 men had left the industry. In the following year, there was the prospect of at least forty more closures. The sheer scale of the run-down, and the fact that the British economy as a whole was in difficulty, meant that in many cases there was no alternative employment on offer. For example, a survey of nearly 1,000 men dismissed from a colliery in Fife showed that of those who had found a job, only 4 per cent had found work that paid them more, and only 8 per cent employment that paid them the same. The rest found themselves financially worse off, but had taken any job on offer because of the fear of unemployment. Of course, the Government offered help to areas affected by closures, but the measures, in a deflationary economy, were inadequate and ineffective. The result was that many men displaced by the closures, and especially the older ones, suffered the degradation of knowing that they had been dumped, as Lawrence Daly put it, 'on an economic scrapheap'.

Many men, though, were trapped in the declining industry. They went to an employment exchange only to be told that their skills suited them solely for mining. 'As a result of this,' said Will Owen, the Labour M.P. for Morpeth, 'the miner will find himself at yet another pit. Eventually, fed up with this moving to and fro, he will apply to the employment exchange again, but will again be told that because he is a skilled worker, he cannot be retrained. He is kept on a treadmill and refused the liberty of choosing employment in another sphere because we need men in the mining industry.' The rewards for staying in the industry were pretty low. 'The mining communities', as Daly said later, 'were suffering more than they had ever done.' Wages had nowhere near kept pace with the increases in productivity. In 1959, there were nearly 700,000 men in an industry producing 190 million tons of coal at about 700 pits. By 1969 just over 300,000 men at just over 300 pits produced about 160 million tons. Productivity had risen by approximately 70 per cent, an achievement which Roy Mason, the Labour Minister of Power, described as 'fantastic'. Yet the rates for both surface and underground workers meant that many were living on or even below the minimum subsistence level laid down by the Ministry of Social Security.

The result was that there was no hope within the industry or outside it. In a debate on the coal industry in the House of Commons in March, miners' M.P. after miners' M.P. rose to lament the state of the industry and its workers. The M.P. for Blaydon, Robert Woof, believed that 'there is nothing more devastating to the human soul than to find that one is not wanted when one is healthy, strong and anxious to gain an honest livelihood. Irritated to the very depths of their being and reflecting on their disappointments leaves men plenty of room to lament the lack of security of their existence.' According to Alex Eadie, who had come only a few years earlier straight from pit to Parliament, miners no longer encouraged their sons to enter the industry: 'Miners whose families were in the industry for generations, and who made great sacrifices, sometimes even losing members of their families, take the view that if the nation is now prepared to let them down, the sons of other people can have a go at the problem.' 'It is not easy to watch miners, who are traditionally proud and loyal, become cynical and without hope,' said Fred Evans, the M.P. for Caerphilly. 'It is not easy,' he went on, 'to watch men who have believed passionately in socialism as the road to a brighter future become disillusioned and look upon themselves as having been betrayed by the cause to which they gave their faith.'

But political changes were taking place in the union which would end the miners' passive acceptance of these changes. The left increased their hold over South Wales, and, as we shall see, strengthened their position in the bellweather coalfield of Yorkshire. At national level, Lawrence Daly, a fiery radical, began his first year as Secretary of the union, beating Joe Gormley in the election that followed the retirement of Will Paynter. Daly, who was only forty-three when he took over, had been brought up in the Fife coalfield and started work at Glencraig Colliery when he was fourteen. He had left the Communist Party before the Hungarian uprising and in 1965 had joined the Labour Party. He had a clear analysis of the problems facing the industry, and saw his election as a mandate for radical action.

Daly attacked the N.U.M.'s acquiescence in the policies of the N.C.B. and the Government. In a pamphlet called 'The Miners and the Nation', published before his election, he wrote: 'If we do not compel the Government to change its policy, jobs will be lost at a very rapid rate; and if we continue to accept the Coal Board's rejection of even the most moderate demands – like, for example, a forty-hour week for surface workers – we shall become ineffective and discredited as a union and make progress, if at all, at a snail's pace.' He recommended short, sharp guerrilla strikes that 'would make the Government realize that the miners' loyalty is not something to be taken coldly for granted, and make the Coal Board realize that a rejection of justified demands in future would meet with an angry and effective response from the miners'. His words raised the expectations of the union for a new course of action, and matched the strong feelings developing within the rank and file.

In fact the angry and effective response from the miners came from an unexpected quarter: the surface workers. These men were the Cinderellas of the industry. Their working conditions were not as dramatically unpleasant as those underground, but they were still gruelling and uncomfortable. Many of them were banished from the more lucrative work at the coal-face because they suffered from pneumoconiosis or other industrial diseases, or because they had been injured in some way. Their disabilities sentenced them to long hours for poor pay. Their rate of £10 a week was so low that overtime was all but compulsory. These men, many of whom had experienced much rougher conditions when they laboured at the face, now saw young lads of nineteen or so working underground and earning much more than they were, for much shorter hours. Their cause became a rallying point for militancy within the union.

And yet there was no action from the national leadership, despite a firm commitment at the 1968 annual conference to improve the lot of the surface worker. Neither the N.U.M. nor the N.C.B. seemed in any particular hurry to discuss ways of achieving this goal. In the new year of 1969, the N.U.M. began negotiating seriously on the issue, but their meetings with the Coal Board were few and far between. Delegates to the 1969 annual conference were clearly angry at the lack of progress. Said Joe Whelan of Nottinghamshire: 'It may stagger you to know that if it was not for the fact that contributions to the union were stopped by the Coal Board, a lot of men would refuse to pay it, because they say, and quite rightly, that this union is not as strong as an aspirin, and a junior one at that.' Outside, surface workers demonstrated in support of their cause. The negotiations went on over the summer until eventually the exclusion of mealbreaks from the forty-hour week became the main sticking point for the N.U.M. By this time feelings were running even higher in the coalfields. The recent strike of dustmen had shown how the relatively poorly-paid could fight and win, and Yorkshire pits in particular were agog with the news that women bus conductors, after a recent pay award, were earning more than the average surface worker. On 9 October the N.U.M. and the N.C.B. met again in London, but their talks ended in deadlock.

The Yorkshire coalfield then seized the initiative. Some pits were already out on strike in support of a separate dispute at Cadeby Main Colliery, but the rest were holding back to see whether anything had been won for the surface workers. By the time the area council met, it was clear that their demands had not been achieved. The area officers presiding over the gathering were largely ignored, as the decision was taken to strike from the following Monday.

The impact of the strike was immediate. By the second day of the dispute, every single pit in Yorkshire was at a standstill, with 70,000 men refusing to work. By the end of the week the strike had spread to Scotland, South Wales and the Midlands. For the first time since 1926, a strike had spread across the boundaries of a coalfield. Mrs Barbara Castle, the Secretary for Employment and Productivity, faced questions in the Commons about the effects of the dispute. Representatives of the wool textile industries sent telegrams to the Government warning that the strike threatened to close many exporting firms 'within days'. Production was cut back at two big steel plants. Sir Sidney Ford, the N.U.M.'s President, described the strike as a 'serious and grievous blow' which could well destroy any hope of achieving a deal on surface hours.

The scale and spontaneity of the strike took the Coal Board by surprise. After all, in August, the rank and file conference of the South Wales miners had decisively rejected a recommendation of the executive committee to strike over the closure of the Avon Ocean Colliery in the Afan Valley. Yet here, within two months, the same coalfield was hit by an unofficial strike over the hours of what was only a small proportion of the union's membership. The Coal Board's bewilderment was intensified when they worked out that if all the N.U.M.'s demands were accepted, only about half the surface workers would benefit. Could this be the real and underlying cause of the dispute?

The N.C.B. decided, rightly, that the surface hours issue was only the symbol of deeper grievances. These, they decided, would be best ameliorated by offering better pay. Even though an unofficial strike was going on, Robens decided to ignore normal practice and continue negotiations. The Board met in emergency session, and in an unprecedented move agreed to give the union every penny they had asked for. They accepted the union's demand for an increase of 27s 6d a week, to bring the minimum for underground workers to £16 a week, and for surface workers to £15. But on the issue of hours, they made no concession. Despite this, the union's negotiating team voted to recommend the deal to their National Executive Committee. It was indeed a famous victory, and Sir Sidney Ford lost no time in appealing for a return to work, saying, 'I have never in all my forty-five years' experience known a wage claim being met in full.'

But his words went unheeded. Far from persuading the men to go back, the timing and scale of the Coal Board's offer had intensified the strike. The N.C.B. maintained that the decision to accept the N.U.M.'s pay demands in full had been made before the strike began, and Robens became very angry if it were suggested otherwise. But the strikers saw the concessions as a direct result of their action and believed that if they only stood their ground, an agreement on hours could also be won. And, anyway, the strike was as much an expression of sheer frustration after a decade of decline and an exuberance at being able to take action, as it was a demand for better hours for surface workers. On both counts, they could see no reason for answering their leaders' call for a return to work.

On Sunday, the four area panels from Yorkshire met in Doncaster and decided to continue with their strike. Two of the panels went even further; they wrote to the N.U.M.'s headquarters asking for the resignations of the President and the General Secretary. Outside Yorkshire, the strike spread even further. In South Wales, the unofficial strike committee decided to visit pits which were still working to try to get them to join in. Defiantly the chairman of the committee said, 'The miners are incensed and they mean business.' By Monday morning, nearly a half of the pits in South Wales and Nottinghamshire were out, about a third of those in Scotland and Kent, and two-thirds of the collieries in Derbyshire. On Tuesday, 140 pits out of a total of 306 throughout Britain were on strike.

The problem for the leadership of the N.U.M. was that they had clearly lost their authority: how could they regain it? A deal with the strikers was ruled out. There had already been a private meeting between the two sides which had achieved nothing. One member of the delegation remembers Sir Sidney Ford's hands shaking throughout, especially after one of the strike leaders called for his resignation to his face. For the sake of his own esteem, Ford could not back down, and at the same time neither could many of the area officials bypassed by unofficial strike committees. They saw no reason to surrender to men who were acting unconstitutionally, for to do so would be to give them a legitimacy they believed they should not have.

On Tuesday, 21 September, the National Executive Committee met to decide what to do. A majority agreed that the Coal Board's offer could not be bettered and they all decided to put it before a special delegate conference to be held later that month. The final word would rest with the membership at a pithead ballot. The decision was greeted with boos and cries of 'sell out' from the crowd gathered outside the union's headquarters. But it was a solution that was correct in terms of the union's rules, and devastating to the power base claimed by the unofficial strikers; for how could they continue to fight against a ballot of the rank and file that they represented?

The unofficial strike began to lose its momentum. There were those who wanted to continue. Delegates to a special area conference in South Wales tried to call a full-scale official strike in the coalfield, but their attempts were overruled. The President and other officials had to push and shove their way out of the hall to shouts of 'traitors', 'bastards' and 'resign'. The Yorkshire area council and Scotland both voted to reject the N.C.B.'s offer and continue their strike, but others were voting to return. By Wednesday, some pits in Nottinghamshire and Derbyshire had gone back to work, and even in South Wales some pits were ending the strike while others were joining in.

In Yorkshire, the Barnsley and Doncaster panels knew that the strike had reached a particularly dangerous phase. If the strike petered out with little sign of leadership, the chances of securing such action again in the future would be damaged. But if they called off the strike would their leadership be discredited, and would anyone follow them again? The panels decided that, even if the issue of surface hours remained unresolved, the strike had at least achieved some very important underlying aims: the miners had proved that unified action was possible, not only within their own coalfield, but also between areas. The problem now was how to save face, and get the men back together.

Lawrence Daly recognized the strikers' position, and off his own bat arranged for them to see Victor Feather, the General Secretary of the T.U.C. As he put it: 'When feelings were running so high, you didn't care who saw them, especially if it gave them something to return to the men with, to let them off the hook.' On Friday, 25 October, a nine-man delegation from Yorkshire went to Congress House and spent over four hours in discussions with Feather. Afterwards, they said that they were so convinced of the justice of their case that they had asked for an independent inquiry to be set up to look at the issue of hours. Feather had agreed to consider their request as a matter of urgency, and as a token of good faith, the strikers said they were prepared to recommend a return to work. Many of the men that they were representing felt let down, but it was difficult to see any alternative. The following day the Yorkshire Miners' Council decided by 66 votes to 22 to recommend a return to work on the Monday. The strike was over.

The strike had shown that Yorkshire had become the engine-house for radical action within the union. Traditionally, the coalfield had been dominated by the right wing, and specifically men from North Yorkshire. They had ensured their dominance by putting up only one candidate in elections, whereas the left, in disarray, would often put up a number. They were also skilled in the intricacies of the single transferable vote. During the sixties, though, the left in the coalfield achieved a degree of unity hitherto lacking, and their tactics, a mirror of those used by the right, reaped rewards: the strike showed that the right-wingers in the union could no longer count on Yorkshire as theirs.

The strike had also demonstrated the organizational capabilities of the 'progressive' elements in Yorkshire. The focus for activity was the panels, the loose-knit committees of branch officials, one for each of the four areas of the N.C.B. in Yorkshire. The Barnsley panel met and coordinated the strike in their area from a room above the White Hart pub, where the landlord had additionally given them the use of the telephone. Some members of the strike committee ensured that everyone in the area knew what was going on, while others tried to spread the strike by establishing contacts with other coalfields. A strike fund was organized, though its resources were pretty meagre, but it was enough to pay the petrol of those who, like Arthur Scargill, used cars, coaches and minibuses to drive to picket other coalfields. They succeeded in keeping some pits in Derbyshire and Nottinghamshire out for over a week, which was quite an achievement considering that the whole movement was unofficial. There was even one incident which has now become part of miners' folklore, when a pit in Nottinghamshire sent out their wives to deal with the Yorkshire pickets; the next day two coachloads of Doncaster women set off for a return bout.

But above all the miners had proved to themselves that they could fight for what they wanted. In fact so strong were the feelings in some cases that it was very difficult to get the men back to work. At Yorkshire Main, near Doncaster, for example, there were five meetings within twenty-four hours to discuss the ending of the strike, all of them stormy. In the view of Ian Ferguson, the lodge secretary, 'It was clear that things would never be the same again. It was the start of 1972 and 1974.'

Although the wage settlement of November 1969 was the highest in the history of the industry, the miners' wages relative to those of other industrial workers continued to fall, and it was therefore not long before pressures began to build up for a new pay increase. This time, though, the national leaders of the union were determined to present a unified front. 'Unless our legitimate demands are met,' Daly told the Northumberland Miners' Gala in June, 'the miners may well be prepared to take industrial action. Should this be so, then it is my preference that such action should be taken officially through the union.' Mick McGahey, the Scottish miners' President, was equally adamant that the leadership should show their mettle: 'October 1969 clearly demonstrated that the miners are no longer prepared to await long-drawn-out negotiations, and if the leaders do not act, they will lose their leadership: the rank and file will take action themselves.' But perhaps the most surprisingly strident speech of all came from the man who had been strongly against the unofficial strike in 1969, but who was preparing his candidacy for the N.U.M. presidency. Joe Gormley, the Secretary of the Lancashire area, told his area conference that the union should fight for higher wages even if it meant that some pits would have to close: 'I am not going to be a miners' leader if I cannot claim a bigger minimum wage for the lads who go underground than the lads carting the dustbins around the streets of London,' he argued. 'I can tell you I'm getting off my knees. I have been on them too long. I don't intend to be on them any longer.'

So it was with a great deal of expectation that the union went about formulating its wage demand at the Isle of Man that summer. The union's Vice-President, Sid Schofield, who was standing in for Sir Sidney Ford, warned the conference against what he called 'adventurers' who were already subverting the union: 'To give the battle cry to our members,' he said, 'takes less courage than the call for restraint and reflection.' But his words could not contain the pressures that had been built up. A resolution before the conference called for a £20 a week minimum for surface workers, £22 for underground workers and £30 for faceworkers, and delegates left no doubt that these demands were no bargaining ploy; they wanted every penny. 'Failure to get this demand will release an anger that will make last October look like a Sunday school picnic,' said Arthur Scargill, proposing the motion. 'We have been told to remain passive. We have remained passive since 1956 and what has it got us? Half the coal-mining industry has been obliterated. If that is what passiveness brings us, we want none of it.' Speaker after speaker rose to support the resolution, and to no one's great surprise it was passed unanimously.

The shock, though, came from South Wales. They put forward a resolution that pledged the union to a strike if negotiations for their wage demand failed. Daly carefully pointed out that under the union's rules there would have to be a ballot before any strike, but nonetheless the motion was put before the conference, and it was passed, though narrowly. As Lord Robens warned a few days later, 'Action on these lines is exactly what will bring this industry to its knees and take the men to the labour exchange.'

The growing militancy across the coalfields was taking place before a backcloth of political change. When the Conservatives won the general election of 1970, the new Prime Minister, Edward Heath, appointed Sir John Eden as Minister of State with responsibility for nationalized industries. He was a man with a reputation as a hardliner, and the change in style and content was immediate. It was not just the broad political context that was transformed, though the impact on trade unionists' attitudes of the industrial relations legislation, for example, was enormous, but also the way in which the Government treated and viewed the coal industry and the miners. In July, the Government decided that the Richborough power station, which took all its coal from Betteshanger Colliery in Kent, should be converted to burn oil. Two other power stations would also be adapted so that they could burn either of the two fuels. The N.U.M. were told by the Coal Board just a few hours before the announcement was made, and on the eve of the Kent miners' holiday. Daly was justifiably furious: 'This makes a mockery of the industry's consultative machinery,' he said, and his fears were even more acute because he knew that other stations were ripe for conversion. The decision, and the way it was announced, harked back to an age they thought was behind them.

The Government were also making it clear that they believed the miners' pay claim was too large. In August they refused to give the Coal Board the full amount of the price rise they were seeking, saying, in effect, that they could ask for more once they had settled with the miners. They made it clear that an 'immediate increase in coal prices should not include an element in anticipation of future wage settlements'. The miners interpreted this as a warning if not a threat, and with this in mind began their negotiations with the Coal Board.

At their first meeting, in August, Lord Robens appeared sympathetic as the union explained their case, and just over a month later the entire executive committee of the N.U.M. went to Hobart House to hear the N.C.B.'s offer. Outside were about 1,000 men from South Wales, Scotland, Yorkshire and Kent, mostly done up in suits, collar and tie, holding placards with such slogans as 'Is £20 too much for a miner's job?' and 'End the scandal of the low-paid miner'. Inside, the Coal Board made it clear that though the miners were claiming increases of up to 33 per cent, they were only prepared to grant an average of 10 per cent. As this was their final offer, the talks broke down, and Daly went outside to denounce the Coal Board's proposals as 'degrading and disgusting'. That evening he attended a battle-thirsty meeting at the Conway Hall in London, organized by the men who had been demonstrating outside Hobart House. 'We are now not only confronting the N.C.B.,' he told them, 'more important, we are confronting the Conservative Government.' The next day the National Executive Committee unanimously voted to recommend a strike, and in accordance with the union's rules announced that there would be a pithead vote on the issue.

It was the first national strike ballot in the history of the N.U.M. And as the membership and their officials contemplated the fact that the necessary two-thirds majority could well be reached, those in the union who had studied a document produced in August by the N.U.M.'s research officer knew that the effects of a total strike would be devastating. Most people outside the industry had not given much thought to the continuing importance of coal, and the ordinary man in the street would probably have thought its role was insignificant. But based on assessments of stocks and the demand for coal throughout the country, the report gave the N.U.M. knowledge of the power they could still exert. All its main findings were pretty well borne out by the events of 1972. This is how it concluded:

> Voltage cuts would be necessary within the first week of a stoppage and within four weeks only priority electricity consumers could be supplied. Within four weeks it is probable that over half the electricity generating capacity of Britain would be lost. This would of course cause a major public outcry and considerable harm to the economy.
>
> Even the importation of foreign coal (moved by H.M. Forces assuming an alliance with the Transport and General Workers' Union) would not prevent power and steel shortages during the time necessary to move large loads to Britain. In effect, Britain's industrial capacity would be drastically reduced to an unbearable level within a month.

'Such,' it finally remarked, 'remains the power of coal.' Would events come to this?

A couple of weeks before the ballot, Lord Robens wrote to Daly to remind him that matters could still be settled by referring the dispute to the National Tribunal for arbitration. He also hinted that the miners' demands could be met, not in one year, but maybe in two. But nothing could stop the ballot, and the feeling was that Robens's remarks were designed only to sway public opinion and weaken the strength of feeling for a strike. In addition, the union distrusted any political interference there might be with arbitration and preferred instead to rely on what they saw as the justice of their cause.

The ballot took place between 12 and 16 October. Meetings were held throughout the coalfields, and Lawrence Daly went around the country urging the men to vote for a strike. Towards the end of the week he told a mass meeting at Doncaster, a particularly volatile area, that there were instances when unofficial strikes were justifiable, but stressed that there had to be the certainty that the men would not end up fighting one another. In many respects, his remarks were prophetic.

On 23 October, the Electoral Reform Society gave the union the result of the ballot. Only 55½ per cent of the miners had voted for a strike, and under the rules it needed a two-thirds majority. But in Scotland, Wales, Cumberland and Kent, more than two-thirds of the vote had been in favour of a strike and in Yorkshire the total had just fallen short. By any normal democratic standards the majority was in favour of action, and unless a strong lead was given these areas were ripe for unofficial strikes. Some indeed were already taking place. In an attempt to preserve unity, the union's leaders appealed for such feelings to be held in check until they had met the Coal Board once more.

The discussions lasted for eleven hours. The union expressed their belief that the ballot result had shown that most miners were dissatisfied with the Coal Board's original offer, and eventually an extra 10s a week was agreed. It was a close thing: the National Executive Committee were split down the middle over whether to accept it or not, but by one vote they decided to put it to a pithead ballot.

The divisions on the National Executive Committee mirrored those in the coalfields, and the unofficial strikes that both sides had been at pains to avoid now began. At midnight that night men working a face at Brodsworth Colliery in Yorkshire went on strike. The next day the rest of the pit went out too, and that evening the Doncaster panel met and decided they would strike as well. At meetings over the weekend, pits in other parts of Yorkshire, in South Wales and in Scotland voted to join in.

What happened in the succeeding weeks is open to two interpretations. According to Robens, the Communist Party who had stirred up the strike now lost control and themselves were attacked by peripheral leftist groups. He alleged that pickets were using intimidation and rough handling to have their way. 'The hooliganism could no longer be denied,' he wrote in his memoirs; 'detailed reports reaching me from all over the country showed the extent to which an influential and determined body of men . . . were prepared to go.' In particular, he was concerned about an incident at Glasshoughton Colliery in the Doncaster area, when, amongst other things, the panels of cars were kicked in. His views were echoed by Albert Martin, the right-wing Secretary of the Nottinghamshire area, who accused outside bodies such as the Institute for Workers' Control as being the cause of a lot of trouble.

The other interpretation is that the union was genuinely split about what to do. After the settlement with the Coal Board had been reached, for example, Mick McGahey, the communist leader of the Scottish miners, went back to Scotland and appealed to his area to remain at work, preserve their unity and campaign inside the union to get the two-thirds rule changed. But the force of opinion from below overtook him, so much so that he commented at the time, 'I have never met such anger on the part of miners in all my lifetime in this industry.' To regain the initiative and control over their members, McGahey and his executive committee called a delegate conference to decide what to do, so that whatever they did, they would at least do it together.

Furthermore, the action by the men who went on strike, although against the union's rules, was not completely mindless. They argued that their case for a large pay rise was a good one, and a year later a Royal Commission was to agree. They could also point to the fact that the democratic parliament of the union, the annual conference, had passed a resolution calling for a strike if their demands were not met. If the union's leaders shied away from a strike, then there were other tactics short of a strike which could be used to enforce their demands, tactics which later · Daly said he had supported. Why, they argued, weren't they being used, especially in the light of the strong speeches at the start of the bargaining season? There was then among the advocates of militant action a feeling not wholly irrational, that the national leadership of the union had let the rank and file down.

Those frustrations spilled over into unofficial strikes. In Yorkshire the panels once more coordinated activities, but this time their effectiveness was limited, mainly because the issue at stake was less clear. At Woolley Colliery, one of the pits that led the 1969 dispute, for example, a pithead vote went against a strike and even a large, intensive and angry picket failed to close the colliery for any length of time. Men were still prepared to run the gauntlet of jeers and go to work because they believed that any action should await the result of the ballot on the pay deal. Woolley Colliery was a microcosm of struggles going on elsewhere in the coalfield: the union was hopelessly split and confused, and as often happens in those situations, men who don't see eye to eye don't always shake hands and walk off in different directions.

All eyes therefore turned towards the National Executive Committee: could they resolve matters? In particular would they, as the left argued, scrap the ballot and instead hold a special delegate conference, where the issues could be openly debated? On the day the executive committee met, there were over 120 pits on strike. About 300 demonstrators gathered outside the union's headquarters, which was guarded by some forty policemen. As they went inside, members of the executive committee were given an angry reception and some were hit or kicked. The executive committee met representatives of the men outside but even so the proposal for a delegate conference was rejected, and by 14 votes to 9 the executive decided to carry on with the ballot and appeal for a return to work. Afterwards Lawrence Daly came out on to the front step of the headquarters to make a statement, but he was forced to retreat inside as angry men broke through the line of police. They would have done a lot of damage had not one leader of the unofficial strike stood on the stairs and appealed for calm: it was their own headquarters after all.

As hopes of changing the N.U.M.'s policy were not destroyed, the strike began to fade away. By the middle of the following week, it was really only pits in South Wales and the Doncaster area that remained firm. And it was in Doncaster that a final confrontation took place with Lord Robens, when he visited the area headquarters of the Coal Board. When he tried to carry out his normal practice of meeting the demonstrators who were waiting for him, he was surrounded by what he called a 'yarling mob' of between sixty and seventy men. They were, he later wrote, 'crude, vulgar and unfit to lead the decent men I know in the pits'. 'But for the presence of the police,' he concluded, 'I believe they would cheerfully have murdered me.' And with that, the strike came to an end. When the Coal Board's offer was finally put to the ballot, it was accepted by 158,239 votes to 82,079.

The disputes of 1969 and 1970 laid the foundations for the victories of 1972 and 1974. The accusations of the Chairman of the Coal Board, Lord Robens, acted as a catalyst for unity: the miners closed ranks. Quite obviously there were some communists involved in the organization of the strike, but as one member of the Doncaster panel put it, 'most of us are firm catholics and card-carrying members of the Labour Party'. It was these sort of men whose attitudes were hardened by Robens's remarks, and who would make sure that next time they went out on strike they would all go out together.

Most of all, the dispute of 1970 provided a demonstration that the rule of two-thirds majority required for a strike should be changed. At the 1971 annual conference, the rule was changed constitutionally by a resolution from South Wales. From then on, a strike would require only 55 per cent of the membership to say 'yes'. The road to 1972 was clear.

9. 1972: The Miners' Greatest Victory

At one o'clock in the morning of 19 February 1972, Joe Gormley came out on to the steps of 10 Downing Street to declare: 'This is the greatest day in the story of the N.U.M.' Lawrence Daly added: 'We've won more in the last twenty-four hours than we've ever won in the last twenty-four years.' Over the previous four months, the miners had proved that with their own hard work and the help of other trade unionists, they could exert a power that no one in the country believed they still had. How did they do it?

The miners' strike of 1972 occurred at a time of radical change in industrial relations in Britain. The events of that period were to dominate thinking not only for the rest of the decade, but also well into the next one. The Labour Government's attempts at statutory reform of trade unions had ended with a voluntary 'solemn and binding' agreement. But the Conservative victory in the election of 1970 created a government determined to take much firmer action. Unemployment was allowed to rise and public sector pay claims were used as a battlefield to secure restraint elsewhere. In the first two years of the new administration, there were strikes by postmen, power workers, railwaymen, health workers and local government employees. In some cases, for instance the power workers, the Government publicly and loudly appealed to public opinion to support them in condemning the strikers, and in two other cases, apart from the miners, they took what up to then had been the comparatively rare step of declaring a state of emergency. All attempts at conciliation by the Government were abandoned, and there were no beer and sandwiches to smooth the way to settlement. Contacts between the T.U.C. and the Government, which under Labour had been close, now all but disappeared, and the relationship between the union leadership and the Government was one of estrangement.

The greatest symbol of this was the Conservatives' Industrial Relations Act. The Act succeeded in making the possibility of achieving some sort of consensus with the trade unions even more remote, and singularly failed to remove industrial relations from politics as the Conservatives had hoped. In fact, rather than decreasing the number of strikes, it added to them, especially in the public sector. Full well could Harold Wilson describe the Act as a 'militants' charter'.

There were also causes of friction specific to the coal industry. At the end of 1970, the Government announced that they would allow coal to be imported to make up for what the N.C.B. failed to produce. Equally seriously, they would continue with the programme of converting coal-burning power stations to work on either coal or oil. Likewise, although the public controversy over the 1971 Coal Industry Act concerned the hiving off of some of the Board's profitable ancillary activities, such as using the spare capacity on their computer for a booking service for hotel rooms, the union were concerned that there was not even a contingency measure to allow the Government to subsidize the C.E.G.B. to use coal, as had been done in the past.

But this was very much high politics. In the coalfields an expectancy of action was building up. The disputes of 1969 and 1970 had changed and intensified a lot of feelings. By the summer of 1971 many more men were turning up to union meetings, and people who would not normally even dream of a strike were now beginning to talk about one. These new attitudes dominated the annual conference in Aberdeen in July, which, incidentally, was the first one to be chaired by Joe Gormley who had beaten Mick McGahey, the Scottish communist, for the presidency. As well as changing the majority needed for a strike, delegates passed a resolution from Yorkshire calling for minimum rates of £26 a week for surface workers, £28 for underground workers and a minimum of £35 a week for men working at the face. It was probably the most important wages resolution the union had ever debated, and contained a clause binding the national executive to consult the membership 'with regard to various forms of industrial action' if there was no satisfactory response from the Board. Gormley welcomed the pressure from below but warned that it must not lead to anarchy: 'The episode of last October when members of the N.E.C. were physically attacked did nothing for the good name of the union, and such actions should be condemned.'

But not only the leadership of the N.U.M. had changed: the composition of the Coal Board was almost entirely different too. Despite offers to stay, Lord Robens left the Coal Board and was replaced in July 1971 by his deputy, Derek Ezra. There was, according to those who were there at the time, a remarkable change in the atmosphere at Hobart House. The style of the one-man band that had characterized the Robens era was replaced by a more democratic approach. There was, as one member put it, 'a feeling of liberation', both himself and his colleagues feeling much freer to say what they wanted. As Ezra told the miners' conference in July 1971, the members of the Board were entirely drawn from within the industry, from people with a 'total professional commitment to the industry'. Of course these men had to prove themselves, and few, if any, at that point appreciated the real decline there had been in miners' wages.

The negotiations for the pay claim began in an extraordinary and unexpected manner. According to Gormley, just two months after his election as President, and one month after the annual conference which had committed the union to a high wage claim, he had a meeting with the Prime Minister, Edward Heath. The arrangements were wholly unofficial: 'I told both Heath and Derek Ezra the figure they would have to come to to get me to a frame of mind to recommend acceptance. I explained that I had become President after years of frustration where we had accepted coppers and I said that it was not going to happen any more. And the figure I put to them was less than was eventually given to us as a result of the Wilberforce inquiry and the strike. I said to Heath, "Ted, you can do the biggest disservice for Britain if you allow a strike to happen because I shall win it." '

On 14 September the N.U.M. had their first full meeting with the National Coal Board. And from the start the two sides appeared irreconcilable. 'Insulting and disgusting' was how the

N.U.M. described the Board's statement that they could spend no more than £25 million on wage increases. Before their next meeting with the union, the Coal Board were informally reminded of the Government's views on pay in the public sector. A civil servant used a graph to demonstrate to the entire Board how the size of wage settlements was being reduced, and pointed to a 7–8 per cent target for the miners. The official was, by all accounts, elated by the Government's defeat of the postmen. For his part, Ezra was strongly of the opinion that the Government's leaden hints had to be obeyed. Many other Board members felt that the time was right to teach the miners a lesson. At the meeting of the Board in early October, Leslie Grainger, the member for science, spoke last and yet was the first to mention the possibility of a strike. He urged the offer of a phoney productivity deal, anything to avoid a confrontation, but his words went unheeded and the Government's informal limits were adhered to.

On 12 October the two sides met again, and the Board offered just over 7 per cent, or £1·80 for the surface minimum and £1·75 for all underground workers. They conceded to the N.U.M. that the Government's views had been made clear to them, but said that these arguments had had no influence on their deliberations. The Coal Board argued that a higher offer would 'mortgage the future' and lead to coal pricing itself out of the market, especially at a time when stocks were high. At this point the difference between the two sides was very great: the N.C.B. offer nowhere near matched the union's demand for rises of up to 43 per cent. Two days later, therefore, the National Executive Committee convened a special conference to decide what to do next.

Special conferences have the reputation of often being inordinately dull. Not this one. Ian Ferguson, the branch secretary at Yorkshire Main Colliery, remembers a television advertisement at the time which showed a man on top of a huge pile of coal urging people to use more of it: 'Our aim,' said Ferguson, 'was to knock him off the top.' The conference met to discuss imposing an overtime ban, withdrawing from the consultative machinery, and balloting the membership to win authority for a possible national strike.

'For the past six months,' Lawrence Daly told the delegates, 'the Central Electricity Generating Board have been pushing coal into every hole and corner they can find in preparation for a miners' strike.' Stocks were indeed much higher than the year before, with 22 million tons distributed to customers and a further 10 million left in the hands of the Coal Board. Because stocks of coal were so high, the C.E.G.B., at the Coal Board's request, had taken all the coal they could, so that in October they held over 17 million tons at power stations throughout the country. 'It is our intention,' said Daly, 'to ensure that the overtime ban makes deep inroads into the stocks so that we can consequently strengthen the bargaining position of our union in coming weeks.'

Daly announced that the Finance and General Purposes Committee, which was later to form the national strike committee, had met and agreed on the guidelines for the overtime ban. Liaison committees would be set up at each pit, each area and at national level to implement the ban. No man would work overtime to cover the job of an absentee, mealtimes would be strictly observed, and the only overtime that would be allowed would be that 'required for the safety of men and the immediate preservation of the mine and plant'. He concluded by reminding the conference that the 'entire trade union movement has its eyes on the miners today. We are in the vanguard, because a whole number of other unions large and small are awaiting the outcome of the miners' struggle and the miners' settlement, because they know that if we cannot break through Conservative wages policy, they may be left isolated and beaten down as the postal workers were earlier this year.' The result was inevitable: the first national industrial action carried out by the miners since 1926 began on 1 November.

The effect of the ban on the men was to harden attitudes considerably. For the first time they could see the real basic rates that they were on, and they did not like what they saw. Overtime had become, in the words of Mick McGahey, a 'cancer in the industry', and its ending helped to harden their determination to win. And of course there was a marked effect on production. All the work that was normally done during overtime stopped, and the many tasks that were done between shifts or at weekends to keep production going came to a halt. The important maintenance done by electricians or fitters, for example, all had to be done during ordinary working hours. In addition, the regulations laid down by the Health and Safety Acts were strictly adhered to.

The operation of the liaison committees, which were supposed to examine requests for safety men, led to positions becoming even more entrenched. These committees were asked to decide on what was a very tricky balance: they could have agreed to the managers' request for men to work over the weekend for reasons of safety, but they only had his word for whether the work was really necessary or not. And if they did agree, they would be able to work normally the next week and the effectiveness of their ban would be reduced. The resulting dichotomy led to all sorts of arguments. One typical reaction was disbelief at the number of safety men required, as 'every week the management seemed to ask for more'. Gradually more and more union officials at pits took the view that safety work should not be done by their members.

At first, the Coal Board seemed to have underestimated the effectiveness of the ban, but when it became clear that deliveries of coal had fallen by about one fifth, and that the decline in stocks at power stations, though not immediately so, was potentially alarming, they began to take a tougher line with the men. For example, at some pits they began to rearrange shifts using private contract men brought in from outside. On 5 November, the area managers met at Hobart House and decided that any action not in accordance with the union's guidelines would result in the men concerned being sent home. The national officers of the N.U.M. also became worried that problems over the implementation of the ban could spark off a rash of unofficial strikes with the situation becoming out of control. With this in mind, they sent out a reminder to the areas that the object of the ban was 'to curtail production outside the normal five shifts while preserving the future of the mine and plant'.

Meanwhile a vigorous campaign was going on throughout the coalfields to secure a 'yes' vote in the ballot on whether to go on strike. There were rallies, meetings and speeches by all the major union leaders. On Thursday, 2 December, the result was declared: 59 per cent had declared themselves in favour of a strike. A week later the National Executive Committee met, and, thrusting aside attempts by the right wing to defer any action, decided to give one month's notice of a strike from 9 January 1972. Preparations began for the first national strike for getting on for half a century. At the end of December, the national strike committee met to discuss how it was to be implemented. They stressed that liaison committees should continue to decide what safety cover should be provided, and that they should seek the support of the transport unions to halt the movement of coal. The N.U.M., they decided, would also assist in ensuring that coal was distributed to hospitals and other similar institutions.

But even then the search for a settlement was continuing. On the very day that the N.E.C. had voted to go on strike, they had also agreed to a request from the Coal Board for more talks. Within hours Gormley and Daly went to Hobart House, and Gormley even put forward the idea of a productivity deal. But the Board did not take up the idea and instead offered slightly higher rises of £2·00 for surface workers and £1·90 for other men. The executive committee turned them down, but asked if they could put their case before the entire National Coal Board. On 21 December the whole of the union's National Executive Committee went to Hobart House for what Derek Ezra, the Chairman, described as 'perhaps one of the most important discussions in the history of the industry'. The union explained the strength of feelings in the coalfields, how their pay had fallen so much behind the rates for much more amenable jobs in other industries, and how a large number of miners were approaching the point where they would qualify for family income supplement. Ezra then stated his belief that on cost-of-living grounds the present offer was a very reasonable one. Higher wages could only be practicable if productivity were increased, as large price rises could not be sustained in the current weak market position of coal. He ended by declaring: 'This is one of the most fateful moments in the history of the British coal industry. If we can go forward in peace we can bring enormous benefits to the industry. If we cannot go forward in peace, the results will be tragic and the recovery distant.' But there had been no material change in the offer, and the National Executive Committee left saying that they would be available for talks at any time.

Over Christmas and the New Year, the negotiations appeared deadlocked. But on 3 January came another chance of a compromise when Ezra and Gormley met at a coal industry lunch and held informal talks. Afterwards, Gormley suggested that the gap between the two sides was not as large as many believed, and so certain were the left wing on the executive that a deal was being hatched that Joe Whelan, the communist from Nottinghamshire, said, 'Judas betrayed Jesus for thirty pieces of silver and the miners are not going to be betrayed for pennies.' That night Gormley and Ezra had an informal meeting at Hobart House lasting an hour and a half. On 5 January, the National Executive Committee met to hear what had gone on. With only a few days left before the strike was due to begin, the N.C.B. themselves joined in the meeting to try to win a last ditch agreement.

For Derek Ezra to lead the Coal Board to the N.U.M.'s headquarters at Euston Road was an act of great courage, as he had faced much opposition from those who said it would be demeaning. But by now Ezra was earnestly desiring a settlement. The unexpected impact of the overtime ban and the result of the strike ballot had made him no longer happy to be an accomplice in the Government's battle for their unofficial pay limit. He was supporting the policy very much against his will. So Ezra went to meet the union believing that he stood a good chance of achieving an agreement, a belief that had quite clearly been encouraged by Gormley.

But he had been badly informed. Ezra made no new cash offer, but did promise an extra five days' holiday as well as holding out promise of great riches from a productivity deal. Having made their point, the N.C.B. then withdrew, and Ezra paced up and down the lobby outside the committee room on the first floor of the union's headquarters. Gormley came out and told him that the National Executive Committee had decided that there was nothing substantially new in the offer and had turned it down. 'Let me talk to them again,' said Ezra. But Gormley replied that it was no good: they had all left and gone to the pubs to celebrate. The Board members were stunned and Ezra was extremely depressed. They made it clear that they had reached their limit, no further offer would be forthcoming, and then they left. Joe Gormley prophesied 'a hell of a lot of chaos in a short time'.

Joe Gormley still believes that the strike should never have happened: 'The gap was so narrow that it was a crime that a strike should have taken place at all.' Since August, he had continually warned that a strike was a very great possibility. In the last few weeks before the strike he had 'held out three or four olive branches to the Government and the Chairman of the Board but none was picked up'. He maintains that he told them he could win agreement for a settlement if they offered £3·50, and even though many on the executive wanted a lot more, he could have sold the deal because he would have believed in it: 'It was so damn stupid of them not to realize that I was bloody serious.' Should they have believed him? It is open to endless speculation whether Gormley could have convinced the membership that the deal was worth accepting. But the build-up of pressure for action in the coalfields, starting in 1969 and culminating in the vote for a strike, make it in retrospect seem very unlikely.

But even if he had been able to sell a deal to his members, would the Government have bought it? For their part, the Government were putting strong pressures on the Coal Board to stand firm behind their unofficial pay limit, while remaining publicly committed to a policy of non-intervention. Many members of the executive committee at the time knew full well that the Government were strongly involved in strengthening Ezra's resolve: 'You'd have a meeting with him and you'd know he'd just come from a meeting with Carr or Heath or someone like that.' This led them to the conclusion that the Government, having beaten the postal workers, were after a showdown with them too. And as one senior minister put it later: 'It is inconceivable that the country would be brought to the brink of the first coal strike since 1926 without the say-so of the Government. A chairman of a nationalized industry just does not make that sort of decision.'

This tough line by the Government was matched by an equally strong line by many members of the Coal Board. Although Ezra joined the small camp of the conciliators, there were more who felt that it would be a very good idea to stem the tide of miners' militancy and teach them a lesson. One member of the Board directly involved in the negotiations agreed with Gormley that the strike could have been avoided – he maintained for 10s – and repeatedly said so, but the rest of the Board seemed bent on confrontation. For the predominant attitude in Hobart House and in the Government, as well as in the country at large, was that the miners no longer counted for anything. After all, the miners had not gone on national strike since 1926, and the economic power of coal had fallen vastly since then. It was also possible to interpret the ballot result not as a symbol of strength but as an indicator of possible disunity, as over 40 per cent of the membership had shown themselves to be against a strike. In short, they did not believe the miners could organize a strike and win.

The Government and the Coal Board were not alone in playing down the threat posed by the strike. Woodrow Wyatt in the *Daily Mirror* said that the miners did not stand a chance: 'Alas it is as if some mystery siren is luring them zombie-like to destruction. They have more stacked against them than the Light Brigade in their famous charge.' *The Economist* believed that the miners 'cannot stop the country in its tracks as they once could have done', and *The Times* predicted that 'coal stocks away from the pits are large enough to withstand a strike for weeks, if it does not spread, with only marginal disruption to industry and commerce as a whole'. For the most part, the press and public believed that coal no longer mattered and the country could get along without it. For this reason, when the real crisis came in the middle of February, most people were left stunned and could only wonder what had gone so very wrong.

On 8 January, the Coal Board announced that they had withdrawn all pay offers made over the previous three months of negotiations, and that any future settlement would not be backdated. The miners realized that they were in for a hard fight. The strike, the first national one in most miners' working lives, began on midnight of 8 January.

From the very first day of the strike, every pit in the country was closed. This gave the miners an immense psychological and strategic advantage. They could by and large forget about intensive picketing of the pits, and concentrate instead on making the strike really effective by halting all movements of coal and other fuels. On the first Monday, the T.U.C. Finance and General Purposes Committee met to consider what coordinated action they could carry out. The miners were hoping for a great deal of practical help, but failed to get it. The committee confined themselves to asking members of affiliated unions not to cross the miners' picket lines. Gormley was disappointed, telling reporters, 'I would have thought this was one time the T.U.C. could have shown itself to be united.'

The failure of the T.U.C. to provide coordinated action dictated the style of the miners' campaign. If no one else would stop all movements of coal, then they would have to do it themselves. If the T.U.C. would only tell its members not to cross picket lines, then they would have to make sure the whole country was covered by pickets. The miners would not win by sitting back and waiting for the apocalypse: they would have to act aggressively.

All the plans of the union were for a rapid victory. On the first Wednesday of the strike, the national strike committee took the crucial decision to concentrate action on an intensive picket of all power stations. Each area of the union was given responsibility for picketing a non-mining part of the country: Yorkshire was given East Anglia, the Kent and Midlands areas were put in charge of London and the South East, and the South Wales N.U.M. was made responsible for the South West of England. The C.E.G.B. yearbook provided most of the information upon which the instructions were sent out to the areas. Each area received a map photocopied from the book, with a list of all the power stations in their area graded according to their importance. Major power stations, the instructions said, should be picketed at all times, while the minor ones should be picketed only if the manpower was available: 'If this strike is to be fully effective and of as short duration as possible, all major coal-users and coal depots must be picketed in view of the assurance given by other unions that their members will not cross N.U.M. picket lines.'

The great strength of the union was that it was still very much a federation. National organization did not matter over much, for the real power of the strike lay with the grass roots in the areas. In the coalfields, action was already being taken and tactics developed which would make the strike famous and give it its hallmark.

In Kent, a tip-off from another union sent a fleet of cars off to stop the movement of coal from Rochester to Croydon power station. The drivers agreed not to move any more coal and pickets were mounted outside each power station. This first incident had shown how important information was about movements of coal and the amount being held in stocks, so during the first week 'flying squads' were sent out to investigate power stations, depots and wharves. Pickets stopped all coal going into power stations at Fulham and Tilbury, and the information they gleaned, as well as the publicity they attracted, boosted morale. From Kent, another group of pickets set off along the south coast to find out what was happening at the docks.

Similar action was taking place throughout the country, and it soon became clear that where there was a strong union organization, only a token picket was needed. But where firms were using non-union labour, and in some cases 'heavies', to drive through the picket lines come what may, a stronger form of picketing was required, and the mass picket was born.

At Grimethorpe in South Yorkshire, for example, a picket line tried to stop lorries going into the coalite plant just down the road from the pit. But as the lorries approached, they accelerated, scattering men in all directions. So cavalier was their approach that one man was taken to hospital with serious leg injuries. The picket line grew to meet this challenge until there were about 300 men present. In the end, they learnt that it was easier to stop the trucks on their way out, heavily laden, and that by pulling a lever at the back the whole thing would tip up, dumping the load in the middle of the road. After a while the manager of the plant gave the pickets a portacabin as shelter from the cold winds and the rain. Eventually the plant was closed, but only after the union and the management had made an agreement that no fuel would be moved unless a driver could produce an N.U.M. docket showing that it was going to an approved destination. These agreements, and there were many of them all over the country, sometimes with the police as witnesses, became another hallmark of the dispute.

Elsewhere in the country, 500 men were picketing the Longannet power station in Scotland, after reports that coal was being moved to Cockenzie station. Power workers later agreed to block the movement of any more coal. By 12 January, there was a picket some 200 strong outside Kincardine power station in Fife. A few days later the Scottish N.U.M. held talks with the transport unions in Scotland, and won an agreement that no picket line should be crossed in any circumstances and that no coal should be moved by road or rail.

In South Wales the miners held similar talks with the leaders of all the main transport unions, and won an agreement that all coal imports through Cardiff, Swansea, Newport, Bristol, Avonmouth and Portishead would be blacked. The Midlands area won an agreement from the power workers to black all coal going into Rugeley B power station. And there was a large picket at the coalite plant at Bolsover in Derbyshire, where the local M.P., Dennis Skinner, and others had to leap into a ditch to avoid accelerating trucks.

But the most important development during the first week was the way in which rank and file miners were showing an organizational ability that in the end would win them their battle. At North Gawber pit in Barnsley, South Yorkshire, for example, the miners' welfare hall was being used as the rallying point for the colliery. From the very first day of the strike, men would turn up, have a talk, maybe buy a drink if they could afford it, and in that way keep in touch with the branch officials and each other. The welfare became the centre of the community for the duration of the dispute, and various socials and sing-songs were organized to entertain strikers and their families. The branch officials divided up responsibility between them for the many tasks that had to be carried out. The Secretary, Albert Frost, dealt with all the claims for social security to support the families of strikers: 'The union decided not to give strike pay. But I told the lads that whatever else they did, they should pay the rent.' They had a great deal of cooperation from the local D.H.S.S. offices, who told them what claimants would require, and helped divide the men up so that they would not all turn up on the same day. The lodge delegate went off to help with the area strike committee in Barnsley, whilst the treasurer and president were responsible for organizing pickets. They had no shortage of volunteers, who were asked to maintain contact regularly by telephone or by calling in at the welfare. So efficient was their system that when a telephone call came through asking for, say, a bus to go to Great Yarmouth, they could usually fill it within minutes. Two committee members travelled with each bus to ensure good behaviour. Said Frost, 'Most people thought we were like Vikings raiding East Anglia, so we didn't want to offer them confirmation of their belief.'

The key decisions about which targets should be selected and how they should be picketed were generally made by the areas of the union, and in Kent and Yorkshire their organization was particularly brilliant. In Yorkshire, the panels which had demonstrated their effectiveness during the disputes of 1969 and 1970 formed themselves into four area strike committees. They held the real power. The Doncaster panel, for example, manned an office at the Brodsworth Home Coal Delivery Service for twenty-four hours a day throughout the dispute. The six-man strike committee virtually lived there, running what had to be a military-style operation. Men would ring in, give their names, where they were and what news they had. All this was recorded in a log, and movements of coal and men were displayed on a large map. There were so many men involved, so many complex arrangements, so much information about coal movements and so on, that the organization had to be strictly ordered. 'What we decided,' said Ian Ferguson, a member of the strike committee, 'was that the main brunt of our attack had to be power stations and stock yards. As long as we concentrated on those issues, we would win.'

The Barnsley committee, with Arthur Scargill as their spokesman, sent exploratory squads of pickets into East Anglia during the first week of the dispute to make contacts and find out as much as they could about the movements of coal. But inevitably, with such a large area, they were spreading their resources too thinly, and so at the end of the week they decided to change their tactics. They agreed to concentrate pickets on fewer targets, and set up a base in East Anglia to coordinate activities. They contacted the Labour Party in Norwich who gave them a room, a map, a telephone and useful contacts. Two committee members went down to man the office on a rota basis, a week at a time. During the day they had the enormous task of arranging the blockade not only of every power station in the area, but also of the innumerable docks and quays that are scattered throughout East Anglia. By night, they would attend meetings to whip up support and money for their cause.

They kept in constant touch with the strike committee in Barnsley, which had by then taken over a room in the miners' offices. There a log was kept, carefully noting the remarks and requests made by the men in Norwich. They saw to it that men were sent wherever and whenever they were needed. On 19 January, a 212-strong flying squad left Barnsley in four coaches for power stations in East Anglia. One by one, the power stations were picketed and all coal movements came to a halt. There was still one outstanding failure, though, at the end of the second week. Despite intense picketing, coal and oil was still being moved through Ipswich docks, and the Norwich H.Q. decided that only by picketing in strength would the docks be closed. Their appeal went out, and on 24 January seven bus loads of pickets, the largest number yet organized, made their way southwards from Barnsley. All movements of coal were stopped and oil tankers were turned away.

During the second week of the strike, similar developments were taking place elsewhere, and it was at this point that the tactic of the mass picket really came into its own. Flying pickets identified targets, and the mass pickets provided the muscle where necessary. The fact that these large numbers of men could be moved around the country so quickly by coach or by car was another of the great organizational successes of the strike. The speed with which this happened bewildered the police, who were quite open in admitting that they were often overwhelmed.

Crucial to the success of the miners' action was the support of other unions. A.S.L.E.F.'s executive had from the beginning of the dispute instructed its members to 'confine themselves to normal working', and not to work extra trains that were put on to carry coal or any other fuel. The National Union of Railwaymen had also sent out instructions to their members not to enter collieries, and not to 'work oil into power stations where, due to the strike, a switch is made from coal to oil'. Later in the dispute at least two areas of A.S.L.E.F. blacked all movement of coal by rail. Contacts between the two unions and the miners were generally very close at area level, and information was passed on about such things as coal movements and the best place to put pickets to stop trains. They even accepted a sign saying 'N.U.M. picket', dangled from railway bridges, displayed on level crossings or waved from station platforms, as an official picket line which trains would not cross.

Other unions helped too. The Transport and General Workers' Union provided information about movements of coal, and their drivers refused to cross picket lines. Generally the only lorries that tried to ignore the miners' action were driven by non-union men, often with police escorts, as in some cases they faced very real threats of dismissal if they did not carry out their firm's orders. N.A.T.S.O.P.A. provided the Kent miners with hotel accommodation and office facilities after they were thrown out of the N.U.M.'s national offices at Euston Road. The lightermen's union lent three boats to make up what became known as the 'miners' navy'. In what was one of the most bizarre methods of picketing during the whole dispute, a pleasure steamer called the *Skylark* went up and down the Thames equipped with a loudhailer and a sign proclaiming 'N.U.M. picket boat'. Dockers and seamen provided information and support to stop the import of coal, and the Miners' International Federation were able to find out where coal shipments were being prepared for the U.K., and try to ensure that they were blacked. But as well as the grand gestures, there were innumerable small ones: a member of the A.U.E.W. who lent his dormobile to some miners' pickets, trade unionists who rang up to tip off national or local officials about shipments of coal, the many, many trade union branches and members that sent donations of money to help the strike, shopkeepers who provided food, and schools which gave free meals to miners' children.

But probably the most important support of all came from

workers at power stations, who provided pickets with information vital to the success of their cause. Pickets would usually arrive at the gates of a power station not knowing quite what to expect. Men at the gates would call the shop stewards, who would generally tell them what stocks there were, what deliveries were expected, and the best place to put pickets. Of course, the power station workers were themselves on the brink of their own dispute over wages, which incidentally was occupying the attention of the media a great deal more than the miners' strike was. But it was they who taught the miners all they needed to know about the generation of electricity, by warning them, for example, that more electricity could be generated by the heavier use of oil and that oil-powered stations often held stocks of coal, so they should be picketed as well. By the end of the second week, it was clear that power stations were burning extra oil and conserving stocks of coal, so on 21 January the order went out from N.U.M. headquarters that all supplies of fuel oil should now be stopped as well. Power stations were put under what the Central Electricity Generating Board called 'a total siege'.

The miners on picket duty had been told by the power workers about the importance of sulphuric acid, so that was turned back, of hydrogen used in cooling, so that was stopped, and of how even in coal-fired power stations small quantities of oil were used for 'sparking' the coal. All these had the added advantage of being very easy to stop, but even so all sorts of tricks were used to try to break the blockade. At Hams Hall power station in the Midlands, the electricity authorities tried to bring oil in overnight down an old farm track, but pickets heard the sound of the motors and stopped them. At Hackney, lorries full of oil were driven at full speed to try to break the picket line. At Thorpe Marsh power station near Doncaster, the C.E.G.B. used helicopters to try to ferry in hydrogen to restart the generators. At one point, the miners ran underneath the helicopter as it came in to land, and the pilot had to climb quickly to avoid decapitating the pickets with the rotor blades. But even if supplies were somehow got into the power stations, the power workers often refused to touch them, saying that they were blacked. There were numerous anecdotes about how the police helped to avoid trouble by supporting the picket line. At Colchester, for example, the police sat in a little hut the miners were using, playing cards and eating bacon sandwiches. As soon as the sound of an engine could be heard approaching, it was more often than not the policeman who was the first to his feet, holding his hand up to stop the traffic.

The N.U.M. were very keen that picketing should be peaceful, and by and large it was. On 19 January, Daly wrote to all areas reminding them that it was illegal to make 'physical contact' with anybody trying to pass through a picket line. But in the main it was the pickets who suffered injuries, especially when lorry drivers accelerated at the lines. There were exceptions, and they often involved disputes within the mining communities themselves. For example, at the end of the second week of the strike, a picket of about 500 men had formed early in the morning across the car park at the N.C.B.'s Doncaster area headquarters. They made a corridor some 200 yards long, down which the staff wanting to go into the building had to pass. An eye-witness account sent by the N.C.B. to Gormley went on:

As they proceeded through the picket lines they were kicked, punched, spat upon. This treatment was given to all, irrespective of age, sex or any apparent union membership. Once inside the building almost every female of the staff collapsed in tears, were hysterical or otherwise physically distressed. They were given first aid and treatment. They cleaned up, for many had been spat upon and bore the marks of tobacco juice, and went to their desks. An hour later, many were still in tears.

Such actions were indefensible, but part of the problem was that some of the office staff who belonged to C.O.S.A., the clerical section of the N.U.M., were alleged to have joined another union during the strike. The same day Daly sent out another circular, stressing that all picketing had to be peaceful and that 'at no time should there be any provocation for any reason on the part of our pickets'. The union further emphasized that all officials should take great care to ensure that at least one N.U.M. member was in charge of a picket line at all times. A week later, Daly expressed his concern that with the deadlock in the dispute, the media would look for any other activity concerned with the dispute to focus their attention on, and for that reason the union should 'guard again infiltration by groups whose only objective is to create maximum disruption to our peaceful campaign in the hope of discrediting our case. Care should be taken that only official N.U.M. literature is distributed by our members.'

Another issue which created trouble on the picket lines was the question of safety. At the beginning of the third week of the strike, the Coal Board wrote to the N.U.M. expressing their serious concern that some pickets were stopping officials, and in some cases managers, attending the pits to carry out inspections and safety work. They said that the 'only possible outcome is that faces, roadways, even entire pits are now threatened'. In spite of directives, the N.C.B. maintained that there were 148 collieries with no safety cover at all. At Cadeby, in fact, sleepers had been put across the road, and no one was allowed through. The N.U.M., however, had been very clear: officials and managers should be allowed to cross the lines, not only for safety reasons, but also to ensure that the union could not be accused of Luddism. Why were these directions ignored? It has already been said that at some pits, according to the union, the managers appeared to want far too much safety work done by far too many men. And then as the dispute went on and accusations grew more acrimonious, the bitterness grew to such an extent that some even regarded officials belonging to N.A.C.O.D.S., the National Association of Colliery Overmen, Deputies and Shotfirers, as legitimate targets, and began in a few cases to picket them too. At various pits they were shouted at, spat upon, pushed and shoved, and often had to be escorted into work by the police. For as one N.U.M. official put it after one such incident: 'Our lads saw red when 68 deputies arrived and tried to do safety work that we knew could be done by only twenty.'

As well as the picketing, each strike committee was instructed to ensure that certain groups like the old and the infirm, and certain organizations like schools and hospitals continued to get supplies of coal. 'The N.U.M. must be seen to be taking all steps possible to ensure that coal is available for priority groups,' wrote Daly. In practice, if a picket organizer decided that a particular group or establishment deserved priority, an N.U.M. man was sent along if necessary to 'ride shotgun' and verify delivery. Each driver was given a docket showing the destination of the coal, and without one nothing would be moved. It was a form of organization unknown since the General Strike.

Throughout the dispute, the miners had the support of the public at large. Offers of accommodation flooded into the N.U.M.'s office at Euston Road, and Nina Stead, the research officer's secretary, sorted them all out. The offers were not only from trade unionists or constituency labour parties, but also from professionals, old ladies, all sorts of people, as well as from many people whose fathers, grandfathers or some other relative had been miners and who still felt in some way a part of the mining community. Yorkshire miners in East Anglia were put up, at one point 1,000 at one time, at the University of Essex, until the university authorities threatened a high court injunction to get rid of them. Speakers' panels were organized so that requests for somebody to put the miners' case could be met promptly. Often men who had never opened their mouths in public before found themselves being whisked off the picket lines to give accounts of their lives and their work to labour clubs, students' unions and other such gatherings. The N.U.M. nationally had already advised each strike committee to make one of their members a spokesman. They issued statements, arranged visits to picket lines, organized interviews with miners' wives and so on. But there was also an extensive campaign of leafleting and pamphleteering. Few, for example, can have forgotten the poster of a miner's blackened face with the slogan in bright red declaring, 'Wanted – a living wage'. Yet not many at the time realized that it had been drawn and designed by a pit-top worker from Kent.

The first three weeks of the dispute were in some ways a phoney war, with deadlock at national level and the effects of the strike still not wholly realized. The House of Commons held the first full debate on the strike during the second week. Several hundred miners and about eighty miners' wives from Kent and Derbyshire came to London to lobby Parliament and hand a letter in at 10 Downing Street. During the debate all the Labour M.P.s and almost every Conservative stressed the loyalty and moderation of the miners, and most of the venom concerned the role of the

Government. Harold Lever said that the Government were displaying a 'dictatorial insensitive attitude', and Tom Swain, the Labour M.P. for North East Derbyshire, described Derek Ezra as the 'highest paid apprentice in the mining industry'. Eric Varley, to Labour cheers, issued the challenge: 'Is the Government's only role in the dispute to whisper to the Board to stand firm? We know, the miners know and I think the country knows that the Government are up to their necks in this dispute.' For the Government, John Davies said the Board's offer compared favourably with recent settlements in both the public and private sector, stating, 'We are witnessing a damaging strike liable to cause great inconvenience and even hardship to the community and great damage to the industry itself.' The Secretary of State for Employment, Robert Carr, said: 'The Government are not seeking a showdown with the miners, we are not seeking to drive the miners into submission or humiliation.' But as for direct involvement in the dispute? Reference to that was carefully avoided.

Instead peace overtures were being left entirely up to the T.U.C. The day following the debate, Vic Feather, the General Secretary of the T.U.C., arranged talks between the two sides at the Charing Cross Hotel. The N.C.B. reiterated that they could offer no more, but Gormley suggested that more money could be found if the Government were to reduce some of the Board's debts. After two hours the talks broke up, with Feather appealing for the Government to intervene, though he admitted it was like 'taking a high dive into shallow water'. That night, Feather went to see Carr to try to persuade him to hold talks. The two sides met Carr the following day but to no avail. Carr concluded 'reluctantly' that there was nothing more he could do to help towards a settlement, as both the N.C.B. and the union showed themselves unable to change their positions. In the Commons, Harold Lever described Carr's attitude as one of 'detached, lofty impartiality', and wondered when he was going to do something positive to end the strike. The failure of this set of talks led to the union issuing instructions to tighten up picketing considerably, stressing that picket lines had to be maintained round-the-clock and that all movements of fuel had to be stopped.

On 26 January the T.U.C.'s General Council met for the first time since the strike began, and agreed that there was no hope of peace unless the Government recognized that the miners had a strong case which had to be examined 'on its own merits not by reference to doctrinaire considerations'. Daly could see no hope of a compromise when he addressed a demonstration in South Wales the next day and, to an ovation, declared: 'Ours will be a victory not only for the miners but for the whole working class of Britain.' The day after, Robert Carr went to open a new employment exchange in Lancashire. He was greeted by a crowd of 400 or so miners and unemployed who shouted and booed and threw eggs at him. According to one report, the Minister was badly shaken.

Then came the first real sign that the miners' action was biting and biting hard. 'General Winter comes to the aid of the miners!' exclaimed the *Daily Express* headline on Monday, 31 January. 'Mr Carr! Mr Gormley! Mr Ezra! Get negotiations started! Get the miners back to work!' For the first time there had been voltage reductions throughout the whole country, and the C.E.G.B., in a remarkably pessimistic statement, forecast power cuts. The prophesy of Gormley had come true, though a little late, and to the majority of people the news came as a considerable shock. The C.E.G.B. put some of the blame on the 'sudden severe weather', but most on the picketing, in some cases by what they called 'extremists', which, they claimed, had prevented the delivery of many of the materials necessary for the safe operation of power stations. They admitted that three power stations had already been closed down.

At the time the mood on the picket lines hardened considerably. On 3 February, Fred Matthews, a thirty-seven-year-old miner from Hatfield Main Colliery in Yorkshire, was killed while picketing outside Keadby power station near Scunthorpe. An articulated lorry carrying materials and driven by a non-unionist had forced its way into the station, where the power workers had refused to unload it. The driver took off the load himself and then drove off at high speed, scattering the police, who tried to tell him to slow down, and the pickets. As the lorry came out of the gates, it swung round to make a turn, but was going too fast. It mounted the pavement and the back end struck Mr Matthews, killing him. Despite calls from the police, the lorry did not stop, so they jumped into one of the picket's cars and eventually caught up with him about a mile from the gates. Up to then the picket line had been peaceful.

News of the death of Fred Matthews stunned the miners and made them more determined to win. And in the House of Commons there were angry and emotional scenes as miners' M.P.s spoke of the new bitterness the death of Matthews would bring. Tom Swain declared: 'This could be the start of another Ulster in the Yorkshire coalfield. I warn the Government here and now that if there is not an immediate statement from a responsible minister, I shall go back to my constituency tonight and advocate violence.' Later that evening the Home Secretary, Reginald Maudling, took the unusual step of making a statement explaining that the police were investigating and expressing his sympathy for the relatives.

Fred Matthews's funeral was, according to one of those present, the biggest demonstration he could ever remember. Ten thousand people turned out, with miners coming from all over the country, and a representative from every pit in Yorkshire. The procession began in thin drizzle, and the pace was set by the muffled beat of a black draped drum. Cards on the wreaths on his coffin expressed the emotions of miners at his death. 'In memory of a gallant miner who fell in his union's cause,' said one.

The inquest was held not in Matthews's home area, but in Scunthorpe, a town with a reputation for antagonism towards miners. The manner of the inquest even now provokes anger amongst Matthews's family and workmates. The coroner directed the jury to return a verdict of accidental death, telling them that the driver's actions had shown him 'doing his best by his employer and if I may say so by his country'. The case of Fred Matthews went no further.

The day after Fred Matthews's death there began what became known as 'the Battle of Saltley Gate'. The Saltley coke depot in Birmingham was the last major depot open, and contained an estimated 100,000 tons of fuel. By the end of January the number of lorries being served each day had almost doubled, to about 650, and pictures in the press and on television showed a 'mountain of coke' which took on a symbolic significance for the miners engaged in making their strike as effective as possible. By the evening of 3 February, seven pickets organized by the Midlands N.U.M. were outside, and the following day they were reinforced by some 200 men from Stoke-on-Trent. Over the weekend, the Midlands area secretary, Jack Lally, was constantly in touch with the N.U.M.'s London office trying to organize reinforcements, and on Saturday when scuffles broke out between police and pickets, the message went around the coalfields that 'they're beating hell out of our lads'. By the Sunday morning men had arrived from South Wales, the Midlands and Yorkshire.

In Barnsley, the response to the call was immediate. The N.U.M. office in London rang the strike headquarters at 4 p.m. and asked for 200 men to be sent to Saltley. The first left within two and a half hours. One branch secretary remembers a colleague coming round to his house with the appeal for help, and as the two walked back towards the miners' welfare in the pouring rain wondering where they were going to get the men from, they saw two empty Wallace Arnold coaches rushing past. Scargill himself drove through the night, arriving in Birmingham at three o'clock on Sunday morning. The Communist Party, the Labour Party, the Transport and General Workers' Union and local students were already organizing accommodation for the pickets, and the Labour M.P., Denis Howell, laid on hot meals in the Labour Party headquarters.

On Sunday, 6 February, about 200 miners picketed the gates from the early morning. They had already established an agreement with the police and the Gas Board that only one of the gates of the depot would be used. During the morning the pickets managed to turn some lorries away until, amidst great jubilation, the Gas Board announced that they would close the gates until the following morning.

On the Monday morning anywhere between 1,000 and 2,000 men were outside the gates, the numbers increasing as the day went by. The relationship with the police changed. One picket vividly recalls seeing phalanxes of police march over the brow of the hill to the depot, and thinking that these were not local men, but the heavies. A superintendent with a megaphone directed them from on top of a wall, like a general commanding troops. During the day, twenty-one people were arrested and just under half the lorries were turned away. Two policemen were hurt and the entire Birmingham police force was put on special alert.

Miners tried all sorts of tactics to stop the flow of coke. In one incident, they let down the tailboard of a loaded lorry and about three tons of coke poured on to the road. Other miners continually used pedestrian crossings to stop traffic, and some lay in front of lorries only to be dragged clear by the police. Fruit, stones, bottles and meat pies were thrown during the fighting. The N.U.M. in London now asked for every available picket to go to Saltley to join in the struggle.

The call was answered, and on Tuesday even more pickets arrived from all over the country. That morning two pickets were injured and three policemen, one of whom, a chief inspector, had his thigh fractured when a lorry pushed its way through the crowd. Every lorry that day provoked skirmishes between the police and pickets, and by nightfall there were a further twenty arrests and a total of eighteen people injured. That day nearly 2,000 Midland car delivery men struck in sympathy with the miners at Saltley, as did workers at the Thorn Lighting Company. On the Wednesday there were a further twenty-five arrests, but the real climax to events came on the following day, Thursday, 10 February.

By mid morning about 15,000 people had arrived at Nechells Place, outside the coke depot. Workers at scores of factories throughout Birmingham had gone on strike and arrived to offer support. The whole area was full of people shoulder to shoulder, with banners, placards and even a Scots piper. The crowd started chanting, 'Close the gate, close the gate!' The roar, according to Alan Law, the Midlands regional secretary of the Transport and General Workers' Union, 'became tumultuous, it stopped the traffic in Saltley Road, which by now was full of shouting workers moving steadily forward towards the gate'. At a quarter to eleven, a Gas Board official turned the key in the lock and closed the depot. The miners had won, and the crowd were jubilant. The police asked Arthur Scargill to disperse the crowd, and he agreed, on the condition that they would allow him to make a speech using police equipment as his was, in his words, 'knackered'. From on top of a urinal, Scargill told the crowd: 'This will go down in trades union history. It will also go down in history as the Battle of Saltley Gate. The working people have united in a mass stand.'

The Battle of Saltley Gate has become legend. For trade unionists, it was the apotheosis of their movement: for those on the right, it was a symbol of political confrontation of potentially frightening proportions. The chief constable who had directed the police, Sir Derek Capper, was, according to this latter view, guilty of surrender. He had never used more than 800 men, whereas had he really wanted to keep the depot open, according to this view, he could have used thousands. But the fact that he did not do so without doubt prevented violence that could well have got out of control. In terms of the miners' union, Saltley put Arthur Scargill firmly into the spotlight as a national trade union figure. The television cameras concentrated on him, and his gifts as a propagandist and speaker guaranteed their attention. In the context of the dispute, however, the victory at Saltley showed that the miners, acting together with other trade unionists, were unstoppable.

At the beginning of the fifth week of the dispute, at the time of the Battle of Saltley, 8,000 people from all over Britain had met beneath leaden skies for a march from Hyde Park to Trafalgar Square, where they stood in silence for a minute whilst a piper played a lament for Fred Matthews. At the same time as the demonstration was taking place there were once again voltage reductions all over the country, and by the weekend it was clear that the miners' stranglehold over the economy was tightening. There were 11,000 pickets on duty each day throughout the country. Most ominously, stocks at power stations had fallen to only three weeks' supply, and there was talk of using troops to move coal.

In the middle of the week in which all eyes were turned towards the visible sign of the miners' struggle at Saltley, the Government declared a state of emergency to 'protect central services and supplies for the community'. The extent of the crisis facing the country was now clear. The Coal Board, the C.E.G.B. and the

Government had all been hoping for a short strike and so had been keen to play down the likely consequences of the dispute. But quietly, throughout January, stocks held at power stations had been falling by 1·6 million tons a week, a measure of the success of the miners' picketing. By 9 February there were less than 6 million tons left, and half of that was at just three power stations in the south of England. The outlook was catastrophic, and drastic steps had to be taken to reduce the consumption of electricity. The fact that the power workers had called off their threatened overtime ban and accepted a pay deal did nothing to alter the arithmetic. On 9 February the Government declared a state of emergency, and on the 11th they imposed a three-day week on industry, with restrictions on office heating, display lighting and daily power cuts first of 10 per cent and later of 15 per cent.

In this atmosphere, the Secretary of State for Employment, Robert Carr, called the miners and the N.C.B. to meet him separately. He suggested that more money could be made available if the settlement was for eighteen months instead of a year, and he asked them whether they would look favourably on a court of inquiry. The miners agreed to have exploratory talks with the Coal Board, but rejected the idea of an inquiry. That night the N.U.M. and the N.C.B. met together under the chairmanship of an official from the Department of Employment. But the new offer put by the Coal Board of between £2.75 and £3.30 nowhere near matched the sort of rises that the N.U.M. needed to settle. The N.U.M. wryly noted that whereas the Board had originally offered a deal amounting to £32 million for twelve months, they were now offering £48 million for eighteen months; the offer would in no way near match inflation and was 'totally unacceptable'.

The N.U.M., however, felt certain that a new and better offer was on the way and so, with some difficulty, they persuaded the N.C.B. to further talks. On Thursday, 10 February, as the Saltley Battle drew to its climax, the two sides met again. Gormley and Daly made it clear that with an offer of between £6 and £7 serious negotiations could start. The N.C.B. went into a huddle and then declared that they thought the union was acting irresponsibly.

For their part, the N.U.M. could see no way that they could accept less, as expectations had risen greatly during the dispute, and for the sake of their own standing neither Gormley nor Daly was keen to be the first to accept a low figure. Once more there was deadlock.

The country now began to realize the full extent of the emergency measures taken by the Government. By Monday, 14 February, the Government estimated that 800,000 workers had been laid off. The following day the number had risen to 1·2 million, and by the end of the week the figure had reached 1·6 million. In a debate on the Government's emergency powers in the House of Commons, John Davies warned that 'the anticipated endurance of the C.E.G.B. is approximately two weeks at present consumption'.

Robert Carr once again summoned the miners to his office, and in a meeting lasting just fifteen minutes told them he was going to appoint a court of inquiry. He asked them to resume work in the meantime, but realizing that to do so would weaken their position, the miners refused. And while they agreed to give evidence to the inquiry, they refused to be bound by its decisions. Meanwhile there were rallies and demonstrations up and down the country, and enormous anger when thirteen men arrested on the picket line at Longannet power station in Scotland appeared in court wearing handcuffs.

But in the quiet surroundings of Church House, Westminster, Lord Wilberforce began his inquiry. Lord Wilberforce sat at the far end of a light oak-panelled room, with John Garnett, the director of the Industrial Society, on his right, and Professor L. S. Hunter of Glasgow University on his left. The atmosphere was restrained and even Daly, putting the miners' case, spoke softly. Much of his statistical evidence had been produced with the help of the Trade Union Research Unit at Ruskin College, Oxford, but Daly put the case with characteristic brilliance. He opened the court's proceedings by declaring:

In speaking to this court of inquiry we are also speaking to millions of people beyond these four walls. We are speaking to, we are appealing to the conscience of the nation . . .

Our pickets have done something more than hasten the course of this dispute. They have acted as ambassadors of the mining community in every city and port of this country. We have enjoyed in practical form, and with steadily growing effectiveness, the solidarity and support of the organized workers of this country. Instead of remaining isolated and alone beside our pits, we have built a unity of action and understanding that has been an immense and positive feature of this strike. It is that and that alone that has forced the Government from the dictatorship that it has been imposing not just on the miners but on all the workers of this country.

The hearings were in public for two days, and they heard evidence not only from the N.U.M. but also from three ordinary miners, the Coal Board, the C.B.I., some academics and an M.P. Their eventual report told the country what they had for so long failed to understand about the miners and their union:

Working conditions in coal-mines are certainly among the toughest and least attractive and we agree that miners' pay levels should recognize this. Other occupations have their dangers and inconveniences but we know of none in which there is such a combination of danger, health hazard, discomfort in working conditions, social inconvenience and community isolation.

They also praised the way in which the miners had watched their numbers decline from over 700,000 in 1957, to under 290,000, and the number of pits fall from over 800 to under 300:

This rundown, which was brought about with the cooperation of the miners and the union, is without parallel in British industry in terms of the social and economic costs it has inevitably entailed for the mining community as a whole.

Wilberforce accepted that productivity over the same period had risen by over 77 per cent, as the N.U.M. had cooperated with the Coal Board by embracing mechanization and learning new skills.

And yet during the period from 1965 to 1970, the pay of the miner fell from near the top rank to a level in the middle of the national pay league.

From a position in which average weekly earnings in coal-mining had stood well above average earnings in manufacturing industry, the industry found itself in 1971 in the reverse situation where its workers earned substantially less, on average, than those in manufacturing.

The adjustment of wage rates since 1966 had meant that some men were 'now earning less than they were five years ago'. In human terms, the impact of this was brought home by the testimony of Jack Collins, a faceworker from Kent, who showed that his pay in 1971 was £5 a shift whereas in 1963 he had been earning £5.10s a shift. 'We are convinced,' concluded Wilberforce,

that the present is a time when a definite and substantial adjustment in wage levels is called for in the coal industry . . . we think it an essential part of the present settlement that the miners' basic claim for a general and exceptional increase should be recognized.

For surface workers Wilberforce recommended an increase of £5, making a minimum rate of £23, for underground workers an overall increase of £6, taking the basic minimum to £25, and for faceworkers an increase of £4.50, taking their basic minimum rate to £34.50. They also recommended that all the increases should be backdated to 1 November 1971, and should run for a period of sixteen months. Wilberforce additionally urged a productivity deal, either a national one or a scheme based on individual pits.

On 18 February, the day that Wilberforce published his report, the National Executive Committee were urgently summoned to London to hear the news. At the same time, the Government told Derek Ezra that the strike had to be settled that very day: he had to reach an agreement come what may. It was a day that was to begin in Robert Carr's office and end at 10 Downing Street.

The National Executive Committee met at the Department of Employment and did the unthinkable. They decided that although the Wilberforce report accepted the principle of the union's case, the amount being offered in cash was not enough, especially as it had to last for sixteen months. By 13 votes to 12 the national executive turned down the report's recommendations. The left had seen the perfect opportunity to push for more, especially for some of the fringe benefits that they had always wanted, and with the pickets still out in force they knew they had the muscle to do so. 'It'll take the Prime Minister to settle this now,' said Gormley. 'And why not,' said McGahey, 'let him earn his seedcorn.'

The news of the rejection shocked the Coal Board and the Government. One member of the Board described it as the worst upset of his life, as he could see no end to the dispute. Carr, equally stunned, arranged for the miners' executive to go to 10 Downing Street.

That evening the entire committee was ushered in through the front door. The three national officials and their staff were taken to meet the Prime Minister while the rest waited in another room, watching television, eating sandwiches, drinking whisky and beer. Once the novelty of being inside Number 10 had worn off, they became very impatient and bored. Eventually Daly and Gormley came out with the final offer. They had won a number of improvements on the Wilberforce offer, including an extra 80p for winding men, an extra five days' holiday each year, the consolidation of the bonus shift payment to give a five-shift basic week, a promise of no redundancies on the return to work, a twelve-month period in which to pay back rent arrears after the strike, and the promise of talks on a subsidized transport scheme. The N.E.C. voted by 16 votes to 9 to recommend a return to work on the terms negotiated, and to put the settlement to a pithead ballot. They also voted to withdraw all pickets while the vote took place. The ballot result was declared on 25 February and showed 96·5 per cent of the membership in favour of the settlement. The Great Miners' Strike was over.

10. The Coal Sheiks and the Election of 1974

In the first few months of 1973, the N.U.M. and the Conservative Government could both reflect that the prospects for coal looked brighter than at any time in the previous sixteen years. The prophets of doom were replaced by those who saw a future for a large and viable coal industry. The Conservatives recognized this new role for coal, and introduced a measure which the Secretary of State for Industry, Peter Walker, believed to be 'the biggest reforming bill the miners had since nationalization'. The miners themselves believed that it showed that the 'attitude towards coal has changed, and its importance recognized'.

Most important, the Act gave the Central Electricity Generating Board money to increase the amount of coal they burnt each year. It also allowed the Government to make grants to 'moderate the contraction' of the industry in areas of high unemployment. The capital liabilities of the industry were reduced by £275 million, and the Board's accumulated deficit was written off. Grants would also be provided to improve redundancy payments, to pay for some of the costs of keeping stocks of coal, to support the production of coking coal for the iron and steel industry, and to help the Board pay for some of the 'social costs' of closing pits and redeploying men. All in all the Conservatives could feel they were doing a great deal for the industry and the Ministers, Peter Walker and Tom Boardman, felt they had every reason to be proud of their efforts.

Confidence about the long-term future of coal increased when the major oil-producing countries demonstrated their power over the economies of the West. In 1973, the prophecies of Lord Robens, E. F. Schumacher, the economic adviser to the Board, and the N.U.M. all came true. The era of seemingly unlimited supplies of cheap oil, which had been the cause of the rundown of the coal industry, came to an end. In 1960, the governments of Iran, Saudi Arabia, Iraq, Kuwait and Venezuela had formed the Organization of Petroleum Exporting Countries (O.P.E.C.). Later on other countries joined, like Algeria, Libya, Nigeria, Indonesia, the United Arab Emirates and Qatar. Their declared aim was to win a greater and greater share of the revenues from oil, and the possibility of their doing so increased during the 1960s as the world's dependence on their product grew. At the same time a perilous imbalance was created for the oil-consuming countries of the West, which with the exception of the United States had no oil of their own to speak of. They began to rely more and more on the supplies coming from a relatively small number of oil-producers in the Middle East and North Africa. For most of the sixties this dependence seemed unremarkable and of little concern, for oil was, after all, much cheaper than coal for most uses. But in 1967, the dangers of this dependence became apparent when the Suez Canal was closed for the second time and supplies of oil on international markets were restricted. As soon as the weakness of the major oil-consuming nations was exposed, O.P.E.C. began to make their demands, not only for a greater share of the revenues, but also for a larger degree of control over the operations of the oil companies in their territory.

Such was the background for the historic meeting of the O.P.E.C. nations at Caracas, Venezuela, at the end of 1970. This twenty-first conference of O.P.E.C. agreed to demand a general increase in the price of oil, with the threat that supplies might be withdrawn if they failed to be given what they were asking for. Two months later, further price increases were agreed after talks in Teheran with the six Gulf states. In April 1971, an agreement signed with Libya in Tripoli pushed up prices still further. Both agreements included provisions to allow the price of oil to rise in stages over the following five years. However, in January 1972 and June 1973 further rises were agreed in Geneva quite apart from the ones already scheduled, because O.P.E.C. wanted compensation for the effects of the devaluation of the dollar. In fact, from June 1973, they decided that prices would be adjusted each month to reflect the changes in the rates of exchange for currencies. Most ominously, though, Saudi Arabia a little while earlier had warned the United States that they would be prepared to use their oil as a political weapon to achieve the kind of settlement they wanted in the Middle East.

Next came war: in October 1973, Egypt and Syria attacked Israel. The areas where the oil came from were not directly affected by the hostilities, but in the middle of October the Arab oil-producers made the political decision to increase the price of oil unilaterally by 70 per cent. A little later they announced that supplies of oil would be progressively withdrawn from countries which they felt were unsympathetic to the Arab cause. A total embargo was imposed on shipments to the United States and the Netherlands. On 1 January 1974, the price of oil from the Gulf was doubled again, though some prices were even higher. The crisis threw the economies of the oil-consuming countries into turmoil, and the world economic order appeared overturned. The assumption which had decided the energy policy of successive British governments had been destroyed. It became clear that it had been short-sighted to expect regular supplies of oil to continue to be available at competitive prices. Most important of all was the realization that the crisis of 1973/4 was only the beginning: the real question was – what happened when the oil ran out?

Within this radically different energy picture, the N.U.M. began formulating its pay claim in the middle of 1973. Earlier, in the spring, the miners had accepted a pay deal within the Government's Phase 2 limits of £1 plus 4 per cent. The Government had fulfilled an obvious and open role in the negotiations, telling the Coal Board to stand firm, and after a pithead ballot that showed over 63 per cent of the membership to be against any form of industrial action, the N.U.M. settled peacefully. But the Union's annual conference at Inverness that summer showed no such inhibitions. The relative position of miners' wages had deteriorated since the Wilberforce report, and a lot of men were leaving the industry, especially in Yorkshire and Nottinghamshire. The drafting of the composite resolution on wages was a particularly long and argumentative affair, but in the end they agreed to a demand for minimum wages of £35 for surface workers, £40 for underground workers and £45 for the men on the coal-face – in other words increases ranging from between £8 to £13 a week.

The conference was clearly in militant mood. Delegates rejected the Government's incomes policy and urged confrontation 'when this stands in the way of legitimate pay demands'. Lawrence Daly was careful to make the qualification that they were not seeking confrontation: 'Confrontation arises only when just and legitimate demands are rejected.' However, the most controversial speech was made by Mick McGahey, the communist President of the Scottish miners. His words were used later, during the strike, to justify the Government's fears that the dispute was politically motivated, even revolutionary in aspiration. According to the official record, this is what he said:

We reject any basis of negotiation with this Government and its so-called anti-inflationary policy. It is not negotiations in Downing Street, but it is agitation in the streets of this country to remove the Government that is required. Ted Heath has laid down the guidelines. He has organized the football match, he has picked the teams, appointed a referee, made sure of the linesmen and has even decided the result, and that is why we say there should be no negotiations with this Government but the need is to defeat it.

McGahey later went to great lengths to insist that he did not mean bringing down the Government by other than democratic means, but his remarks were interpreted otherwise, and even within the union there was a great deal of feeling that they would lose public support for their cause.

The obvious militancy of the conference was reflected by the growing discontent in the coalfields. But this time, unlike in the early seventies, the leadership were far more responsive to such pressures. The 1972 strike had unleashed the miners' strength and potential. At the same time, it had destroyed once and for all the belief that the nationalization of the industry had created the need for a special response from the union. The 'new morality' was finally dead, and the N.C.B. was seen as much like any other employer. In elections after the strike, men who recognized these changes were put into important positions in the union. At the 1973 conference McGahey was elected Vice-President, but he retained his vote on the National Executive Committee, unlike the Secretary, who had none, and the President, who had only a casting vote. His old seat on the N.E.C. was taken by another left-winger. The strengthening of the left was completed when Peter Tait, a communist from Yorkshire, took up his seat after the conference. By this time, Arthur Scargill was also on the National Executive Committee. There had been an election for the job of area compensation agent after the 1972 strike, and he had won it easily. His organizational abilities and talent for public speaking earned him the confidence of a lot of people in the Yorkshire coalfield, but there was more to his rise than just that. The same forces that had made Yorkshire the centre of the disputes in 1969 and 1970 propelled Scargill forward. The cloth-cap-and-muffler trade unionist who had hitherto dominated the coalfield and maintained at area level, at least, the ascendancy of the right wing, was being attacked by a groundswell of opinion from below. What better symbol of the new, confident, articulate miner than Arthur Scargill? He was undoubtedly the right man, though also in the right place at the right time.

A fortnight after the conference, on 16 July, Gormley was summoned to a secret meeting with the Prime Minister, Edward Heath, at 10 Downing Street. The conversation was highly confidential, and no one else in the Cabinet or the union's National Executive Committee knew about it until a long time afterwards. The only other person present was Sir William (later Lord) Armstrong, the head of the civil service, and because the weather was so hot the three of them sat outside in the garden of Number 10 and talked about the prospects for industrial peace in the coming winter. Gormley told Heath that he thought things were going to be 'bloody difficult', because after the victory of 1972 the 'lads' chests were a mile wide and they thought they were the kings of the castle'. But he pointed out that there were other ways of settling the miners' pay demands, for example increasing the payments for unsocial hours. Gormley left the meeting believing that he had won the Prime Minister's accept-ance of the miners' case, and convinced that although he had told Heath that things would be difficult, there would still be enough concessions to give the miners the deal that they wanted. He believed then, and still believes now, that confrontation could have been avoided.

Over the summer, the Government worked out the details of Phase 3 of their anti-inflation policy. On 8 October it was published as a Green Paper. Pay rises would be limited to 7 per cent of the average pay bill per head, or £2.25 per person per week. With a nod and a wink in the direction of the miners, the policy allowed for a premium payment to be introduced or increased for any hours worked between 8.00 p.m. and 6.00 a.m., as long as the payment was not more than one-fifth of normal rates. The pay limit could also be increased by 1 per cent for such things as better holiday pay or sick pay. There were additional provisions for improvements in holidays, efficiency schemes and threshold payments, whereby, after a certain point, pay could increase by 40p a week for every 1 per cent rise in the cost of living.

Two days later, the Deputy Chairman of the Coal Board, Norman Siddall, told the union that although the details of Phase 3 had only been published as a consultative document, they nonetheless felt constrained by them. Their offer was, as he put it later, 'an unusual and interesting policy – like a Christmas tree with a lot of presents on it'. They proposed an increase of £2.25 a week for surface workers, and £2.50 for men underground. In addition, they offered a rise of 17p an hour for men on night shift, as well as a productivity scheme which could be worth another 3½ per cent on their basic rates. The N.U.M. had been expecting a lot more, and told the Board so. They also said that the Board should tell the Government what they wished to offer and not merely accept the proposals in the Green Paper. Gormley was genuinely surprised, after his secret meeting with Heath, to see the payments for unsocial hours actually written into the document, as he had thought it would be produced as a trump card later in the negotiations. McGahey told Siddall that he ought to defy the Government's policy, and if they both ended up in gaol, at least they could keep each other company.

The next day the union's executive met to discuss what to do. Outside the headquarters in Euston Road, pickets gathered to press for a militant response to the offer. Inside, the offer was unanimously rejected, though they did not rule out further negotiations. However, it was equally clear by this time that the only people who could make concessions were the Government, and accordingly, they asked for a meeting with the Prime Minister.

It was not a very unified delegation that went to Number 10. Already there had been a public rift between Gormley and McGahey. A few days earlier, Gormley had told an N.U.M. summer school that he believed a strike by the miners might precipitate a general election: 'If they could go to the country when there was an energy crisis, they might possibly go to the country on that one issue and win it, and we would be castigated by the whole trade union movement for having given them the opportunity.' It was a characteristic ploy, often used by Gormley to polarize feelings and push people to the brink in the hope that they would then pull back. As a strategy, it has the unfortunate risk that sometimes people jump over. However, the effect this time was to prompt an angry response from McGahey, who accused Gormley of 'playing into the hands of the Tories'. He believed it was a calculated statement designed to weaken the resolve of the miners.

The sixteen-man negotiating team met Heath for about two hours, and by all accounts it was a friendly enough occasion. The Prime Minister outlined his Government's economic objectives, and told them that the offer was a good one and would give the miners more under Phase 3 than any other group of workers. The miners were unimpressed and said so, stressing that the lead they had established after the 1972 strike had been eroded. Lawrence Daly warned that there could be industrial action in support of their claim, prompting Joe Gormley to comment that 'you don't go in to the Prime Minister threatening action if you don't get your own way'.

Two days later, the National Executive Committee met for three hours, but no one suggested a strike. Instead they argued about the extent of an overtime ban which they all agreed should be put before a special delegate conference arranged for the next day. In the end they unanimously agreed on a resolution authorizing 'a complete overtime ban if and when necessary in the light of further negotiations which the N.E.C. will undertake'. Significantly, no firm date was fixed for the ban to begin.

The special conference the next day approved action to make the ban even more powerful than in 1972, by insisting that no safety or maintenance work was done during overtime. In the meantime, the union's leaders had scoured the final Phase 3 pay code and found nothing new which could provide a solution to their grievances. At a meeting on 8 November, the executive decided to start the overtime ban on the following Monday. They set up a four-man team to deal with any emergencies which might arise during the dispute. Said Gormley: 'The decision was taken in the knowledge that this will cause a lot of disruption. It is my estimate that if the overtime ban is properly applied, there will be very few pits working after the first week.' The miners once again found themselves confronting the Government head-on.

What had gone wrong? How had a Government which had built its pay policy around the avoidance of confrontation with the miners ended up on a collision course with them? For a start the union were keen to get the negotiations over as soon as possible. The wages resolution passed that summer said that the new deal should be implemented by November, even though their award was supposed to last until the following March. Of course, the miners preferred to have a settling date in November, not only for traditional reasons but also because a strike would have a great deal more impact in the middle of the winter than in the early spring. Wilberforce, in his report, had recognized at least the first part of the miners' desire for a November settlement when he said that 'there is nothing to prevent the parties getting back to this timing at the next settlement'. The problem was that the unilateral return to a November settlement pushed the miners to the front of the pay queue. The Government could therefore not afford to be over-generous to them lest it set a trend, and the miners, because they were so early in the pay round, were not in a position to see themselves doing better out of the pay policy than anyone else.

For the nub of the matter was that the miners had not been made enough of a special case. When Heath met Gormley in July both men believed that they had made a deal which would give the miners what they wanted. But whereas the Government claimed that the increase the miners had been offered would add 13 per cent to the N.C.B.'s wages bill, the union preferred to see the increase as only 7 per cent on the basic rate. This was no idle debating point. It would indeed have totalled 13 per cent if all the miners had worked on night shift all the time. But only about 14–15,000 of them did and therefore qualified for the full payment. Others who worked only some unsocial hours during the week would get less, and those who worked none at all would be firmly on the basic rate of Phase 3. As Eric Varley put it at the time: 'Miners will not be attracted back into the pits by being told what they could earn if they worked all the unearthly hours that God sends.' To put all the miners back to the Wilberforce level needed almost £5 a week more for everyone. The fact that the pay policy could not allow this created the very inflexibility the Government had been so keen to avoid.

This inflexibility was reinforced by the tactics adopted by the Coal Board during the negotiations. At the first session, they gave the union all they possibly could under the pay policy, so that there was literally nothing else left to argue about. As their evidence to the Pay Board eventually showed, the Coal Board were in no mood for confrontation and indeed supported many of the miners' claims. But once they had made the maximum possible offer under Phase 3, the union was left with no alternative but to negotiate with the Government from a very early stage.

For their part, Heath and his ministers expected too much from Gormley. Gormley exuded confidence in his own abilities as a negotiator, a coal-face Mr Fixit, with the aim of 'getting the best deal for the lads'. But what was there for him to sell? If the unsocial hours provision was meant for the miners alone, then how come the firemen and the railwaymen were also looking to it as a way of winning more money? Gormley had to be seen to be fighting like a dog to win all he could, and then much later pulling a deal apparently out of thin air. But the drafting of the pay policy had made that course of action impossible. Gormley was wily and shrewd enough to know that there are times to lead and times to follow. With others pulling on the oars and setting the pace, he preferred to bide his time and at the right moment push the tiller in the direction he wanted to go. It was for that reason that Heath and his civil servants by all accounts found Gormley such a difficult character to deal with. They had expected Gormley to lead from the front and attempt to sell the deal on unsocial hours. The reason why he didn't was not hard to find.

Far from there being a carefully orchestrated militant plot in the union that autumn, there was in fact a good deal of rank and file support for radically better pay. Surprisingly, it was some of the so-called moderate areas that appeared most vociferous. At the special delegate conference in October, for example, the Secretary of the Lancashire area, Sid Vincent, spoke of an advertisement in a local paper that offered £40 for a forty-hour week: 'I'm telling you,' he said, 'they'll recruit the manpower out of the mining industry.' Another delegate, from the Midlands area, pointed out that whereas they were demanding £45 a week for a coal-face worker, 'In our local paper, there are no end of advertisements for unskilled labour with minimum rates of £45 per week, with transport laid on, food vouchers, fluorescent lights above them, God's fresh air to breathe, no pneumoconiosis, no broken backs. Even our young girls are being enticed to London on the Coventry train to get special training facilities and wages considerably in excess of this £40 to £45 a week we are talking about.' This desire for strong action was particularly argued by Len Clarke, the normally 'moderate' leader of the Nottingham-shire miners, whose men had done particularly badly out of the rationalization of wages in recent years. It was Clarke who forced agreement to a much tougher version of the overtime ban, believing it to be a 'twentieth-century approach' to industrial relations which tightened the screw on the employers without the individual worker losing too much pay. The combination of Clarke and the left secured a majority for action on the National Executive Committee.

But as the miners' comparative position caused grievance, there was also a realization in the coalfields that the Yom Kippur war had made coal king once more. They could not help but compare their treatment by the Government with the way the Arabs were getting whatever they asked for their oil. As one collier from Ireland Colliery told Eric Varley: 'I wish my pit was in the Persian Gulf – then we would get whatever we asked for, and even have a say in the Government's foreign policy as well.'

On Monday, 12 November, the miners' overtime ban began. Within twenty-four hours the Government had declared a state of emergency. The Home Secretary, Robert Carr, said that the move was necessary to safeguard the community and to ensure that a reasonable level of industrial activity was maintained. He also announced that an information centre had been established at Scotland Yard to help the police coordinate information on picketing. To the miners, the declaration both confirmed their powerful position, and made the Government appear bent on confrontation. Its timing was interpreted as a political gesture designed to turn the public against them; why else, they wondered, should such drastic action be taken against them when stocks of coal at power stations were at the very high level of around 17 million tons?

At that point in the winter, though, the declaration of a state of emergency appeared both necessary and expedient to the Government. The shortage of oil which was leading to queues outside petrol stations and fears of rationing was also affecting the supply of oil to power stations. The Central Electricity Generating Board believed that they could deal with a halving of their oil supply, especially as stocks of coal at power stations in England and Wales were, at the beginning of the winter, at the high level of 18½ million tons, but what they had not expected, and could not cope with, was a miners' overtime ban at the same time. They needed all the coal they could get to replace the oil they were losing because of the shortage. Their worries became acute when they calculated that the overtime ban was cutting supplies to power stations by up to 40 per cent, as they were particularly concerned to avoid a repetition of the events of 1972 when stocks had become so low that the viability of the whole generating system had been threatened. The miners' action tipped the scales in favour of action that might well have been necessary anyway. It was the beginning of the most critical period that the British economy had faced for a generation.

The state of emergency and the overtime ban intensified the search for a settlement. The Coal Board put forward some marginal improvements that would, amongst other things, have increased the deal by 5p a week for surface workers and 7p a week for those underground. But this was really scraping the barrel, and it became clear that no amount of further scraping would yield more.

The Prime Minister then made a dramatic intervention in the negotiations and invited the entire executive committee of the N.U.M. for talks at 10 Downing Street. They met in the cabinet room, with the miners double-banked down one side of the table, and the Prime Minister, Sir William Armstrong, Tony Barber, the Chancellor of the Exchequer, Maurice Macmillan, the Employment Secretary, and Tom Boardman, an Industry Minister, down the other. Gormley broke the ice by remarking that the security men obviously trusted them, as they had been allowed inside without a search. On the Government's side, only Heath spoke. He stressed that he had no quarrel with the miners and underlined that the wages negotiations were a matter for the N.U.M. and the N.C.B. to settle within Phase 3. He pointed out that the Wilberforce settlement and the wages deal that spring had given the miners an improvement of 26 per cent compared with a 15 per cent increase in prices during the same period. Finally he warned that just as the Arabs could push things too far, so could the miners: and he stressed that he could countenance no breach of the pay policy.

On the union side, everybody and anybody had a say. Gormley laid great emphasis on the fact that the union was not trying to change the Government. And he shattered Heath's hopes that a pithead ballot would vote for moderation, by stating clearly that in his opinion a ballot would declare the union in favour of a strike: 'Are you prepared to accept the consequences of what that means?' he asked. Another miner went to the heart of the matter when he asked why the Government were prepared to pay the Arabs whatever they wanted for their oil, when they turned down a similar request from the miners about their coal. But the real antagonism came towards the end of the morning, when McGahey intervened to say that he would personally like to see the end of the Government, and made no apologies for it. Heath looked aghast, and his growing feeling that the strike was politically motivated began to gain hold. The meeting ended with some well-prepared attacks on the Government's policy from Joe Whelan, the communist from Nottinghamshire. And Gormley concluded, 'On that happy note we will end.'

After a lunch of beef stroganoff, the National Executive Committee met in another room at Number 10 to decide whether to hold a pithead ballot of the membership, an action the Prime Minister hoped they would take to test grass roots response to the Phase 3 offer. Gormley took the view that the time was right for a ballot, which he believed would considerably strengthen his hand in negotiation. But he could not carry the meeting, and the Government failed to understand why. In fact it was simply that most of the N.E.C. believed that the overtime ban was working and would lead to a settlement without a strike. With this in mind, they voted overwhelmingly to continue as they were.

The deadlock in the talks now prompted one of the most intricate, in some respects bizarre, and in the end fruitless series of negotiations the coal industry had probably ever undertaken. The whole business made the defence of incomes policy increasingly obscure, and began with the appointment of William Whitelaw to replace Maurice Macmillan as Secretary of State for Employment. To the miners, this change seemed like a significant shift in the Government's attitude. Macmillan's standing had not been very high within the Government, whereas Whitelaw was riding high on his reputation in Northern Ireland. His appearance on the scene was greeted with a feeling of relief, that at last there was someone who could talk the language of reasonableness and conciliation. The fact that he had been in a job far removed from the tides of industrial relations was quietly forgotten. Instead attention surrounded what at the time seemed the best hope for peace: extra pay for 'washing and waiting' time.

It was estimated that a miner took on average about twenty minutes to change from his clean clothes to pit clothes, collect his lamp and make his way to the pithead, where he would wait for a cage to take him down. After coming up from his shift, each man spent an average of another twenty minutes returning his lamp and having a bath before leaving for home. None of this had up until then been paid for, and some form of compensation had been a longstanding claim at conferences.

At first the Board dismissed a proposal for payment as too expensive. But later, in private conversation, Gormley mentioned the idea to Harold Wilson. Wilson then brought the whole matter up in the House of Commons and the idea was killed stone dead. Gormley was livid, believing that, but for Wilson's intervention, he could have achieved a deal with the Government on washing and waiting time.

When Whitelaw took over, the idea was raised again. In mid December he and Gormley met at Brown's Hotel, off Piccadilly, one Sunday evening for a private conversation. Gormley left late, with the impression that the idea of buying off the miners with a deal on washing and waiting time was one which was attractive to the Government. But, as events were to show, he had misunderstood what the Government were thinking.

On 20 December, the misunderstandings deepened. After a meeting that ended up in an Italian restaurant because of a bomb scare, the N.U.M.'s representatives left with the feeling that Whitelaw had indicated some areas of the pay code that they might have another look at. They believed that they had been given a 'nod and a wink' that washing and waiting time might provide a solution. Gormley was convinced that something was being offered: why else would Whitelaw tell them to talk to the Pay Board, whose job it was to interpret the pay code?

The next day the N.C.B. and the union began a series of meetings with the Pay Board. The miners tried to exploit the clause in the policy that allowed standard working hours to be reduced to forty hours a week. They believed that if they could prove that they normally worked considerably more than forty hours a week, then they could claim more overtime and win extra money. But it was very difficult for the N.C.B. and the N.U.M. to provide the evidence that the Pay Board needed. At one point, for example, the Coal Board used stopwatches to discover that a man coming up from the pit took between eight and nine minutes to have a wash and shower with a bar of carbolic. The union, specifically Joe Gormley, replied that such a finding was wholly arbitrary as in reality it took a man much longer to get all the dust out of his ears, eyes and nose.

The miners also tried to show that they spent more time travelling down the shaft each day than they were paid for. But again it was almost impossible to produce the firm evidence the Pay Board needed. Quite simply, the time spent winding varied from pit to pit, and on where you happened to be standing in the queue to ride in the cage. And so the esoteric discussions went on, further complicated by the fact that the Pay Board saw itself as merely giving legalistic interpretations of the pay code, whereas the two sides saw them much more as negotiators. In the end the Deputy Chairman of the Coal Board, Norman Siddall, told the N.U.M. that he was prepared to submit evidence supporting the idea of forty minutes a day waiting time, which would have produced payments of between 40 and 70p extra a week. He could provide no evidence in support of an additional allowance for winding time. But the Pay Board, after considering their submission, rejected it as insufficient. They gave a simple legal judgement on the basis of evidence, but part of the trouble was that in the framework of industrial relations the very act of calling for evidence can imply a willingness to find an excuse for settling.

With the failure of washing and waiting time to provide a solution, the deadlock seemed complete. On 9 January, the full executive committee of the union met Whitelaw at his request. Stressing that he had no intention of delivering a lecture, he argued that Phase 3 offered the miners a settlement in excess of what was being offered to all other groups. If the union would accept a settlement under Phase 3, the official minutes record, 'the Government were prepared to sit down to immediate discussions with the union and the N.C.B. on the future of the industry, which would include manpower problems and pay involved in a modern industry'. The union, however, emphasized that the limit had to be broken. They left the talks feeling that Whitelaw did not understand the industry, and, to make the point, one member of the N.E.C. asked him if he knew how much fish and chips cost: Whitelaw, of course, hadn't a clue.

On the same day as the fruitless talks with Whitelaw, the T.U.C. intervened in a dramatic fashion. At a routine meeting of

N.E.D.C. ('Neddy'), Sid Greene of the National Union of
Railwaymen made an offer that took everyone, including the
Government, by surprise. The idea, which amounted to a major
concession by the T.U.C., had been given the unanimous support
of the economic committee that morning, but they had kept it
quiet – not even telling the miners, who had anyway failed to
appear at the meeting – fearing that the initiative, once leaked,
could founder on political squabbles in the House of Commons.
On behalf of the General Council of the T.U.C., Greene said
that if the Government allowed the miners to make a settlement
outside Phase 3, they would not use it as an argument when
negotiating their own deals. The element of surprise was one of
the reasons why the Government's initial reaction, voiced by the
Chancellor of the Exchequer, Tony Barber, was so swiftly against:
they thought it might have been an attempt to outsmart them.
Nonetheless, the next day, Heath met the T.U.C.

They talked for two and a half hours, and the Government
remained very sceptical. Could they be certain the rank and file
would accept such an agreement? Could the union leaders
guarantee that they would hold their members back? Would they
give a firm indication to the miners of what they should settle
for? As they came out of the talks, the five-man delegation
appeared content that their initiative had not been rejected out
of hand. But Whitelaw was less encouraging, and so was the
N.U.M. Gormley said that if he were negotiating he would take
no notice of a T.U.C. agreement for restraint.

The Government's final meeting with the T.U.C. was on 21
January. It was clear by then that the strong resistance to the
proposals epitomized by the attitude of Tony Barber had won the
day. Heath appeared glum and apparently said little. The T.U.C.
could offer no more, though they had been given the near-
unanimous backing of a special meeting of trade unionists a few
days earlier. Heath recognized that the T.U.C. had gone further
than ever before, but still believed that the offer made to the
miners was a very good one. In addition, the changed economic
circumstances brought on by the oil crisis, and the fact that 4
million people had already settled within the limits, were beginning to make even the original Phase 3 policy look over-generous.

Fundamentally, though, there was the memory of 1972 and the power of the miners; other groups had a similar ability to disrupt the life of the nation and there was nothing in the T.U.C.'s statement that would prevent them from following the miners' example. As Heath told the Commons the following day, 'They would not cite the miners; they would cite their own special circumstances and use industrial power to achieve their ends. They could cause equal damage to this nation as any other group.' In other words, the miners had shown what a determined and powerful group could do; what was to stop others doing the same? It was a fundamental issue that went to the heart of the democratic system.

As the talks foundered on mistrust, so the country experienced its third week of short-time working. On 13 December Heath had announced a new series of measures to restrict severely the use of electricity, the centrepiece of which was a decision to put industry on a three-day week from the new year. He told the Commons that the measures were needed because the miners' overtime ban was causing a sharp fall in the amount of coal being delivered to power stations, a drop in fact of some 40 per cent. To conserve coal, the Government told the oil companies to increase the supply of oil to power stations, but the market for oil was still tight, and to carry out their instruction would mean taking oil from other consumers. At the same time Heath claimed that the ability of the electricity authorities to cope was being hampered by the decision of the power engineers to restrict their own hours of work. In this situation, the Government judged that they needed to cut consumption by about one-fifth.

But was the three-day week really necessary, or was it being used by the Government to woo public opinion from the miners? It was an issue that caused great controversy in the winter of 1973/4. These fears were most forcefully put by Tony Benn on New Year's Day, when he called the three-day week 'a calculated deception' intended to turn the working class against the miners, and accused Heath of 'gravely misleading the nation'. The statistical evidence for his views was attacked as suspect. The *Sunday Times*, for example, concluded that 'the three-day week and emergency power laws, far from being politically motivated, were an absolute necessity, delayed for political reasons well beyond the date thought necessary by the C.E.G.B. Were they not in force it is certain, given coal stocks at power stations, that normal life would have ceased before the end of January. Disease, famine, darkness and death would have been the typical British condition.'

Information reaching the miners gave them a very different perspective. They believed by the new year that the overtime ban was cutting back the production of coal, but its impact on coal stocks was less dramatic than had earlier been thought. It appeared to them that by implementing the three-day week the Government were hoping to ride out the winter, trusting that the miners would not go on strike. The evidence for this belief came from a survey completed by the Electrical, Electronic, Telecommunication and Plumbing Union during the second week in January. They examined every power station in Britain, and the overall picture was one of full bunkers and stocks. The difficulties involved in getting the information were revealed in one entry concerning a station in the North East: 'Shop steward was stopped by management when checking stocks and forbidden to give any information. But information from another source says the station is fully loaded.' The conclusion of the whole report was that there were nearly 14 million tons of coal at power stations and nearly 4 million tons held in N.C.B. hands; 'without a further ton being dug there is now over ten weeks' supply'. No previous action by the miners, it declared, had brought about 'such a drastic Government response'.

The final confirmation for the miners that the three-day week was a nonsense came from the Government themselves, when they announced that they were considering putting industry on a four-day week. Just a few days before the union met to decide whether to strengthen their action, the Government declared that there were sufficient stocks of coal to last through to the summer. The consumption of coal had fallen to about half of what it had been, and the production of coal had not decreased further. Equally important was the substitution of oil for coal, as a vigorous round of Middle Eastern diplomacy by the Government improved the supply of oil to Britain. The Central Electricity

Generating Board's figures show that by mid-January oil consumption was increasing, so much so that by the end of the dispute, usage had nearly doubled. Stocks of oil had also risen dramatically. But why announce this changed position at a time when the union were contemplating an all-out strike? Maybe they were trying to make the N.U.M. realize that they could resist the miners' onslaught. And it is possible that they were trying to ensure that if the miners did go on strike, the blame would rest firmly on the N.U.M. for preventing a return to normal. Unfortunately for the Government, all they succeeded in doing was convincing the miners that they would have to take sterner measures if they were to succeed.

On 24 January, the National Executive Committee met and concluded that their recent experience had shown that the Government had 'no intention of seeking a position where the trade union could honourably reach a settlement with the N.C.B.'. They considered a letter sent by Edward Heath which appealed to them to settle: 'We now have before us the possibility of a return to more normal working for industry. The extent to which we can realize this possibility, and with it all the benefits to which it would lead, depends upon the decisions of your executive and your union.' But after much discussion, the National Executive Committee voted by 16 votes to 10 to recommend a strike to a ballot of the membership. As the meeting broke up, the news was shouted to some Welsh miners waiting in the lobby at Euston Road, who greeted the decision with cheers. Late that night the Cabinet met for a second time that day, and decided that the three-day week would have to remain after all.

But on the very same day, Heath was offered yet another chance of settlement. The Pay Board published a report which recommended the setting up of a body to look at pay relativities: if it was clear that a group of workers had suffered a fall in their pay relative to other workers, this body could award wage rises beyond the limits of incomes policy. This new procedure appeared tailor-made to let the Government off the hook and give the miners what they were asking for. But they missed their chance. When, later that day, Ezra went to lunch at Number 10, Heath virtually ignored him and certainly failed even to mention the Pay

Board report. Instead conversation turned to what initials the new ministries of Energy, Employment and Environment should use to avoid confusion.

In fact, the report of the Pay Board was partly responsible for the Government's myopia. It stressed that the procedure could not operate under the threat of a strike, because there would be a temptation for those trying to form a judgement to distort it in order to settle the dispute. Heath himself took this view, insisting that the miners would have to end their strike before their case could be examined. But the pressures on him to use the report to settle became intense. The Vice-Chairman of the Pay Board, Derek Robinson, said publicly that the new machinery could be brought into operation quickly enough for it to represent a real chance of peace. Then the Coal Board, too, approached the Government, using similar arguments. But Heath was adamant, and in a letter to Harold Wilson, who had also urged use of the procedure, made clear why: 'We are not thinking in terms of a one-off, seven-day procedure,' he wrote.

That would, it seems to me, have many of the disadvantages of the ad hoc type of inquiry, even if it was conducted by the Pay Board. Those disadvantages are, as we have seen in the past, that the industry considers the claim of a particular group only in the context of settling an individual dispute and without considering the consequences for the claims of other groups whose relative position is thus affected.

By now the Government had rejected every possibility of compromise, and had shut themselves tightly into a corner. Heath and Sir William Armstrong were entrenched in Number 10, and defence of Phase 3 had become paramount. Gradually, the issue of a statutory incomes policy had become transmuted into one of maintaining the authority of Government itself. The calls from within the Conservative Party for an election to decide 'who governs' became louder, and the fear within Downing Street that the dispute was politically motivated increased.

On 5 February, Joe Gormley told the miners' executive that 81 per cent of the membership had voted in favour of a strike. The meeting lasted for four hours, and there was an attempt by some representatives from Durham to postpone the strike until later in the month. But Len Clarke, the miners' leader from Nottinghamshire, put paid to that idea and they decided to strike from midnight of 9 February. Two days later, on 7 February, Edward Heath called a general election.

The next day, the miners' National Executive Committee met in emergency session. Gormley explained that as Parliament had been dissolved, there would be no effective Government for them to negotiate with for about a month. The Prime Minister had therefore written suggesting that there was little point in starting the strike during a period when no progress could be made. But the view of the majority was that the postponement of the strike would weaken the union's bargaining position once the election was over, and that as the strike was in no way politically motivated, it would be wrong to call it off in support of any political party.

The 1972 strike had perfected the miners' organization; by comparison the running of the 1974 dispute was almost effortless. But there were some differences. For a start, there were no liaison committees at pit level to discuss questions of safety. The union decided not to carry out safety work, and to leave it instead in the hands of men belonging to the British Association of Colliery Management. It was agreed, however, that where there was a threat to a pit because of some emergency, the area and national officials would decide what to do. The national strike committee also had a great deal more control than in 1972. Picketing would only take place after they had given their agreement, and the numbers on any particular picket line would be voluntarily restricted to six. Each area was asked to establish close liaison with the Chief Constable, as the police would have considerable powers to decide whether the methods being used by pickets were lawful. The national strike committee decided that the targets would be coal dumps, power stations, ports and docks, and steel works. Once more, lists of power stations were sent out to the areas, though this time the information was much more extensive than before. Old contacts for pickets travelling outside their own area – notably in East Anglia – were once again revived. Contacts with other unions, which had been so valuable during the 1972 dispute, were renewed at both national and local level. Most valuable of all, on 11 February a special meeting of the National Joint Council for the Electricity Supply Industry decided that they would impose a complete ban on all deliveries of coal, from whatever source, at home or abroad. In addition, they agreed not to permit the substitution of oil or alternative fuels for coal, and generally to do nothing that might be detrimental to the strike. This agreement helped the miners' action to be as effective as in 1972, with fewer pickets.

In Yorkshire, activities were coordinated once more by the area, though this time Arthur Scargill was firmly entrenched in the miners' offices at Barnsley as President of the area. Once more, the panels established themselves as strike committees, though the emphasis on picketing changed to include steel works. Most notable was the picketing of the giant Anchor complex at Scunthorpe, which was British Steel's most important bulk steel producer. Earlier in the year, British Steel had made it clear that there was a growing steel shortage which could rival the power shortage for its effects on the economy. Arthur Scargill decided to capitalize on this and direct the pickets towards steel works to stop the flow of coking coal. Steel production began to fall off still further.

Generally speaking, though, the picketing never reached the intensity of the 1972 strike. It was altogether a less dramatic affair, as everyone knew more or less what to do. But that is not to deny its impact: even with a voluntary agreement to have only six pickets on each line, the miners' action was as effective as before. As long as they had the support of other trade unionists in refusing to cross their picket lines, it did not matter whether there were six pickets or sixty.

Even during the election to find out 'who governs Britain', the issue of the relativities report refused to go away. On the day after the election was announced, Whitelaw decided to refer the miners' case to the Pay Board. It was a most eccentric decision, which appeared to contradict the very reason that the Government had given for going to the country. What was more, as the inquiry went on it became abundantly clear that the miners' case for a rise over and above Phase 3 was exceedingly strong, and was supported by the Coal Board. In their evidence the N.C.B.

pointed out how the numbers employed in the industry had fallen so much that a change in the terms and conditions of service was essential: 'There is no evidence that marginal improvements in the relative position of miners will have an adequate effect on manning levels. A major shift in the relative position of miners (compared with other workers) appears essential.' The Coal Board also made it clear that they envisaged an award higher than that given by Wilberforce, because of the 'new importance of the coal-mining industry'. All this, incidentally, must have been known to the Government when they refused to consider giving the miners an increase beyond Phase 3 of the incomes policy. The new role of coal, concluded the Coal Board, meant that 'corresponding improvements in the wages and conditions of the workforce are vital so that the challenge of this new role can be met successfully'.

Worse still for the Government's case was the disclosure, on 21 February, of new statistical evidence prepared by the Pay Board which suggested that the miners had been entitled all along to at least 8 per cent more than the Government and the Coal Board had thought. The controversy surrounded the question of which set of figures was used to assess miners' earnings, as one table made the miners look comparatively better off than they really were. The discovery marked a turning point in the election campaign. Wilson rose to the challenge and accused the Government of blundering incompetence: 'The nation now knows,' he declared, 'that the hundreds of thousands of pounds of lost wages, the thousands of millions of lost hours of production from which workers and their employers suffered for the past eight weeks, was never necessary. The Government have brought Britain to the edge of ruin – and now they have to concede that the miners have had a stronger case all along than they would ever admit.'

Just before the polls closed on 28 February, the Pay Board completed their report on miners' pay. They concluded that 'the main limit over the next few years on the maximum size of coal output will be the physical capacity of the industry. Provided that world oil prices remain at about their present level, and that the costs of coal production do not rise to an exaggerated extent, the N.C.B. will be able to sell as much coal as it can produce.' They decided that wages should be improved to end the shortage of manpower, as recruits would only join if the 'pay of the mineworkers is improved relative to that of other workers'. They suggested that the Coal Board's offer should be increased by a special allowance of £1.20 a shift to underground workers, and that extra money should also be set aside for adjusting relativities within the industry. They also recommended a productivity deal based on targets set for each pit. The report conceded a lot more than the miners or the Government could have dreamed of during the negotiations in November. Yet the Government which might have benefited from its own invention was no longer in power.

The new Secretary of State for Employment in the Labour Government, Michael Foot, summoned the miners' leaders to meet him. He asked them to reopen negotiations immediately, unfettered by either the previous Government's dictates, or the report of the Pay Board, and put forward the idea of a wider review of the industry in all its forms.

The next day was spent in negotiations at Hobart House. The N.U.M. made it clear that they would not accept the Pay Board's proposal for the differential between underground and surface workers. Following an initial offer the talks adjourned, until in the end the Board offered £45 for faceworkers, thus conceding that part of the claim in full, a minimum of £36 underground, and £32 on the surface. In addition there were a lot of other trimmings, such as an increase in the allowance for working night shift to 19p an hour. After a lengthy discussion, the National Executive Committee decided to 'strongly recommend acceptance', and to resume normal working on the first shift of Monday 11 March. Only Arthur Scargill and Jack Collins, the Kent miners' representative, voted against. The miners' strike was over. But the final irony was that the total cost of the settlement was about the same as the total cost of the Phase 3 settlement and the relativities report recommendation added together.

Did the miners bring down the Government? There can be little doubt that the N.U.M.'s decision to ask for more than incomes policy allowed provided one of the conditions that led Heath to believe an election was necessary. But of greater importance was a rigid incomes policy backed up by law. Time and time again the Government asked themselves what would happen if the miners were allowed to break that policy. Would it open the floodgates for greater and greater wage claims? In the end they felt that they could not make an exception and at the same time achieve their aim of reducing inflation. Yet the Government had shown no consistent line of support for incomes policy. They had begun by publicly emphasizing that the policy was designed to give the miners more than anyone else, and finished by refusing and then accepting the reference of the claim to the Pay Board. In the end their ambivalence was exposed. The public, while not supporting the miners to the same degree as in 1972, were apathetic when it came to fighting any battle and enduring any hardship for the sake of the defence of pay policy. The Government were offered many escape routes, olive branches, call them what you will, which most politicians would have seized upon. But Heath, for what might have been the best of reasons, didn't. And in the end he brought his undoing upon himself.

11. The Second Coming of King Coal

'King Coal is back on his throne again,' said the Labour Government's new Energy Secretary at a private meeting with the National Executive Committee in 1974. 'He is firmly established on it. No one can knock him off. The only way he can lose it is by abdication.' For their part, the miners recognized that the bad days of the sixties were over and the coal they produced would now sell. What was more, there was a Government in power that was committed to coal and was deserving of their support. It was in a sense their own social contract. Yet at the same time, after the strikes of 1972 and 1974, 'the lads' chests', in Gormley's words, were 'a mile wide'. There were understandable pressures to achieve new improvements in their conditions, the most important of all being a reduction in the retirement age. But would these demands for better pay and conditions threaten the union's support for the Government? The big strikes had made the answer to that question of interest beyond the confines of the coalfields. And the second coming of coal had only enhanced its importance.

From all over the world came recognition of the new value of coal. The United States launched 'Project Independence', to achieve energy self-sufficiency by 1985. In 1977 President Carter told the nation in a fireside chat that they faced 'a problem unprecedented in our history', and that because supplies of oil and gas were limited, they would need the production of a new Texas every year just to stay where they were. The answer was a massive switch to coal. His proposals, however, ran into serious difficulties with Congress. The European Economic Community also supported the expansion of the coal and nuclear industries to reduce the dependence of the Common Market on imported energy supplies. In 1976, the Community published guidelines to help achieve this objective, including a system of aids to help coal-fired power stations, a subsidy to assist the conversion of oil stations to coal, and a subsidy to assist the construction of new coal-fired power stations. The European Commission also put forward a plan to use E.E.C. funds to subsidize the holding of stocks of coal. But these fine words produced little action.

At home, though, the miners long-standing dreams of an energy policy which recognized coal's importance were coming to fruition. The new Labour Government were committed to coal, and in their first year of office they set up a steering committee composed of the Coal Board, the Government and the unions to examine the future of the industry. The committee endorsed the N.C.B.'s 'Plan for Coal', maintaining that the output of the industry had to be stabilized and then increased. Simply to keep output at its existing level was quite a task, because the pits were on average eighty years old and many were therefore nearing exhaustion. The industry was suffering, and would continue to suffer, from the lack of investment in the sixties. Between 1 and 3 million tons were lost each year for that reason alone. The committee set a production target of 150 million tons by 1985, which would mean the creation of 42 million tons of new capacity. About half of that would come from new mines, most of the rest from major improvements at existing collieries, and some from extending the life of otherwise exhausted collieries. The Government pledged themselves to help with any special financial problems. To this end the borrowing powers of the Board were extended in 1976, and at the same time the Government were empowered to make grants to finance stocks of coal and coke, so protecting the industry from short term fluctuations in demand. The Government's Energy Act offered additional help in checking the penetration of oil and gas into traditional markets for coal.

In February 1976, the Government, the C.E.G.B., the Coal Board and all the unions involved in the two industries met to discuss the future use of coal for the generation of electricity, a meeting which, according to the N.U.M., was the most 'significant event of the past year'. In June 1976, another meeting of even greater importance took place. The new Energy Secretary, Tony

Benn, organized a conference of over 400 people, representing energy producers, consumers, trade unions, academics, political parties and environmental pressure groups. It was the first such gathering of its kind, and proved hugely successful in encouraging the various interests to explain their forecasts and objectives. There was a general consensus that decisions would have to be taken quickly to ensure that there would not be another energy gap in the middle of the 1990s. And it was also agreed that more rigorous planning procedures were required, involving all parties discussing their plans at an early stage. The result of this was the setting up of the Energy Commission as an advisory body for the Secretary of State, with the objective of seeking an agreed view of major energy policy issues.

In 1977 the coal industry tripartite group produced a new report, entitled 'Coal for the Future'. This recognized that the Government remained committed to a target of 120 million tons of deep mined output by 1985, but accepted that less of this would now come from new mines, mainly because of the delays in winning planning permission for new sites to be opened up. To compensate, more money would have to be spent on collieries with a long life ahead of them. They forecast an annual loss of production of around 2 million tons between the 1970s and the end of the century, and reckoned that an additional 80 million tons of new capacity would have to be created after 1985 if the industry were to meet their target for the year 2000. To help the industry meet this enormous challenge, the Government reaffirmed their commitment to protect the industry from short-term fluctuations that might damage its ability to meet longer-term demands.

Within the union there was a widespread feeling that as long as the industry was secure and jobs were preserved, there could be no repeat of the strikes of the early seventies. This goes some way towards explaining why the miners agreed to support the social contract between the Labour Government and the trade union movement in the years after 1974. But even their loyalty to Labour failed to make that support as unequivocal as some would have liked. And the reason was that the lesson of the sixties had been that quiescence did not preserve jobs. These twin, and contradictory, influences battled with each other in the years following 1974.

The relationship between the trade union movement generally and the new Labour Government was a close one, arguably closer than at any time previously. When the Government came into power it was in no position to continue the pay policy of the Heath Government, and anyway did not want to. But gradually, in the first few months of office, the fulfilment of the terms of the social contract became linked to an equal commitment on the side of the unions to responsibility and realism with wage settlements. In June 1974, the T.U.C. formalized their views in a document setting out the guidelines for wage negotiations. The document recognized that the 'scope for real increases in consumption is limited', so pay rises should do no more than claim compensation for the rise in the cost of living. Priority should be given to achieving the T.U.C.'s target of a minimum basic rate of £30, and to settlements which would 'have a beneficial effect on unit costs and efficiency'. 'In general', there should be a twelve-month interval between major increases, and the General Council of the T.U.C. should be consulted and informed about their level.

If the policy was to have any success at all it had to have the backing of the miners, especially as an election in the autumn began to look more and more likely. All eyes turned towards the N.U.M.'s annual conference in Llandudno. The importance of their vote was underlined by the appearance of the T.U.C.'s General Secretary, Len Murray, who called on the delegates to remember their obligations to the Labour movement as a whole, as well as to their members. But the divisions in the union over the social contract ran very deep. Its supporters defeated a resolution from Yorkshire calling for pay increases of up to £20 a week, but only by a hairsbreadth of 4 votes. But a resolution from Nottinghamshire, leaving out all mention of figures and instead calling merely for 'substantial increases', was carried by an equally slender majority.

The uncertainty, even outright hostility, felt by many delegates was demonstrated only too clearly when the union debated the social contract itself. The Scottish area put forward a motion calling for 'total opposition to all forms of incomes policy whether statutory or voluntary, so long as the capitalist private-profit-making character of British society remains unaltered'. The proposer declared that whatever terminology was used, the social contract meant wage restraint: 'the working class have bought apples from that cart before and they know that it is not on'. Lawrence Daly, the Secretary of the union, defended the idea of the social contract. 'Who can be in opposition to an agreement which says that real wages should be maintained, as well as insisting that the incomes of the lower-paid workers be improved?' he argued. 'We would be accused, having fought for and welcomed a Labour Government . . . of having kicked them in the teeth.' But his arguments were in vain, and the Scottish motion was accepted by the conference as union policy. The N.U.M. were now committed to oppose any wage restraint contained within the social contract.

How then could the N.U.M. find itself not only supporting but actually proposing the motion that approved the social contract at the Trades Union Congress that September? It was a train of events that was to cause controversy for a long time afterwards. At the T.U.C., Daly made a brilliant speech supporting the social contract, claiming that the Labour Government were committed to a radical programme of reform including the large-scale redistribution of income and wealth, a massive increase in house-building, vastly improved social services, substantial increases in public ownership, and a wide-ranging and permanent system of price control. And he believed that they had been given evidence of that commitment in Chancellor Denis Healey's first budget. All that, in Daly's view, composed a Government programme that was worth supporting. But Daly still had to reconcile his deeds to the conference decision to reject the social contract. He did this quite simply by drawing attention to the final part of the motion, which said that 'in the event of the implementation of the social control and planning of Britain's resources in the interests of the ordinary common people, the N.U.M. will contribute its full cooperation'. That, said Daly, gave him the authority he needed. But what of the section of the social contract that urged wage restraint? Daly made it clear that he believed in a 'sensible, voluntary incomes policy' to help overcome inflation and assist the lower-paid, provided it was 'one part of a socialist economic strategy'. In other words, while the Government were pursuing economic and social policies designed to increase the living standards of trade union members, how could the trade union movement refuse to recognize certain limitations, and vague ones at that, on their scope for negotiating wage increases?

Even so, winning the agreement of the union to restraint was no easy matter. Later that year the N.U.M. rejected a productivity deal which would have increased their wages, and for a while the social contract looked imperilled. But the following spring, after two and a half days of tough negotiations, the N.U.M. settled for sizeable increases for underground workers which were justified under the social contract's guidelines on pay restructuring, and for equally large rises for surface workers which were, according to the Coal Board, 'slightly outside' it. The national executive recommended acceptance by 16 votes to 11. Joe Gormley thought that the agreement fell within the 'spirit' of the social contract, whereas Arthur Scargill welcomed it only to the extent that it broke it. Their increase averaged 31 per cent, and was on a par with other workers in the public sector.

By the summer of 1975, the meaning of the social contract had changed, and changed dramatically. The Government had become increasingly concerned about the high level of public sector wage settlements during the previous winter, and the Treasury had begun to push hard for a statutory incomes policy. By May, the T.U.C., worried about rising inflation, conceded the need for an incomes policy of some kind and were looking very favourably on the idea championed by the Secretary of the Transport Workers' Union, Jack Jones, for a flat rate across-the-board increase. At the end of June, a financial crisis provided the spur to action: the pound lost heavily against the dollar, and in an atmosphere of panic, the Government, on 11 July, announced its intention to reduce inflation to 10 per cent in a year by limiting pay settlements to £6 a week.

From Gormley's point of view, while he might not like the remedies the Chancellor was putting forward, he believed that action had to be taken to end a serious economic emergency that affected everyone – the old, the sick and the retired – as the value of their money fell rapidly: 'While we may spend our time arguing as to who is responsible for this position as the whole position is deteriorating from hour to hour and if we, as a trade union, can be seen to be giving a lead to other trade unions in Britain by saying that we are determined to help as far as is humanly possible, we can set an example to those vocal critics of the trade union movement, who by their own actions may have caused the situation to deteriorate.' In the summer of 1975, therefore, the union had to be won round once more to support the Government and the T.U.C.'s social contract.

One of Gormley's tactics was to rule by vagueness, abhorring fixed targets for wage increases, which tied him down in negotiations and reduced his ability to reach agreement. In July 1975, Yorkshire put before the conference just the sort of resolution that Gormley disliked, demanding a rise to give faceworkers £100 a week. This resolution, which in the run-up to the conference had considerable support, would have committed the union to destroying the new version of the social contract. During the weekend before the conference began, there were repeated attempts to get Scargill to compromise and amalgamate his resolution with another from Nottinghamshire, which vaguely called for 'substantial increases'. But no deal was forthcoming. Joe Gormley, in his opening address to the conference, appealed to the delegates not to 'tie the hands and feet' of the N.E.C., acknowledging that some members of the union had over the past few years become a 'little drunk with power' and were trying to endanger the life of the Labour Government. But the real broadside came from the Prime Minister, Harold Wilson, who told the conference that the battle against inflation was a battle for full employment. High wage rises of the sort being considered by the conference would only be paid for out of the money that had been set aside for expansion; 'such an act would be crazy, even suicidal with all that means for future employment in the industry'. In conclusion he made his famous appeal: 'What the Government is asking for the year ahead, what the Government has the right to ask, the duty to ask, is not a year for self but a year for Britain.'

But the speech got a lukewarm reception, and the motion calling for £100 a week was still not withdrawn. Then, only a few hours before the debate on wages was due to begin, Scotland, Wales and Kent withdrew their support, believing that there was not sufficient backing for the resolution either within the union or outside it. Scargill felt isolated and betrayed. He went up to the rostrum ostensibly to propose the compromise resolution, but instead he rounded on what he called the 'social con trick' and declared angrily that whatever the motion might say, he still believed that they should demand £100 for faceworkers then and there. Len Clarke, who seconded the motion, was annoyed at what he believed was Scargill's abuse of his position as proposer of the motion, and another speaker accused Scargill of carrying out 'an exercise of grammatical con tricks'. But the compromise had nonetheless become official union policy.

The right wing on the national executive then made moves to cement the union's support for the Government and the T.U.C. A week after the conference, Len Clarke asked the N.E.C. to support the £6-a-week flat rate increase. He insisted that a lot of changes had taken place since the conference: 'The N.E.C. had not only a responsibility to its members but to the nation as a whole in the present economic crisis. The membership would support strong action against inflation, and were not in favour of high wage settlements regardless.' The whole matter was put to a ballot, and by a majority of 3 to 2 they voted to accept the limit. It was not only an endorsement of the N.E.C.'s policy, but was also seen as a significant test of rank and file opinion generally in the country. The support of the T.U.C. in September for the policy was overwhelming.

By this point in the affairs of the national union, the dominance of Gormley was pretty well complete. At the beginning of October 1975, the General Secretary Lawrence Daly was seriously injured in a car crash in Scotland. His brother, his sister-in-law and a close lifelong friend were killed in the accident. It left Daly a sick man. But the crash was not only a personal tragedy for him – it was also a great loss for the union, for, in the opinion of many, Daly could have been the greatest General Secretary the miners had ever had. Instead, from that time on, the burden of running the union was taken on almost entirely by Gormley, and it was no mean feat.

In the first half of 1976, the T.U.C. and the Government sat down once more to work out a second phase of incomes policy. The economic crisis showed no sign of abating: unemployment had risen to 1·2 million, the rate of inflation was well into double figures, and there had been a first round of cuts in public spending. In an innovative move, the Chancellor announced that he was prepared to cut income tax if wages were restrained to a level, he initially suggested, of 3 per cent. Despite opposition to the cuts in public spending, and the ending of food subsidies, the T.U.C. agreed to a limit of 4½ per cent. But would individual unions ratify the agreement and give it the backing needed at a special T.U.C. conference to be held in June? The support of the miners was vital, not only because they had a history of undoing incomes policies, but also because any ballot they were bound to hold would represent a major, and quite probably the only, test of shop-floor opinion. The omens were not good, showing a union deeply divided about continuing support for wage restraint.

For a start there were renewed demands for £100 a week for faceworkers. Indeed, such was the influence of the miners in this period that when the South Wales area conference declared their objective of achieving this figure, the pound fell sharply on the foreign exchanges. In the period before the ballot, which the N.E.C. decided to hold by a very narrow majority, Kent, Yorkshire, South Wales and Scotland all campaigned vigorously against further pay restraint. And as the vote took place, the general belief was that the vote would be close, with drastic implications for the Government's economic strategy. In the end just over 53 per cent of the votes cast were for accepting the policy, less close than expected, but close enough for Gormley to warn that a third year of restraint would not be on.

But the miners did pose a challenge to the second year of formal restraint, though from a rather unexpected source. The achievement of earlier retirement for miners proved to be an issue which could unite the coalfields as much as a struggle for higher pay. But it also threatened to bring the union directly into conflict with the Government and the T.U.C., as both insisted that any deal had to be paid for within the 4½ per cent limit.

Compared with his European counterparts, the British miner was particularly badly off. The arduous nature of the job, the dust, the fear of accidents, were some of the reasons why men felt perfectly justified in wanting to retire before they were sixty-five. Many did not think they would make it to sixty-five and wanted to 'live a bit' and 'see the clouds' before they died. At the annual conference of 1976, a resolution from Nottinghamshire was passed calling for retirement at sixty from the new year, and then progressively down to fifty-five by 1980. The unholy alliance of Len Clarke and the left wing of the union ensured that this demand was unstoppable. And of great concern was the fact that the resolution called for an all-out strike if no settlement was forthcoming.

A meeting with the Prime Minister left them in no doubt that the Government would not finance a scheme for early retirement. And the T.U.C., too, stressed that they would countenance no breach of pay policy. The Coal Board, while opposing the demands on the grounds of 'astronomical cost' and the shortage of manpower any concessions would cause, also made it clear that giving in to the claim in full would drive a coach and horses through the 4½ per cent limit. At the end of November, the union held a ballot of the membership to test support for the claim, and the result showed that 78 per cent were in favour of a tough stance in the negotiations.

When the talks resumed, the Government told the union that they could see no objection to a limited scheme, to begin that summer, even though it would technically break the social contract. But they argued that the surface workers could not be included, in case there were similar claims from other industries. After the T.U.C. insisted that early retirement for surface workers would 'alienate the rest of the trade union movement', the N.U.M. decided to settle. Men who had twenty years of underground service would be able to retire at sixty-two from the summer of 1977, and at sixty two years later. In spite of widespread resentment among surface workers, which led to a stoppage by one group in Yorkshire, the deal was accepted by 55 per cent of the membership in a ballot.

By the summer of 1977, opposition to the pay policy was almost total within the union. In September 1976 at Brighton the T.U.C. had voted overwhelmingly for an 'orderly return to free collective bargaining at the end of Stage 2'. It was clear, even by then, that the tensions caused by restraint could be held back no longer. By 1977 they were even greater. The injustices and anomalies usually associated with broad incomes policies were causing problems, as were the reductions in differentials between the skilled and the unskilled caused by the flat-rate increase allowed under Stage 1. Tensions began to grow between the union leadership and the rank and file. The cuts in living standards showed no signs of abating, and by mid 1977 prices had outstripped wages by some 8 per cent. And whereas, at the beginning, wage restraint had been seen as a way of avoiding rising unemployment, it was clear by the middle of 1977 that unemployment was rising regardless: men were not 'pricing themselves into a job'. The mix was inevitably explosive, and all the T.U.C. felt it could offer was a pledge that there would be a twelve-month gap between wage settlements. In the face of this, the Government insisted that they would hold public sector wage rises to 10 per cent. The Chancellor made it clear that he would not tolerate spurious productivity agreements, and would blacklist private firms who disobeyed the limit and paid more.

In March, Gormley, after formally accepting the Stage 2 increase for the miners, declared that there was 'not a cat in hell's chance' of them accepting another round. He believed the Government were in grave danger of losing the next election because 'thousands of our members who have made sacrifices are not prepared to take any more'. And, as he told the Nottinghamshire miners, 'we have not received our part of the bargain because we explicitly told our members that the contract was not exclusively about wages'. At the annual conference in the summer, Daly appealed for the union to support what was left of the accord between the Government and the T.U.C., warning that a return to free collective bargaining would be rather like a return to free collective motoring: 'It would give drivers the chance to drive on any side of the road they liked and ignore the traffic signals if they wished.' But despite his speech, the conference rejected any extension of the social contract because it had 'limited pay increases and at the same time allowed prices to spiral out of all proportion, so creating disillusionment in the labour and trade union movement'. And at the T.U.C. conference, the miners even voted against acceptance of the twelve-month rule.

The problem facing the right wing in the union was how to win more money without destroying the Government's 10 per cent pay limit. It appeared to Gormley, Clarke and Ken Toon, the member of the National Executive Committee from South Derbyshire, who was to become one of the leading proponents of a productivity scheme, that the best way forward would be through a productivity deal. But it was an emotional issue, one which was seen as a potential destroyer of the unity of the union. What was more, an attempt to achieve a productivity agreement had been tried in 1974. After a great deal of blood-letting, it had failed.

The Coal Board pushed hard for a scheme. In the last half of the seventies, they were in charge of an industry that was rapidly contracting. True, they were putting a great deal of money into investment. Since 1974, they had driven ahead with new projects for winning coal and new schemes for using it. In 1975 they won approval for opening up the new Selby coalfield. At the same time they began searching for new reserves of coal, in an intensive and important programme of exploration. But the majority of these plans could not be realized in less than a decade. What then of the short term?

Throughout this period of unprecedented expansion and optimism, the industry was dogged by the problem of meeting the targets set for it. Even though the Coal Board had to run very hard to keep standing still, the results were disappointing. In 1975, just under 115 million tons were mined in Britain's pits. By 1978/9 the figure had fallen to about 107·5 million tons. The industry was still suffering the effects of the cessation of investment in the previous decade, when coal had been judged obsolete. But as the Energy Secretary, Eric Varley, had warned as far back as the autumn of 1974, 'excuses cannot be burned'. The union cooperated with drives to increase production, but their lack of success in achieving startling results added support to the view that some better way had to be found to win more coal. Against much opposition from those in the N.U.M. who prophesied 'blood on the coal' and much else, the panacea was seen to be a productivity scheme.

The idea of a productivity deal had been supported by the Wilberforce report and by the Relativities Board after the 1974 dispute. Then, after the election, the tripartite committee looking into the coal industry recommended a 'sound and effective incentive scheme'. This, according to Daly, himself no enthusiast for such ideas, meant that they had to give it a try.

Within the union, Len Clarke of Nottinghamshire was the most avid supporter of the idea. His men had had to stand still in terms of pay during the late sixties and early seventies, while other areas caught up as part of the changeover to a national wages structure. This was partly the cause of the militancy displayed by this traditionally moderate area during the great disputes and in the period after. They also stood to gain the most from an incentive scheme, as their pits were among the most lucrative.

But the support of the Nottinghamshire area was not enough. The Coal Board and the miners' leaders came up with a scheme, but it created havoc in the union, and the National Executive Committee could not make up their minds what to do. They rejected a motion rejecting the scheme, and then voted down a motion accepting the scheme. In the end they decided to hold a ballot of the membership, and in the meantime discuss their lack of progress with a conference of delegates from the coalfields. This caused another row, culminating in Arthur Scargill leading his Yorkshire delegation from the hall in protest at Gormley's refusal to allow the conference to decide on the scheme one way or another. But the conference also showed that even delegates from areas which were supposed to back the deal were very suspicious, so the N.E.C. postponed the ballot to allow for further talks with the Coal Board.

By the time the executive committee of the union met again a week later, it was clear that an incentive scheme of the sort that the Board had been hoping for stood no chance of acceptance. The idea of a national productivity deal had been proposed, but the N.C.B. were not keen 'because of the impossibility of individual men identifying their efforts with the national achievement'. Nevertheless, by the end of October the Board had, in the words of the union, 'conceded all the amendments the union had put forward'. But in a move that the Board's Deputy Chairman described as 'bloody staggering', the National Executive Committee narrowly decided to recommend rejection of a productivity scheme to the membership. The turning point of the whole meeting came when Josh Ellis, from North Wales, threatened to take his shirt off to show the blue scars on his back caused by working under a piece-rate system. It was no great surprise when the membership voted by roughly 3 to 2 to reject the deal.

But three years later, in 1977, they tried again. This time the circumstances were even more critical. The Government's pay policy made a productivity deal look like an attractive way of winning more money, legitimately. And this coincided with mounting concern within the Coal Board about output. A national productivity scheme, salvaged from the 1974 talks on such arrangements, had singularly failed to achieve better results. In July 1977, Sir Derek Ezra told a National Consultative Council meeting that output had fallen off badly, and, most serious of all, there had been a fall in the number of shifts worked at the face. Ezra said he was profoundly disappointed that, despite so much investment, they had missed their target of doing no worse than in the same period of the previous year. And he warned that 'in the absence of an incentive scheme, it was just not possible to pay the kind of wage that would attract enough of the available men to do the facework that needed to be done'.

Earlier in the year a fact-finding team, including Ken Toon of South Derbyshire, went out into the coalfields to examine ways of increasing output. They met a great deal of indifference, not to say hostility. Afterwards they drew up a productivity scheme which was accepted by the National Executive Committee as a basis for negotiation. To the proponents of the idea, it seemed a fail-safe way of winning extra money.

But the annual conference did not share this view. They threw out a resolution from South Derbyshire demanding a 'meaningful incentive scheme', and accepted a motion from South Wales which asserted that such a deal would destroy the unity of the union. This left the right wing of the union with a problem: how could they introduce an incentive scheme despite a resolution of the union's governing body, the annual conference?

By this time Gormley, Ken Toon and Len Clarke were regarding the achievement of a deal as something of a personal mission. At the September meeting of the National Executive Committee, there was a lot of pressure to reopen negotiations. It was even suggested that the decision of the annual conference did not reflect the real feelings of the membership. Poor productivity figures from the Coal Board provided the excuse for starting talks once more, and by the middle of October the terms had been settled. Each pit would have a standard performance, assessed at pit level in negotiations between management and N.U.M. officials. Once three-quarters of this standard performance had been produced, men would start earning a bonus, and once the full figure was achieved a faceworker would expect to get a weekly bonus of £23.50. The scheme won the approval of the National Executive Committee by the narrowest of majorities, and the matter was put to a pithead ballot.

The opposition to the deal was strong. The Kent miners went to the appeal court to try to win an injunction stopping the ballot, on the grounds that it was unconstitutional after the annual conference had rejected the idea of a productivity deal. But the Master of the Rolls, Lord Denning, said that the conference might not have spoken with the true voice of all the members, and in his view a ballot was a reasonable and democratic proposal.

During the campaign, the opponents of the deal had tradition on their side. There was a long-standing mistrust of anything that smacked of the old piece-rate system. Men would cut corners, ignoring safety regulations. They would be prepared to work with more dust than was safe, simply to win more coal. As work underground was so interdependent, any failure elsewhere in the pit would lose them their bonus. In short, it would set man against man, and divide the power of the union. The national unified wage structure had only recently been won after a great deal of struggle and sacrifice; why give it up when the rewards from such unity had been amply proven earlier in the decade? Productive areas, which would do well out of the deal, would be loath to strike to help their colleagues in areas which were less well-endowed. The dream of one rate for the job had inspired the men at Tonypandy in 1910, it had been at the centre of 'The Miners' Next Step' published 2 years later, and it had underpinned the miners' struggle in 1926. They were not going to give it up so easily.

In addition to the natural distrust of an incentive scheme, there was the 'Arthur factor'. Scargill conducted a vigorous campaign throughout the coalfields. He said that men would have to work 62 per cent harder to reach the maximum bonus – an exaggeration – and used an advertising campaign which distorted the scheme greatly.

If the opposition was strong, the supporters of the scheme were far from united. Len Clarke, for example, one of the staunchest proponents of the deal, actually voted against it at the October meeting of the National Executive Committee, because he wanted a number of points cleared up. By the time the Coal Board had agreed to most of them, they had lost a lot of campaigning time as well as a certain amount of credibility. Tony Benn, who as Energy Secretary had initially sold the deal to the Cabinet in glowing terms, kept very quiet until well into the campaign. It was only after a great deal of prompting by the Prime Minister that he issued a statement, calling for the scheme to be given 'a fair trial' as it had been devised 'to avoid the evils of past piecework schemes, which set men against men and lowered safety standards'. His intervention demonstrated only too clearly how seriously the Cabinet were taking the ballot.

For their part, the Coal Board appeared reluctant to recommend the scheme in case enthusiasm on their part made the rank and file suspicious. Most important, they could not say publicly that the scheme would bring an immediate pay rise to at least half the industry, and the deal was so complex that it was difficult for anyone to work it out for themselves. The low profile of the Coal Board was demonstrated by the departure of Sir Derek Ezra on a business trip to Australia. Gormley went with him, leaving the supporters of the scheme in disarray. Add to the confusion the fact that the edition of *The Miner* which was supposed to explain the deal carried out-of-date facts, and the rout of the scheme was complete. The final vote showed 87,901 in favour, but 110,634 against.

The right wing in the union were livid. They accused Scargill of gross disloyalty, and even won the N.E.C.'s approval to take advertisements in the national press denouncing all that he had said. But they didn't stop there. Ken Toon of South Derbyshire suggested that as many areas had voted in favour of the scheme, they should be allowed to introduce their own schemes if they so wished. Within a month, Lancashire, Leicestershire, the Midlands and Nottinghamshire had all taken votes asking to be allowed to make area deals. At the N.E.C. meeting in December, it was decided to give them permission. President Joe Gormley refused to declare the move out-of-order, and the matter was agreed. Even Gormley's most ferocious critics on the left agreed that this move was tactically brilliant. He had rescued a débâcle a month and a half earlier, and achieved his aim of a productivity deal. There was an attempt to stop him in the courts, but that failed. One by one, areas arranged their own productivity schemes, until eventually even the areas that had been stalwart opponents capitulated.

Two years later the fury unleashed by the deal had still not calmed down. When asked about the impact of the productivity schemes, the secretary of one N.U.M. branch simply pointed to the line of box files on the window-ledge of his office: 'Those are full of the complaints I've had to deal with since the scheme was introduced. For example, we're now getting cases of men in their forties with a bad dust problem. But it would be a brave man who would end the system: there's too much money in it.' Miners' wages have indeed risen greatly. The average gross weekly earnings in 1975 was £75.20. By 1977, it was £84.80, but by 1979 the average for an underground worker had risen to £125.80 a week, of which about one-fifth was made up from productivity payments. These figures are Gormley's justification for giving the miners the incentive schemes they had so long abhorred. In terms of results, therefore, Gormley might well pride himself on being a negotiator first and foremost. But has the cost been the weakening of the miners' industrial muscle? So far, the answer must be 'yes'.

12. The Future

The future of coal in Britain should be a dazzling one. The World Coal Study, or W.O.C.O.L., published in 1980, estimated that the demand for coal in Britain will be between 133 and 179 million tonnes by the year 2000. Obviously power stations will be an important market for coal. The N.C.B. predicts that after the recession of the early eighties, the demand for electricity will once more pick up again; almost certainly it will grow more slowly than previously, but it will nonetheless increase. Coal's main competitor to generate this electricity will be nuclear energy. The Conservative Government committed themselves to start building one new nuclear station each year from 1982, and most of them would be American pressurized water reactors of the kind used at Three Mile Island in Pennsylvania, U.S.A. These stations account for the fall in coal usage at power stations, predicted by the Department of Energy. They estimate that whereas 89 million tonnes of coal were burnt at power stations in 1979, they will use only between 65 and 78 million tonnes by the year 2000. But will nuclear energy be able to fill this gap?

The Coal Board assume that as all plans for nuclear power stations have in the past been revised downwards regularly, the nuclear contribution by the year 2000 will be much less than is currently being expected: for a start, according to Sir Derek Ezra, the capital cost of nuclear stations is at present very high, as is the cost of the capital needed to finance them. Planning applications alone will take a long time, as was shown by one inquiry into the N.C.B.'s plans for expansion in the Vale of Belvoir, which were nowhere near as emotive as the siting of a nuclear power station. In terms of running cost, the argument between nuclear and coal is much less clear. The tendency with costing of nuclear power stations is to forget the capital outlay, which is much higher than

239

for coal, and then, because the station is projected to run all the time to provide the baseload of electricity, it looks like a very cheap source of energy. These advantages are not given to coal-fired stations, whose running costs are inevitably higher. But despite that, the Coal Board believe that the technological improvements with coal-fired stations are such as to make them very competitive indeed on any reasonable comparison of costs. New ways of burning coal are being developed. For example, the United States is embarking on a large-scale programme of expanding its coal-fired capacity, and that will give a boost to new technologies. It is possible to introduce a lot more coal-fired stations at low cost by refurbishing old coal-fired stations instead of building new nuclear ones. Methods are also being developed to produce a mixture of coal and oil to burn in oil-fired equipment, because to convert totally to coal-firing would be too expensive. But will the Central Electricity Generating Board, avowed advocates of nuclear power, and the Government demonstrate their faith in coal by commissioning new coal-fired stations? At present it remains to be seen.

It could well be that nuclear energy is in a stronger position than the Coal Board publicly believes. What would happen, for example, if the demand for electricity failed to grow? The very serious problems which have dogged the development of the advanced gas-cooled reactor (A.G.R.) will not keep them out of action forever. A number of them are still not contributing to the national grid, but when they do, that will lessen the market for coal. And in addition, the designs of reactor now being preferred, like the pressurized water reactor (P.W.R.), are more tested and tried and less guilty of pushing technology too hard. These factors could weaken the contribution of coal and bring its share of the electricity generating market to the level being suggested by the Department of Energy. If this turns out to be the case, then the larger future for coal could well turn out to be in areas where it has a higher value.

Perhaps, then, the greatest expansion of the demand for coal will come in the industrial market. More efficient boilers will make coal more attractive for bulk heating, and with the substantial price advantage coal could have over oil, the industrial demand for coal is expected at least to treble in size and maybe even expand by as much as five times.

In this field, one of the most important new developments is a new technique for burning coal. Realizing that the industrial market offers a good opportunity for expansion, the Coal Board has, for some years, been developing what is called 'fluidized bed combustion'. This method involves burning coal in a bed of its own ash, which is kept in a state of continuous agitation by air blown through it, so that it behaves rather like a liquid. Potentially, the advantages of this type of boiler are enormous: the cost should be lower, any grade of coal from waste upwards can be used, and the system can be adapted to reduce sulphur dioxide pollution. Boilers and furnaces using this method have already been put into daily use at selected industrial sites, and commercial versions will soon be on the market. A large test plant, to assess its potential for electricity generation, was being commissioned in 1980 at Grimethorpe, South Yorkshire, funded by the U.S.A., the U.K. and West Germany.

In the home and in the office, future developments are more difficult to predict. In those situations the advantages of net-worked fuels such as electricity and gas are very great: they present no problems of ordering, storage, or handling. Neverthe-less, new highly efficient coal-burning appliances are available for the home, which burn ordinary domestic coal but produce no smoke. A lot of people are also opening up fireplaces once more, to rediscover the delights, and the labour, of a 'real fire'. But perhaps the greatest potential for coal in this market is its use for district heating or in combined heat and power schemes. These schemes would provide heat for a residential or commercial area either from a single plant, or from the waste heat generated in power stations. A report by a committee under the chairmanship of Sir Walter Marshall, the Deputy Chairman of the U.K. Atomic Energy Authority, recommended that one or two pilot schemes should be set up as soon as practicable. The United Kingdom has a large number of relatively old, inefficient power stations in urban areas, which are due for replacement and would provide perfect testing grounds for such schemes. Even though the idea has met with success in France and Germany, the Government in this country has remained cautious in its response. In the meantime, the N.C.B. is continuing research into better ways of handling coal and ash, coupled with increased automation of boiler systems to try to reduce the overwhelming advantage other fuels have in terms of convenience.

In the longer term, the potential for coal is enormous. The last Labour Government in general, and Alex Eadie at the Department of Energy in particular, provided a great deal of support, financial and otherwise, for new developments. Schemes that only a couple of years earlier would have been dismissed as pure Walter Mitty, from 1978 onwards became established orthodoxy. In this respect, the report of a working party into coal technology, with Eadie as chairman, provided the biggest boost the industry has had since 1973. The Coal Board, in turn, became messianic in their advocacy of coal. At an international energy conference in 1980, Sir Derek Ezra predicted that 'before the end of this century, the British motorist will be filling up with petrol from coal, and British aircraft will be jet-fuelled by coal'. In fact, the N.C.B. and B.P. have been running a standard A.A. patrol van on oil-from-coal for some time, and it has been running just like a normal petrol-powered vehicle.

The liquefaction of coal is of course not new. It was used by the Germans during the last war to obtain a high degree of independence from crude oil. In South Africa, 'Sasol' plants for producing petrol from coal use a similar technique. But the Coal Board and the Department of Energy, however, believe that they have a potentially cheaper and more efficient method of liquefying coal. The coal is heated to break down its structure, and then hydrogen is added: the result is synthetic crude oil, or 'syncrude' as it is commonly known. At present the Coal Board is looking at three ways of doing this.

In the first of these processes, coal is treated with a hot liquid solvent, itself derived from coal. The resulting thick, tarry solution is filtered and then hydrogenated to produce synthetic crude oil, and a solvent which can be recycled back into the process. The site for two pilot plants using this process has been chosen at the Point of Ayr Colliery in North Wales. Another method uses high pressure gas, instead of a liquid, to dissolve the coal. The product 'shows promise', according to the joint coal industry and Government study, as a chemical feedstock for the manufacture of plastics, resins, rubber, artificial fibres, and paints. The final process, 'pyrolysis' as it is called, involves the heating of coal in a vacuum, which breaks it down into solid, liquid and gaseous products. This system is being studied by the N.C.B. with international cooperation, and a judgement as to its large-scale practicability is still some way off. But all these processes, in their varying stages of development, make the N.C.B.'s vision of commercial scale coal refineries, or 'coalplexes', by the 1990s look very possible. The hope is that by then liquefied coal will be able to do everything oil does now: but unlike oil, coal will not be running out.

For the same reason, work is going ahead on finding substitutes for natural gas, as it too has a very limited life compared with coal. As the report on coal technology declared in 1978, 'a substantial market for substitute natural gas (S.N.G.) may be envisaged in the long-term future post 2000 A.D. representing a demand of several tens of millions of tonnes of coal'. The widescale use of substitute natural gas would be particularly important, as coal, though converted, would once more be given substantial access into the domestic and commercial market. The British Gas Corporation have already proved that coal can be converted to S.N.G. on a commercial scale, but they have also developed what is known as a 'slagging gasifier', in which ash is removed as a liquid slag. A demonstration plant in Fife is being considered as the basis of a prototype in the United States. The gasifier would produce a range of other products as well as gas, and the feeling is that both it and the gas it would produce will become economic some time after the end of the century, when supplies of natural gas from the North Sea begin to dwindle.

So much for the potential uses of coal: but where is all the coal going to come from? 'Plan for Coal' started a major programme of exploration for new reserves. So successful was this that in 'Plan 2000', the N.C.B. point out that the geological surveys which they had carried out do not support the view that all the best coal has been worked, still less that the remaining recoverable reserves will not be as productive. Quite the contrary in fact. The evidence points to very substantial reserves, comparable in terms of thickness and low geological disturbance to those being worked at present in the productive coalfields of the Midlands and Yorkshire. Some of the recoverable reserves can be won by extending the life of existing pits beyond the point where they are economically viable: a judgement is made that the coal that could be produced is more important than the cost. Other reserves of coal can be won by extending and increasing production at pits with a long life ahead of them. But in the last resort, the future viability of the coal industry depends on the development of new reserves which can be worked at new collieries.

The newest coalfield in Britain is to the north of Selby. Such is the time it takes for a new scheme to come on stream that although permission was given in 1976, it will not be at full production until 1987–8. But after Selby, what then? A feasibility study is being undertaken of the area of South Warwickshire between Coventry and Leamington Spa. Boreholes in Oxfordshire, south of Banbury, north-east of Woodstock and east of Witney, have proved coal of workable thickness, though it is unlikely that any feasibility study would be made before the middle of the eighties. Reserves of coal have also been proved at Kesteven in Lincolnshire, and in the area between Lincoln and Newark known as the Witham Prospect. In the past few years valuable reserves have been shown in Yorkshire, in the area south of Selby, and between Kellingley and Goole. But none of these coalfields generates as much excitement at Hobart House as the North East Leicestershire project in the Vale of Belvoir. According to the N.C.B., it represents the next best site for exploration in the U.K. after the Selby coalfield. At the public inquiry into the Coal Board's plans, the Deputy Director-General of Mining, Mr K. Moses, summed up the importance of the Vale of Belvoir's reserves in this way: 'Their general disposition and quantity, together with their known quality and the relative ease of access in mining engineering terms, means they form a highly attractive investment prospect for the U.K. coal-mining engineer which is unlikely to be bettered as exploration continues in this country.'

But the development of the Vale of Belvoir and the Selby

coalfield shows an important constraint on the speed of expansion of the coal industry. Such new projects create understandable concern amongst local communities in areas with no history of coal-mining. There are worries about the integration of miners into local society, and fears that pits will wreck the countryside and create havoc on the roads. In this respect, the Coal Board have had to make great efforts to select sites carefully to create the minimum disturbance, and to pay attention to the visible aspects of colliery workings by using trees, banks and so on to form an attractive landscape. In the Selby project, for example, 10 million tons of coal will be mined at five collieries in 100 square miles of coalfield. But the pits will all be linked underground, and the entire output will be brought to the surface from two drift mines. All movements of coal will take place by railway, to create the minimum disturbance. Very little waste will have to be brought to the surface, so large pitheaps will be avoided. Subsidence is designed to fit into a coherent pattern for the area's water drainage. Even the stone of the buildings has been chosen to blend into the locality. All this adds to the time taken to bring a colliery into production. In the case of the Vale of Belvoir, exploration was finished in 1975 but the public inquiry did not begin until 1979. Against strong local objections, the Board had to prove that the nation needed the coal and could win it in no other way. Robert Alexander, Q.C., acting for the Board, put the position simply and starkly: 'Unless new capacity is developed, of which the production from this field is an essential element, the coal industry will decline. We are not arguing here about expansion, however desirable that might be, but rather about maintaining the industry's capacity.'

New mines in existing coalfields, and new schemes at existing pits, are also vital in the campaign for more coal. At the end of the seventies, the N.C.B. were winning only 13 per cent of their output from pits sunk after the Second World War, and more than half the collieries in operation had been sunk before the First World War. It was hardly surprising that there were productivity problems. In addition, nothing had been done during the late sixties to remedy the situation, as oil was cheap, and coal was seen to be obsolete. The big capital projects which would have been necessary to provide a buoyant industry in the late seventies were simply not undertaken. The adoption of 'Plan for Coal' in 1974 was therefore vital, but as with every investment in the coal industry, its effects take a long time to work through.

However, there are signs that the benefits of that plan are coming to fruition. As Sir Derek Ezra put it: 'We are fast rebuilding a new industry from the old.' Well over 100 major projects were, in 1980, being carried out at operating collieries throughout the country. For example, whereas previously the amount of coal a colliery could produce was restricted to the amount that could be wound up the shaft, the Coal Board is now turning towards the use of sloping tunnels from the surface into the coal reserves, 'drifts' as they are called, to speed the movement of coal and supplies. Some collieries have been linked up underground, so that in the Barnsley area, for example, three giant drifts will surface at Woolley, South Kirkby and Grimethorpe Colliery, each drawing coal from 'satellite' pits around about. Then there are also the new mines, drifts like Royston, near Barnsley, or Betws in South Wales, which are making important contributions towards increasing the industry's productivity.

Although the automated minerless pit is a very long way off, the N.C.B. has been developing new underground technology to make collieries safer and more efficient. In the mid sixties the Coal Board suffered a severe setback with what was intended to be the world's first remotely operated pit, at Bevercotes. The technology was too unreliable, and finally came unstuck on an unforeseen geological fault. Since then the Coal Board has concentrated on more modest forms of automation in fields other than coal-cutting. At Bagworth Colliery in the Leicestershire coalfield, for example, a computer controls underground bunkers and conveyor belts, and at Rawdon it controls a coal preparation plant. The computer system, called M.I.N.O.S., or Mines Operating System, is being developed to take on more and more tasks to do with getting the coal out of the pit, and is now being installed in many collieries.

As well as work into developing better machines, research is also going on into ways of getting men to the coal-face quicker.

And most important, methods of cutting down the amount of dirt produced with the coal are being examined. One of the projects contributing towards this goal involves the automatic steering of face machines, using natural gamma radiation. In the longer term, research is going on into ways of remotely controlling mining operations from the surface. A powerful robot underground would work according to the instructions and actions of a miner seated safely on the surface. He would have all the information he would need on a television screen in front of him, and his movements would be echoed by the robots way below underground. Another idea for the future is the gasification or liquefying of coal in the seam. Coal could then be pumped much more conveniently to the surface. Another advantage would be that much less coal would have to be left in the seam for safety reasons. The N.C.B. has concluded that for the present such methods are not practicable or economic. But they would, at some time in the future, allow the exploitation of deeper deposits of coal either inland or offshore, thus providing an even greater source of energy for a long time to come.

But at a time of enormous promise for coal, there was, in Britain, a great deal of uncertainty about the Government's attitude towards the industry. According to the Labour Party's spokesman on energy at the time, Dr David Owen, 'it is an industry in which there should be no fears, but there are fears'. The cause of the worries was twofold: the Conservatives' new Coal Industry Act, and their attitude towards imports.

According to the Secretary of State, David Howell, the Act had three broad objectives. It recognized that the industry was in the process of replacing old, relatively uneconomic capacity with new highly efficient faces and collieries, and to that extent would need continuing support from the Government to finance new projects. The Act therefore increased the Board's borrowing powers for three years, and allowed the Government to make what are called 'deferred interest loans', whereby the Coal Board would not have to pay interest until the new projects started earning money. The Government also decided to continue to support the system of grants to help the industry change. Some of these so-called 'social grants' were even improved, such as those covering the transfer of men from pit to pit, and they additionally put extra money into the scheme to help victims of pneumoconiosis. But the final and most controversial objective of the Act was to declare that by 1983–4, all operating grants given to the Coal Board would be ended and they would have to make a profit. David Howell noted that the Board's dependence on grants had been growing, and as such would provide 'no basis for a secure and prosperous future in any industry'. In the years up to that date, the Government would continue to pay operating grants, but the method of paying them would change. They would instead be paid in the form of 'a single explicit deficit grant' which would 'make for better accountability and will enable the industry's progress towards financial viability to be clearly seen'. All in all, the aim of the Act was, according to Howell, to create a 'viable, profitable industry, accepting change and determined to make its own way in a competitive market'.

The Act won criticism from almost every quarter. For a start, the Government had undertaken their strategy of making the industry more self-reliant at a time when the general economic situation was worsening greatly. Since the financial targets were first discussed with the Coal Board in the summer of 1979, the demand for coal had fallen because of the economic downturn. British Steel, for example, was taking much less coking coal, and the high exchange rate was making imported coking coal appear cheaper. The Central Electricity Generating Board faced a dramatic drop in demand, and there were severe doubts whether it would need all the coal it was committed to. The result was to pile the cost of this unwanted coal – from both industries – onto the Coal Board. According to Alex Eadie, the man who had been responsible for the coal industry throughout the period of the Labour Government, to remove all operating grants within three years in such circumstances was to put the Coal Board into an economic straitjacket.

The Act caused grave concern, not to say depression, within the industry. Sir Derek Ezra made it clear to the Government that he was seriously worried about the practicability of phasing out operating grants within three years. It was very difficult indeed to make the coal industry responsive to short-term market considerations, which was what the Act sought to do. When the N.C.B. started on its programme of expansion in 1974, it was made clear that the industry would need some cushioning against vagaries in demand until the new investment was complete. The industry was investing at a much faster rate than normal, to make up for a virtual cessation of investment in the fifteen years prior to 1974, and to meet the Government's objective of a growth in capacity from the mid 1980s onwards. But whereas the industry had been addressing itself to long-term problems, it now faced the hazards of the short-term. And this metamorphosis, desired by the Government, from an emphasis on targets of output to short run profitability, was to be attempted as the entire economy lurched into recession.

There were other issues also raised by the Act and the Conservatives' policy. Late in the day, the Department of Energy introduced the concept of 'deficit financing', rather than paying grants, and the Board could not help but feel that the object was simply to show the Board in a bad light each time they declared their results. Furthermore, there was great concern in Hobart House lest finance for schemes to test the practicability of new uses for coal was not forthcoming. In many fields, the N.C.B. undoubtedly has great expertise, but the lead looks like being lost to the Americans: technologies for the 1990s will in all probability have to be imported.

At the same time, there was considerable scope for arguing that the Coal Board was being treated badly and unfairly in comparison with other industries and other countries. British production costs were the lowest in Europe, but so were the subsidies. What was more, if the Coal Board had to compete, it should at least be allowed to compete freely. It should be allowed to borrow from private institutions at lower rates, rather than being stuck with the high cost of loans from the Government's National Loan Fund. Like private industry, it should also be allowed to lease equipment, which in some cases would work out cheaper than buying it outright. And there was also concern that as council-house building had slowed almost to a halt, the Coal Board would have to pay to have new houses built by new pits.

Alex Eadie believed that the consequences of the Bill would be twofold. The first was that there would be pit closures: 'If the N.C.B. does not achieve its target within three years, while it is shackled by cash limits, it will be told to have an accelerated programme of pit closures.' By doing so they would be reducing coal production, which would be an act of 'sheer vandalism when all the coal-producing nations of the world are calling for increased production'. His thoughts were supported by the British Association of Colliery Management, which declared that 'the financial objectives in the Bill are . . . too stringent and cannot be achieved within the given timescale without seriously undermining the healthy growth of the industry'. They concluded that 'by asking the coal industry to break even so soon, the Government is putting no monetary value whatsoever on the strategic necessity of greater indigenous production. If security of supply within the U.K., within the E.E.C. and within the western world is as important as the Government and Western leaders maintain, they should be willing to back their commitment with cash.'

The uncertainty about the future which the Coal Act is likely to cause is matched by the insecurity resulting from imports of coal. On their election in 1979, the Conservatives rescinded the ban on imports of Australian coking coal for the steel industry. Later in the year, the British Steel Corporation announced a large-scale closure programme which further threatened the market for South Wales coking coal. At the same time, the Central Electricity Generating Board entered into contracts to more than double the amount of coal they were importing. And at the public inquiry into the Vale of Belvoir coalfield, they revealed that they were looking at the feasibility of building new deep water port facilities to enable them to increase the amount of coal they could import to 10 million tons a year by 1985. The N.U.M. believed that an increase in imports of coal would greatly exacerbate problems of unemployment and economic decline, add to our balance of payments deficit, and make British industry reliant on sources of supply that might not be secure. It appeared to be a repeat performance of the rundown of the 1960s for the sake of a temporary price advantage. And just as in the 1960s, if the price of imported coal shot up again, there would be no mines left producing indigenous supplies.

The union faces what could well turn out to be its most dangerous decade. The big strikes of 1972 and 1974 arose out of a feeling of injustice, at a time of great insecurity for the industry. The relative peace in the coalfields since then has existed partly because the necessity of keeping the miners at or near the top of the wages league has been recognized. But of equal importance in maintaining peace has been the feeling that the importance of coal has been recognized, and that the industry could look forward to a period of security: jobs would be maintained. Up until the present day a consensus existed that coal should be supported as an exception, but what would happen if that consensus came to an end?

The lesson of the 1960s was that quiescence and low wages do not preserve the coal industry or jobs. The union faced an avalanche of closures so overwhelming that it became impossible to pick on one and say 'thus far and no further'. Yet the argument that if they pushed for higher wages they would create unemployment and lose more pits had been proved demonstrably untrue: the turbulence of the period from 1969 to 1974 won them a return to their position as high wage earners, with little impact on the rate of closures. The 1960s also proved the wrongheadedness of trying to run the industry on a basis of short-term profitability. Pits were closed in the 1960s which within ten years could well have been profitable once more. The cost was not only in terms of coal lost to the nation: it was also the cost in terms of hardship and insecurity to miners and the destruction of many of their communities. And of course the culmination of these pressures were the epic struggles of 1972 and 1974. The miners today are keenly aware that those mistakes must not be repeated.

Ostensibly, coal is once more king, and the miners need no longer worry about their future. Yet the future looks very much more uncertain. A visit to the Yorkshire coalfield in the summer of 1980 left me in no doubt that uppermost in many miners' minds is the fear of closures. At every single pit there was uncertainty. Straws were being clutched at to show that closures were coming: why else, I was told, would the N.C.B. announce new improved terms to encourage men to move; why else would pits starved of manpower refuse to take men on? The belief was gaining ground that the consensus of support for the industry was coming to an end. By the end of 1980 many in the coalfields were predicting that the possibility of closures could lead to conflict.

Postscript: Victory without Tears (*March 1981*)

It was an extraordinary and unexpected reversal. Faced with the threat of a national miners' strike in February 1981, Margaret Thatcher's Conservative Government totally changed their policy towards coal. Whereas previously they had aimed to end most subsidies to the National Coal Board and make the whole operation more 'competitive', the Government committed themselves to funding an expensive programme of support for the industry. The miners' industrial muscle had for the third time within a decade won them what they wanted. The threat of pit closures appeared at an end.

The right-wing press went wild. 'Surrender to Old King Coal', declared the *Daily Express*. 'The Big Climbdown' was the headline in the *Daily Mail*. The *Mail* went on: 'Mr Gormley and the miners have dealt the most damaging blow to her [Mrs Thatcher's] authority that she has suffered in nearly two years as premier. The implications could be devastating for the Government's battle to hold the line on the rest of the industrial front.' One miners' M.P. described what had been achieved as 'greater than the victories of 1972 or 1974'. How had this massive capitulation come about?

It was by no means inevitable that the threat of pit closures would lead to conflict. The experience of the sixties proved the difficulty of such action. For a start, in an extractive industry like mining there would always be closures, and geological difficulties could sometimes make that event occur relatively unexpectedly. It follows that the miners would have to make sure that they picked the right closure to fight. Furthermore, it was believed until very recently that it would be extremely difficult to ensure that the union took unified action, even if the right case could be found. The example of Langwith Colliery in 1976, when the

National Executive voted for an overtime ban to force the N.C.B. to keep the pit open, only to rescind their vote a few days later when support appeared to be less than hoped, demonstrated the difficulty of successfully carrying out such a campaign. A later attempt to save another colliery, Teversal in Nottinghamshire, also failed. Furthermore, in the five years up to April 1980 the N.U.M. had acquiesced in the closure of twenty-seven collieries, with the loss of about 14,000 jobs. Opposition to individual pit closures was a lot more problematic than rhetoric at conferences might allow.

But during 1979, attitudes in the coalfields changed. The new Conservative administration appeared ready to break the consensus of support for the industry. Publication of the Coal Industry Bill, as was explained in the previous chapter, confirmed that that was their aim. And for the Government to insist on withdrawing a good deal of their financial support at a time when the industry needed it most meant only one thing to the miners: a return to the dogmas of the sixties, and pit closures. But this time, in contrast to the position in the sixties, the miners had confidence in the future of coal, and a knowledge that time had proved the veracity of the arguments put forward by the union during that decade. Any attempt at pit closures on the scale of the Robens era was likely to meet with strong resistance.

Symptomatic of this new mood was the campaign to save Deep Duffryn pit at Mountain Ash in South Wales during the summer of 1979. The N.U.M. and the communities of the Cynon Valley were united in their opposition to the closure. They took the campaign into the rest of the South Wales coalfield and into the other areas of the union. The arguments were similar to those of the sixties, with the Coal Board maintaining that the pit faced overwhelming geological difficulties, and the N.U.M. alleging that the colliery was being deliberately run down. But what was new was the confidence with which the arguments about the importance of coal, and therefore of their pit, were being put forward. In the end, after Gormley had intervened, the Coal Board gave the pit a six-week reprieve to see whether the miners could prove its viability. They failed, and agreed that there was no alternative to closure. But their success was to make an issue which ostensibly concerned only one part of the country into one of national concern.

Fears of an accelerated programme of closures grew during the year that followed. The position was most acute in South Wales. The loss made by that coalfield rose dramatically during 1980, to almost £60 million in one year. Twelve pits were held responsible, and the closure of one of them, Tymawr-Lewis Merthyr, was announced. Once more a campaign was mounted to save the pit, and the fight took on a symbolic significance for the union. Why, they asked, should a pit with what they believed to be fifteen years of easily worked reserves be closed when imports of coal were rising so rapidly?

At the miners' annual conference of 1980 in the sedate surroundings of the Grand Hotel, Eastbourne, the rostrum was decked out with posters supporting the men at Tymawr-Lewis Merthyr. And while much attention concentrated on the demand for, among other things, a 35 per cent rise, the delegates also had strong words to say about closures. A sign of the mood came when a resolution from Nottinghamshire, calling for improved redundancy payments, was thrown out. Delegates argued that they should not make it any easier for closures to take place. But a resolution from the Kent coalfield which promised 'any action necessary' to oppose pit closures, other than those due to proven seam exhaustion, was unanimously accepted. Mick McGahey declared: 'We must tell the Government and the Coal Board that there will be no massacre of this industry as there was in the sixties.' This emotional debate was followed by the annual address to the conference by the Chairman of the Coal Board, Sir Derek Ezra. He was given a rough ride, and faced such repeated heckling that Joe Gormley had to intervene four times from the chair to restore order. Sir Derek denied a claim made by Arthur Scargill that the Coal Board had a list of fifty proposed closures, at which point Scargill himself shouted, 'That's a lie.' Nevertheless, Ezra went on to insist that the future of each colliery would continue to be reviewed according to procedures agreed with the union. But at the same time he made very clear his own concern at the implications of the Government's policies towards the coal industry.

To put the fears expressed at Eastbourne into some perspective, it must be said that there were some respects in which the Coal Board was doing very well in 1980. Deep mined output rose during the year by over 4½ million tonnes. There were fewer men employed than ever before, absenteeism had fallen, and productivity was rising. In addition, exports of coal had increased by over 70 per cent. The industry also had some security in the knowledge that the Central Electricity Generating Board had agreed to take a minimum of 75 million tonnes of coal each year for five years. And, after a bout of public duelling, the British Steel Corporation had agreed to limit imports of coking coal to 4 million tonnes a year in 1980. The problem was that at a time when the industry was doing better than ever before, demand for coal was falling.

The recession was more severe than anyone had predicted. During 1980, the use of coal by industry fell by 15 per cent, consumption in homes dropped by nearly 20 per cent, and usage by commerce and public bodies was down by over 10 per cent. Only power stations burnt more coal in 1980 than in 1979, despite an overall drop in the demand for electricity. The major problem area, though, was the steel industry. The Government's policies towards steel had led to a rapid contraction in the demand for coking coal. The steel workers' strike, the closure of older, less efficient steel-making plants, and the ready availability of top quality imported coking coal all added to the problem. And the fall in demand really was quite dramatic. Whereas over 15 million tonnes were used in all coking ovens in 1979, a year later the amount was down to just over 11·5 million tonnes, a fall of almost a quarter. Significantly, in the light of what was to happen in the first few months of 1981, the area most directly affected by this slump was the South Wales coalfield.

At the same time as British pits were producing more than they could sell, imports of coal were rising. In 1980, they rose by nearly 70 per cent, to over 7 million tonnes. To an industry passing through a recession, these imports represented jobs. Some of the coal brought from abroad was undoubtedly cheaper. Australian coal, for example, was dredged out of open cast mines at low cost, South African coal was mined by black Africans on low wages, and American coal was subsidized by the state and mined by non-union labour. But was it really the best policy to sacrifice British pits and jobs for the sake of imported coal that for the present was cheaper? For even if these countries were producing coal at lower cost than Britain, few, if any, other countries were producing it more efficiently. In 1979, the cost of producing a tonne of coal in Belgium was £58, in France £45, in West Germany £41, whereas the comparative figure for Britain was only £29. Yet subsidies from foreign governments meant that their coal could enter Britain at a price that undercut the home-dug product. In fact subsidies in West Germany, at about £38 a tonne for coking coal, were high enough to make the price of domestic and imported coal the same. In Belgium the subsidy was £33.90 a tonne, in France it was £18, whereas the comparative figure for the United Kingdom was £1.50. The British Government were clearly not only refusing to match such generous subsidies, but were also, through the 1980 Coal Industry Act, withdrawing much of what help there was.

The mood at the Coal Board was of intense gloom. Despite a vigorous campaign, they had failed to win the argument with the Government over the Coal Industry Act. They had also failed to gain help to counteract the short-term effects of the recession, as had been agreed with the previous Government under the 'Plan for Coal'. The Government refused to ease the cash limits on the industry, or even to postpone their aim of making the N.C.B. break even by 1984. Cherished schemes for the future, where Coal Board expertise was ahead of the rest of the world, were held in abeyance. As one Coal Board member put it: 'The Labour Government were a relatively easy touch in a way, but the Conservatives were impossible.' There was at least one point when the arguments with the Government reached such an impasse that Sir Derek Ezra very seriously considered resigning.

Gradually, the miners became aware that the crisis so long predicted was now upon them. During the wage negotiations in the autumn of 1980, it was spelt out that pits and jobs were threatened by the drop in demand for coal. The eventual acceptance of a 13 per cent deal after a pithead ballot showed that the message had been understood. By the New Year of 1981, it was clear that the Coal Board had no alternative but to close loss-making pits. The Yorkshire miners jumped the gun and held a ballot asking for authority to take industrial action to ensure that pits were kept open. Overwhelmingly, the Yorkshire miners gave their leaders the endorsement they wanted.

On 10 February, the entire executive committee of the N.U.M. went to Hobart House to hear what closures were planned. The occasion was a regular consultative meeting between the Coal Board and the three mining unions. Ezra's address gave only the broadest outlines of the scale of retrenchment required. He told them that they could not afford to keep adding to stocks of coal, which they reckoned would reach 37 million tonnes by the end of March. But most frustratingly for those present, he refused to give details of the pits to be closed, preferring to leave that job to the twelve area boards. Instead he said that the aim was to reduce the output of coal by 10 million tonnes a year. When he finished speaking there were questions about the numbers of pits involved, but he still refused to be drawn. Not surprisingly, this led to some bawling and shouting, as after three hours the miners still knew very little. Eventually Gormley turned to Ezra and said, 'You might as well tell them, Derek. You must know the numbers.' With great reluctance, Ezra said that between twenty and thirty pits could go through exhaustion, bad geology and similar problems. Beyond that, and over a longer period, the total could reach between twenty and fifty. By all accounts, when Ezra left the meeting, he looked depressed. Gormley went outside and told reporters: 'I am not going to allow this industry to be raped in this way in my last year as President.'

The miners began to prepare their campaign of war. The National Executive Committee were scheduled to meet within forty-eight hours, on Thursday morning. But the evening before, the fourteen members of the so-called 'progressive group' on the executive met in a bar in London to discuss tactics. This caucus composes the right-wing majority on the N.E.C., or, as they prefer to style it, 'the group that makes decisions'. Over some drinks, they decided that even though some of them were not keen on a strike, they had to steal the thunder from the left. One of their members, the secretary of the N.U.M.'s North Western area, Sid Vincent, drew up a resolution that called for talks with the Government, with the rider that if they failed, there should be a ballot for a strike.

The meeting at the N.U.M. headquarters on Euston Road the next morning was lobbied by about 500 delegates from eight coalfields, including some traditionally labelled as 'moderate'. The slogans on the banners they carried were reminiscent of the rallying cries of the sixties: 'Invest in Britain's future', and 'Subsidize our coal now'. Inside, the 'progressive group' put forward their motion, proposed by Tommy Bartle of the Durham Mechanics, and seconded by Trevor Bell, the Secretary of C.O.S.A., the clerical section. In an unprecedented display of unity which was to impress the Government deeply, the Executive Committee voted unanimously to oppose totally all pit closures, and warned that 'if any attempt is made to put these plans into effect either in individual areas or collectively, the National Executive Committee will recommend through a ballot vote that the members take national strike action'. They decided to press for talks with the Government to argue their case for subsidies and a halt to imports, and to meet again in a week's time to discuss the results. If, by then, they had not achieved what they wanted, they would ballot the membership to gain authority for a strike. Ominously, the N.E.C. warned that strikes could nonetheless start before then in some areas, and Gormley told newsmen, 'We'll have difficulty holding the lads back.'

The strength of feeling was shown at a rally held after the meeting, across the road at the Friends' Meeting House. There was a determination that the treatment meted out to the steel-workers was unacceptable to the miners, as well as a very real edginess – if there were to be redundancies, there would be little chance of finding work elsewhere at a time of such high unemployment. Both Arthur Scargill and Mick McGahey won standing ovations for their speeches. Scargill declared: 'We are in a battle to save our jobs and in the process bring about the condition for an early general election in Britain, and an end to the Tory Government once and for all.' McGahey encouraged his audience to make arrangements to ensure that the triple alliance, formed earlier in the year between the railwaymen, the steelworkers and the miners, worked effectively at local level when the strike came, as come it would: 'I'm not warning of industrial action. I'm predicting it is going to happen. The union could be balloting for industrial action with the miners already on strike. If the Scottish miners come out against the threat of closures, I'll not be telling them to go back, I'll be leading them out.'

On Friday 13 February, the details of the closures began to emerge, area by area. In South Wales, the area director Philip Weekes announced that five pits were to close with the loss of 2,800 jobs. He added that the future of three or four more would be reviewed during the following year. The President of the South Wales Miners, Emlyn Williams, said: 'If we do not move quickly, we will face annihilation of the coalfield in the next five years.' The same day, miners in Durham were given notice of the closure of four pits with the loss of nearly 2,000 jobs, and Kent miners were informed that Snowdown Colliery was to cease production. In all three coalfields, it was made clear that alternative work would be available for a large proportion of the men, but that many, usually the older ones, would still be made redundant.

By the middle of the following week, all the areas had heard their fate. Overall, twenty-three pits were to close, with a combined output of about 4¼ million tonnes, nowhere near the 10 million tonnes Sir Derek Ezra had initially said he wanted to lose. They also showed, with the exception of the closures in the North East, a concentration on the left-wing dominated coalfields of Wales, Scotland and Yorkshire. There were widespread suspicions that this was a deliberate attempt by the Coal Board to split the union, but if it was, it backfired badly. The Board's technique of announcing a national programme of closures area by area, far from softening the blow, made sporadic, unofficial action even more likely.

The catalyst for the unofficial strikes was South Wales. At the executive meeting on Thursday, Emlyn Williams, leader of the South Wales miners, warned that there would be unofficial strikes in his area, and the final resolution agreed by the N.E.C. had recognized this. For Williams and his officials, it had been a hard year. Twelve months earlier the South Wales membership had voted overwhelmingly against a strike to protest about imports of coal and steel closures. The leadership, as they put it, had been 'constitutionalized out of action'. But they had also learnt a lesson. Subsequently, they spent enormous amounts of time and energy at meetings, trying to patch up the damage so that whenever they next called a strike, they could carry the membership with them. They knew that South Wales was bound to be hit hard by any closures and, through their contacts with other areas, knew that once they came out on strike, others would follow. And that's exactly what happened.

On Saturday, men at one of the pits threatened with closure in South Wales, Coegnant Colliery near Maesteg, voted to strike. They also decided to send pickets to other pits in the coalfield to press for an immediate stoppage. Gradually, the strike began to spread. On Monday, delegates from throughout the coalfield met at Bridgend to discuss tactics. It took them less than half an hour to vote to go on strike. Despite a plea from Gormley to hold fire, at dawn the following day all thirty-four pits in South Wales were at a standstill.

By Wednesday, the miners of the Kent coalfield had joined in, even though they had originally intended to wait until the beginning of the following week. Pits in the normally 'moderate' Durham coalfield had also stopped work, as had all the collieries in Scotland. Some pits in Yorkshire and the Midlands were at a standstill too. With the entire Yorkshire coalfield committed to joining the following Monday, the word from almost every other area was that they were also prepared for action. In addition, the impact of the strike was beginning to be felt beyond the colliery yard. South Wales miners, for example, began picketing power stations, and the railwaymen, so crucial in the disputes of 1972 and 1974, were among the first to pledge their support. The Government seemed doomed to a head-on confrontation with the miners and some powerful allies.

It was clear that the Energy Secretary, David Howell, had completely misread the situation. He had been given ample warning of what was likely to happen by the miners themselves, and by Sir Derek Ezra. He should also have been aware that the N.U.M. itself was in a sensitive state. The election campaign to find a successor to Joe Gormley as President had to all intents and purposes begun, sharpening attitudes considerably.

But none of this seems to have been appreciated by Howell and his team. Instead, they appeared to take comfort from the fact that as winter drew to a close, stocks of coal were at a remarkably high level. Furthermore, they appeared encouraged by the more 'moderate', quiescent climate of industrial relations following the defeat of the steelworkers, and following the miners' own settlement the previous autumn. But above all they subscribed to the tough view of the Treasury, which maintained that with a cash limit of £834 million for 1980/81 and £882 million for 1981/82 the Government was being quite generous enough in its support for the industry. To underwrite any increased borrowing by the Coal Board would only add to the Public Sector Borrowing Requirement, which was already substantially higher than they had hoped. The proponents of this view seemed unaware of the dangers they faced, as did most of the rest of the Cabinet, including the Prime Minister herself.

On the day that the Coal Board met the miners to discuss the closures, the Prime Minister faced Mr Michael Foot at question time in the House of Commons. Foot declared that it was utterly contemptible that the N.C.B. should contemplate closing pits which still had coal left in them. Mrs Thatcher replied that such matters were for the Coal Board to decide: 'It would be quite wrong for the Government to attempt to manage each separate nationalized industry.' When Foot again intervened, she answered him even more firmly: 'I am not directing that industry. It is for the management of the N.C.B. to make these arrangements.'

Two days later, Foot once more pressed the Prime Minister to do something. 'Is the right honourable lady seriously saying,' he asked, 'that in this critical situation she will refuse to call together the tripartite meetings which we had on the coal industry and which saved the coal industry following the experiences of 1974? . . . Will she not decide to do it now, instead of being forced to do it later?' Mrs Thatcher's retort was brief and to the point: 'No, sir, and I am not forced to do many things.'

Meanwhile, the National Executive Committee had made it clear that they wanted to talk to the Government. But whereas they wanted to discuss subsidies, and a ban on imports, the Government appeared still to believe that better redundancy terms might save the day. In addition, Howell showed no sense of urgency in organizing a meeting with the miners. Even as the unofficial strikes spread through the coalfields, he picked a day that was still over a week away. He seemed unconcerned that by the time the meeting took place, the National Executive Committee would have met, and having achieved nothing, would have been committed to a strike.

But over the weekend the potential scale of the crisis became clearer, and Howell, as the *Daily Mail* put it, 'came blinking into the sunlight like some mole out of hibernation'. The most important influence on him was the rapid spread of unofficial strikes, coupled with pledges of support from other members of the triple alliance, the railwaymen and the steelworkers. As one N.U.M. official remarked: 'All the signs were of a very broad dispute indeed, with the possibility of it reaching almost general strike proportions.'

By the morning of Tuesday 17 February, with the South Wales coalfield at a complete standstill, some rapid and decisive action was required. That morning Joe Gormley, Lawrence Daly and Michael Foot met at Westminster. Their strategy all along had been to press for an immediate meeting between the Government, the N.U.M. and the Coal Board. Once more, their solution was passed on to Howell. He, meanwhile, was at Downing Street talking to the Prime Minister about the strike. She seized on the idea, and demanded that talks be arranged for the following day. Howell went off to do her bidding, and arrange what was called a 'listening session'.

That evening, Mrs Thatcher set about consulting a close group of ministers. The Cabinet was not involved, and neither was the Cabinet's economic committee. Instead she talked to Jim Prior, the Employment Secretary, Sir Geoffrey Howe, the Chancellor of the Exchequer, Francis Pym, the Leader of the House, and William Whitelaw, the Home Secretary. They confirmed her view that the union looked united as never before and ready for a long dispute. They were also keen to avoid an early test of the new code on picketing. Prior, whose relationship with Gormley was a good one, was particularly anxious to settle quickly and avoid confrontation. The Trade Secretary, John Biffen, in a remarkably frank television interview after the event, summed up the Government's view by saying, 'I think the spectre which frightened them was the very clear evidence that there would be massive industrial action on this issue.' For good measure, he added, 'I didn't come into politics to be a kamikaze pilot.'

The following morning, Howell, Prior and the Chief Secretary to the Treasury, Leon Brittan, met the Prime Minister, and decided the details of what would be said to the miners later in the day. By lunchtime on Wednesday, barely twenty-four hours after involving herself personally in the crisis, the Prime Minister had avoided the normal procedures of Cabinet and turned her Government's policy on its head.

To those outside Mrs Thatcher's small circle of confidants, the Government's about-turn came as a complete surprise. Even civil servants in the Energy Department were said to be shocked. When Howell met the miners and the Coal Board at his office on Millbank, he told them that the Government were prepared 'to discuss the financial constraints with an open mind, and also with a view to movement'. He invited the industry to 'come forward with new proposals consistent with the Plan for Coal', and said that he would look at what could be done to reduce imports. Specific details of the Government's support would have to wait for further talks, and it was not at all clear whether the Government were fully aware, or prepared to admit, how costly their climb-down was going to be. Certainly Sir Derek Ezra, according to one report, took some convincing before he was prepared to withdraw the planned closures. But Gormley was certain that they had won a major victory, declaring: 'The closure programme no longer exists and there is no need for any strike action.' Joe Whelan, the Secretary of the Nottinghamshire miners, summed up the feeling of euphoria when he told reporters: 'The Lady said she wasn't for turning, but now she has become an expert in double somersaults.'

The next day the miners' executive met to discuss the break-through. Splitting along traditional lines, they voted by 14 to 8 to accept the outcome of the talks as a 'victory for N.U.M. policy and commonsense', and to recommend a return to work. The left, including Arthur Scargill, were suspicious of the vagueness of the Government's promises, did not trust anything the Conservatives did anyway, and generally wanted 'copper-bottomed' assurances before a return to work. For a while it looked as if some areas would continue on unofficial strike, but eventually, after a great deal of contact by telephone, they too went back.

In the Commons on the afternoon after the capitulation to the miners, the Leader of the Opposition, Michael Foot, congratulated Mrs Thatcher on what appeared to be a 'great victory for the miners and the nation'. 'I assure the right honourable lady,' he went on, 'that every time she turns she will get a nice bouquet from me.' For her part, Mrs Thatcher maintained that her action had been 'swift, decisive and realistic', but made it clear that she still believed in a 'competitive coal industry' that would put 'the least burden on other parts of the economy'. It was a theme continued by the Energy Secretary, David Howell, when he told the House: 'Unless we can get competitive coal, we cannot get competitive electricity and we shall not have the jobs that we want for our people. That is a lesson that has to be learnt.'

The decision to settle with the miners provoked some bitter criticism in the Conservative Party. At a meeting of the Tory backbench Energy Committee there were calls for the resignations of Howell and Ezra. There were angry noises about the climbdown itself, the cost of the deal, and the apparent suddenness of the crisis which seemed to have taken the Government and Howell so much by surprise. There was also an attempt to blame the Employment Secretary, Jim Prior. He had undoubtedly had a central role in the crisis, but the *Daily Express* alleged that he had had a secret meeting with Gormley at which he had undermined the bargaining strategy of the Department of Energy. Prior furiously denied this report as 'untrue and disgraceful'.

Another target was Sir Derek Ezra. One Conservative backbencher, Eric Cockeram, went so far as to describe him as an 'I.R.A. bomber' who had tossed his closure plan into the industry after first lighting the fuse. 'Is it not apparent,' he asked, 'that Sir Derek has achieved his objective of squeezing more money out of the British taxpayer?' His suspicions were shared by many

Conservatives and even by members of the miners' union. The suggestion was that Ezra deliberately designed the package of closures to provoke the miners into a conflict which he knew they were bound to win. Proponents of this view cited Sir Derek's longstanding and well-known dislike of the Government's policies towards coal, and the fact that the likelihood of his coming retirement as chairman meant that he had little to lose. Furthermore, they questioned his handling of the dispute, especially the leaks about closures that had dripped from the Coal Board since early in the year. And they also wondered why, at the initial meeting with the miners, Sir Derek had told them that he wanted to close 10 million tonnes of capacity, whereas by the end of the dispute it had emerged that the twenty-three pits earmarked for closure would save only 4¼ million tonnes. Was this an attempt to soften the blow or to stir up the miners? Joe Gormley aired his suspicions in the *Daily Mail*:

> I have been in coal a long, long time . . . I have to ask myself how it is that these 'figures' about closure, the blackest picture, are being fed back to me from my areas, information that is coming out from the Board through the back door in bits and pieces. I have to assume that the Board well knows that if it does this, it is going to create a lot of passion. I think we have become the nut in a nutcracker. I think the N.C.B., knowing the impossibility of meeting the financial targets the Government have set, saw a way of using the miners. They want to use our strength to force a change in the Government's approach.

Sir Derek vigorously denied any charge that he engineered the dispute, and maintained that his action had been designed to limit it. The strategy behind letting the information out area by area was one of forestalling united action by the N.U.M., and he was said to be genuinely dismayed by events. One member of the miners' executive committee, who had a close relationship with the Coal Board, was equally emphatic: 'They had no part in trying to use us.' Either way, such a conspiracy would at present be impossible to prove, but the rumours remained. Joe Gormley's role as a negotiator in the dispute was, by all accounts, unsurpassed. The miners' victory marked a golden end to his career as President.

Faced with the undoubted power of the miners, and in the light of the events of February 1981, it seems appropriate to conclude with the remarks of two very different men. The first are the thoughts of the Trade Secretary, John Biffen, who, while admitting that the Government had given in to the miners' muscle and not to their arguments, said: 'Certain sections of organized labour hold the capacity to exercise an extra-parliamentary authority which is almost baronial.' He went on: 'There are limited numbers of people in key areas of the economy, vital minorities, who can exercise this strong impact.'

The other person was the greatest economist the Coal Board ever had, Dr E. F. Schumacher. He used to tell a story that encapsulates why the Government and the country should be prepared to support the coal industry and the men who work in it. It was about an American in Britain who wrote home to his girl, saying, 'I'm finished with you. I have a girl in England.' She wrote back asking, 'What's she got that I haven't got?' And he replied: 'Nothing . . . but she's got it here.'

Select Bibliography

Alexander, K. J. W., 'Wages in the Coal Mining Industry since Nationalisation', *Oxford Economic Papers*, 1956.

Barrett-Brown, Michael, 'Determinants of the structure and level of wages in the coal mining industry since 1956', *Bulletin of the Oxford Institute of Statistics*, 1967.

Barrett-Brown, Michael, *The Background to the Miners' Strike*, Nottingham, Institute of Workers' Control, 1972.

Benson, John, *British Coalminers in the 19th Century*, Dublin, Gill & MacMillan, 1980.

Berkovitch, Israel, *Coal on the Switchback*, London, George Allen & Unwin, 1977.

Bodey, Hugh, *Mining*, London, Batsford, 1976.

Burton, Anthony, *The Miners*, London, Futura, 1976.

Buxton, Neil, *The Economic Development of the Coal Industry*, London, Batsford, 1978.

Coates, David, *Labour in Power?*, London, Longman, 1980.

Coates, Ken, *Democracy in the Mines*, Nottingham, Spokesman Books, 1974.

Crossman, R. H. S., *Diaries of a Cabinet Minister*, Hamish Hamilton and Jonathan Cape, London, 1976.

Daly, Lawrence, 'The Miners and the Nation', Scottish N.U.M. pamphlet, 1968.

Dennis, Norman, *et al.*, *Coal is Our Life*, London, Tavistock Publications, 1969.

Eatwell, Roger, *The 1945–1951 Labour Governments*, London, Batsford, 1979.

Ezra, Sir Derek, *Coal and Energy*, London, Ernest Benn, 1978.

Foot, Robert, 'A Plan for Coal', Mining Association of Great Britain, London, 1943.

Forsyth, D. J., *Studies in the Coal Industry*, Oxford, Pergamon, 1969.

Francis, Hywel, and Smith, David, *The Fed*, London, Lawrence & Wishart, 1980.

Fuel Policy, H.M.S.O., 1965, 1967.

Gregg, Pauline, *A Social and Economic History of Britain*, London, Harrap, 1965.

Griffin, A. R., *The Miners of Nottinghamshire*, London, George Allen & Unwin, 1962.

Hobsbawm, E. J., *Industry and Empire*, London, Penguin, 1969.

Hughes, John, and Moore, Roy, *A Special Case*, London, Penguin, 1972.

Horner, Arthur, *Incorrigible Rebel*, London, MacGibbon & Kee, 1960.

House, J. W., and Knight, E. M., *Pit Closure and the Community*, Report to the Ministry of Labour, 1967.

Jevons, Prof. H. S., *The British Coal Trade*, Kegan Paul, 1915.

Kirkby, M. W., *The British Coalmining Industry 1870 to 1946*, London, MacMillan, 1977.

MacFarlane, Jim (ed.), *Essays from the Yorkshire Coalfield*, University of Sheffield, 1979.

McCormick, B. J., *Industrial Relations in the Coal Industry*, London, MacMillan, 1979.

Moffat, Abe, *My Life with Miners*, London, Lawrence & Wishart, 1971.

Morris, Margaret, *The General Strike*, London, Penguin, 1976.

National Coal Board, Annual Reports, 1947–79.
  'Plan for Coal', 1950.
  'Investing in Coal', 1956.
  'Report of the Advisory Committee on Organization (The Fleck Report)', 1955.
  The First Ten Years, 1957.
  'Revised Plan for Coal', 1959.
  'Plan for Coal', 1974.

Nev, J. U., *The Rise of the British Coal Industry*, London, Routledge, 1932.

National Union of Mineworkers, Annual Reports of National Executive Committee, N.E.C. Minutes, Conference Reports, *The Miner* newspaper.

Page Arnot, Robin, *The Miners: A History of the Miners' Federation 1889–1910*, London, George Allen & Unwin, 1949.
   The Miners: Years of Struggle, London, George Allen & Unwin, 1953.
   The Miners in Crisis and War, London, George Allen & Unwin, 1961.
   The Miners: One Union, One Industry, London, George Allen & Unwin, 1979.
   A History of the Scottish Miners, London, George Allen & Unwin, 1955.
   The South Wales Miners, Cardiff, The Cymric Federation Press, 1975.
Pay Board, Special Report, *Relative Pay of Mineworkers*, H.M.S.O., 1974.
Paynter, Will, *My Generation*, London, George Allen & Unwin, 1972.
Pelling, Henry, *A History of British Trade Unionism*, London, Penguin, 1963.
Political & Economic Planning, *Report on the British Coal Mining Industry*, London, 1936.
Pitt, Malcolm, *The World on Our Backs*, London, Lawrence & Wishart, 1979.
Report of a Court of Inquiry into a dispute between the National Coal Board and the National Union of Mineworkers, Chairman Lord Wilberforce, H.M.S.O., 1972.
Robens, Lord Alfred, *Ten Year Stint*, London, Cassell, 1972.
Ryhope, A Pit Closes, H.M.S.O., 1970.
Samuel Commission, H.M.S.O., 1926.
Sankey Commission, H.M.S.O., 1919.
Scott, W. H., *et al.*, *Coal and Conflict*, Liverpool University Press, 1963.
Select Committee of the House of Commons on Nationalized Industries, various reports, H.M.S.O., 1958, 1966, 1967.
Townshend-Rose, H., *The British Coal Industry*, London, George Allen & Unwin, 1951.
Williams, J. E., *The Derbyshire Miners*, London, George Allen & Unwin, 1959.
Wilson, Harold, *A New Deal for Coal*, London, Contact, 1945.

Index

More about Penguins
and Pelicans

For further information about books available from Penguins
please write to Dept EP, Penguin Books Ltd,
Harmondsworth, Middlesex UB7 0DA.

In the U.S.A: For a complete list of books available from
Penguins in the United States write to Dept CS, Penguin
Books, 625 Madison Avenue, New York, New York 10022.

In Canada: For a complete list of books available from
Penguins in Canada write to Penguin Books Canada Ltd,
2801 John Street, Markham, Ontario L3R 1B4.

In Australia: For a complete list of books available from
Penguins in Australia write to the Marketing Department,
Penguin Books Australia Ltd, P.O. Box 257, Ringwood,
Victoria 3134.

In New Zealand: For a complete list of books available from
Penguins in New Zealand write to the Marketing
Department, Penguin Books (NZ) Ltd, P.0. Box 4019,
Auckland 10.